LEEDS COLLEGE OF BUILDING LIBRARY
CLASS NO. 640 SHE
BARCODE T 34834

D0504634

LEEDS COLLEGE OF BUILDING
WITHDRAWN FROM STOCK

LEEDS COLLEGE OF BUILDING

T34834

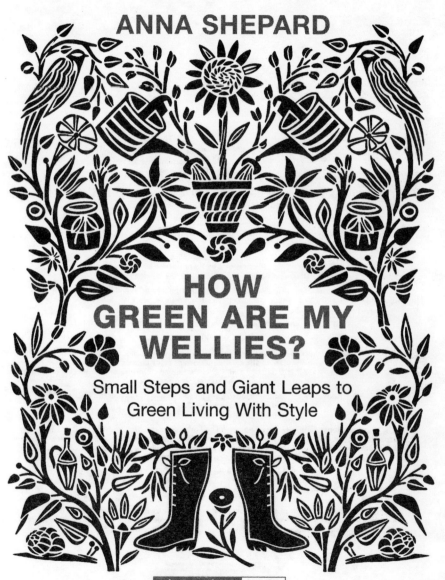

ANNA SHEPARD

HOW GREEN ARE MY WELLIES?

Small Steps and Giant Leaps to
Green Living With Style

eden project books

TRANSWORLD PUBLISHERS
61–63 Uxbridge Road, London W5 5SA
A Random House Group Company
www.rbooks.co.uk

First published in Great Britain in 2008 by Eden Project Books
an imprint of Transworld Publishers

Copyright © Anna Shepard 2008

Anna Shepard has asserted her right under the Copyright, Designs
and Patents Act 1988 to be identified as the author of this work.

Design by Julia Lloyd
Illustrations by Petra Borner
Diagrams on pp. 115, 117 and 118 © Patrick Mulrey

This book is a work of non-fiction based on the experiences and recollections of the author.
The author has stated to the publishers that, except in such minor respects not affecting the substantial
accuracy of the work, the contents of this book are true.

A CIP catalogue record for this book is available from the British Library.

ISBN 9781905811205

This book is sold subject to the condition that it shall not, by way of trade or otherwise, be lent,
resold, hired out, or otherwise circulated without the publisher's prior consent in any form of binding or
cover other than that in which it is published and without a similar condition, including this condition,
being imposed on the subsequent purchaser.

Addresses for Random House Group Ltd companies outside the UK
can be found at: www.randomhouse.co.uk
The Random House Group Ltd Reg. No. 954009

The Random House Group Limited supports The Forest Stewardship Council (FSC), the leading
international forest-certification organization. All our titles that are printed on Greenpeace-approved
FSC-certified paper carry the FSC logo. Our paper procurement policy can be found at
www.rbooks.co.uk/environment

Typeset in 10/14 pt Charlotte Book by Falcon Oast Graphic Art Ltd.
Printed in the UK by CPI Mackays, Chatham, ME5 8TD

2 4 6 8 10 9 7 5 3 1

Every effort has been made to obtain the necessary permissions with reference to copyright material,
both illustrative and quoted. We apologize for any omissions in this respect and will be pleased to make the
appropriate acknowledgements in any future edition.

Mixed Sources
Product group from well-managed
forests and other controlled sources
www.fsc.org Cert no. TT-COC-2139
© 1996 Forest Stewardship Council
FSC

To my mum, the master of making the new from the old

Contents

Acknowledgements

MY SPECIAL THANKS TO SUSANNA WADESON FOR HER SUPPORT, HUMOUR AND GOOD sense, along with many other things which would take too long to list. I am also grateful to everyone at Transworld and Eden Project Books who played a part in bringing this book to life, including Petra Borner, Aislinn Casey, Geraldine Ellison, Vivien Garrett, Manpreet Grewal, Julia Lloyd, Phil Lord, Patrick Mulrey, Mike Petty, Mari Roberts, Miriam Rosenbloom and Claire Ward.

Thank you, too, to my agent Lizzy Kremer for hooking me up with a fantastic publisher and making sense of my ideas, and to my editor at *The Times*, Hilly Janes, who has always supported me and encouraged my eco-worrying. I owe Erica Wagner a mention for reassuring me that writing a proposal is often the worst bit.

It is thanks to a great number of green-minded individuals who took time to talk to me so that I have been able to include their ethical advice and eco-adventures. They include: Holly Aquilina, Josephine Fairley, Martin Gibson, Kira Jolliffe, David Lort-Phillips, Celia Lyttelton, Toby Mason, Donnachadh McCarthy, Thomasina Miers, Karen Patrick, Paul Stott, John Wright and Anne Yarrow. Paul Waddington also deserves a mention for his part in assisting my vegetable growing efforts, along with Hugh Fearnley-Whittingstall for providing hedgerow recipes.

And a big thank you to my friends: Patrizia, for inspiring me for the past ten years; Martin, for sound horticultural advice; Livvy, my worm ally, and many others, including Lou, Tom, Coco, Jo, Nicole, Rosie, Xav and Charlie for letting me write about their weird and wonderful habits – even though they don't all know it yet.

Lastly, I want to thank my family for their love and support, and, most importantly, Gervase, who has been – and I hope will continue to be – remarkably tolerant.

Introduction

I DOUBT THAT ANYONE IS BORN GREEN BUT I HAD A PRETTY GOOD START. I WAS A kitchen baby. The first few years of my life were spent in a large squishy armchair, from where I could observe the sights and smells of my new world. It was a place where nothing was wasted. Saucers of leftovers cluttered the worktop; jars of honey were propped up on the Aga to soften the final scrape, and there was always a saucepan of stock on the go, a resting place for unfinished glasses of wine.

For the thrifty habits that have seeped into my life today, I therefore hold my mother entirely responsible. She is – I hope she won't mind me saying – spectacularly frugal, still prone to dashing around the house drawing curtains the moment it's dark to conserve the heat, and diluting the ketchup with a splash of vinegar. Not, I might add, because we were ever seriously hard up, although saving money certainly comes into it, but because she believes in making things go further.

She, in turn, was brought up under the 'eke eke' philosophy of my grandmother, an expression that still makes me giggle. It describes being sparing with resources, and would be muttered when a modest lump of meat was required to feed a large number of guests for Sunday lunch, or when we were expected to hold back at an expensive restaurant. To make ingredients – sometimes money, more often food – stretch, the powers of eke eke would be summoned.

All this probably explains why I find myself inclined to turn a stale teacake into bread and butter pudding and cram the washing machine fuller than anyone I have ever met believes is possible.

But it was not always so. There were many years before I made peace with my resourcefulness. It wasn't easy having a slice of yesterday's quiche in my school lunchbox instead of a packet of Monster Munch, or having to tell friends to bring their thermals when they came to stay. At first, quite naturally, I rebelled, wondering if I could override my genes to become someone who skipped frivolously through life, consuming resources with abandon. But I came to realize that resisting was pointless. My family's thrifty values were here to stay. And they were good ones. Over the years, the embarrassment has fallen away. Much of my gradual shift towards a greener life has been about nothing more than getting back in touch with the values I grew up with. In the 21st century, they are surprisingly relevant.

Three years ago, when I started writing the Eco-Worrier column for the Saturday *Times*, giving advice on green dilemmas, I was amazed how often I recycled the sort of nuggets of wisdom that my granny would have passed on to my mother. In my grandmother's day, it would have been called 'good housekeeping', the aim being to keep down costs and make the most of what you have. Today, it is served up as eco advice, to reduce our impact on the environment.

In this new world order, it is climate change and disappearing fossil fuels that motivate us as much as economizing. Whatever the reason, an attitude of conserving, rather than wasting, resources – which makes sense however the environmental challenges ahead unfold – is being revived. What was innate to most people in Britain just forty years ago is having to be relearned. The focus may be different today and there may be new things to worry about (it would not have occurred to my mother, for instance, to consider the chemicals used in household products or the distance food has travelled), but at its heart it is the same 'waste not, want not' message.

As I see it, there is no secret to being green. It revolves around consuming less and more carefully, whether that is energy, food, water, clothing or any other raw material. But it's not only about the details – about whether your fridge is full of organic produce and there is a wind turbine on your roof. Green is also a state of being. It is a way of interacting with the world, from the moment you wake up. It encourages you to question what really makes you happy and to strip away the bits that don't.

What I hope to prove in *How Green Are My Wellies* is that being green doesn't deprive you of life's pleasures – it introduces you to them. Or that's what I found. As I tweaked my daily routine to include more green touches, my life became richer, fuller and more satisfying. I became more creative, potion-making at home instead of buying cleaning products, and holding clothes-swapping parties with friends rather than bothering with the high street. The benefits of a simpler, slowed-down life were revealed. The fact that cycling to work keeps me fit and healthy became as much of a selling point as the thought of reducing car emissions – although that helps with the all-round glow. In the same way, it is the taste of a nourishing bowl of homemade soup that encourages me to use up vegetables more than the waste implications.

Along with my upbringing, two other factors have helped me over the past few years. The first is the Eco-Worrier column, which has allowed my green leanings to flourish, largely because I am uncomfortable suggesting a solution to a reader unless I have had a go at it myself. Until you have struggled with a leaky water butt or nurtured a row of lettuces, how can you possibly advise anyone on how to cut through a drainpipe or dispose of dead snails? And there's nothing like giving advice to other people to leave you with little excuse for not taking it yourself.

This has worked both ways. My column – and also the Eco-Worrier blog – has generated an enormous amount of feedback, and the advice and tips I get from readers on all subjects of eco-friendly living have helped with the writing of this book and with my own attempts to live lightly.

Then there are my worms. Around the same time as starting the column, I became the proud owner of a wormery containing over a thousand wrigglers that survive on my kitchen scraps. Its success and my flourishing relationship with these new pets marked a shift in my attitude. When I harvested the first tray of rich compost, it was a turning point. Setting up the wormery was by no means the first domestic alteration I had made in my attempts to be a greener individual, but it was – and still is – by far the most satisfying. After it, nothing seemed out of reach. Doors opened to greener pastures.

For some it might be their first successfully home-grown organic tomato, or a decision to take the ferry to go on holiday instead of the plane. For me, it was watching my waste magically transform into something useful. This simple act framed future green endeavours.

And once I started seeing eco-actions as life-enhancing, rather than difficult, expensive and just another thing to do when I got home, I overcame the reflex that kicks in telling me not to bother. I realized it was simply a question of changing habits rather than doing anything particularly tedious or abstemious.

At no point have I turned my life upside-down. I upped my green commitment step by step. It's not that I wouldn't love to go the whole hog and live in a yurt somewhere remote and muddy, with maybe a few hogs of my own to eat, but, as with most people, there's a job and a flat in the way. There's also a boyfriend firmly rooted in city life to think about, and he's enough without any livestock to look after.

But before we get to Gervase – who deserves a special mention since he pops up all over the place – let me explain how the book works. It is part memoir, part manual. Whether you read it cover to cover or dip in for seasonal inspiration is entirely up to you. (However you tackle it, I hope you enjoy it.) It was a daunting task to try to cover all aspects of eco-friendly living, so instead I focused on the ones that have inspired me and that I have found most life-enhancing. I may wander off a little – usually into the kitchen to report on some novel way of reviving stale bread or reusing jam jars – but the idea is to stick to seasonally themed subjects. It just makes things easier. Working with, not against, the rhythms of the natural world enables the transition to a greener life to be more harmonious.

As you will discover, not everything I try works, and not everything I mention would I expect you to try. But my hope is that everyone should find something, however small, that they can do each month.

Please don't expect instant transformation. I believe gradual change is more likely to become permanent. Small steps to green living are more my style. Achievable little shuffles with lots of time for cups of Fairtrade tea in between.

And don't be disheartened by imagining that these steps won't make a difference. When you're perched on a wobbly stool trying to fit an energy-saving light bulb, I know how easy it is to feel dwarfed by the challenge ahead. Or to put off tackling it until another day. Everyone has moments when we doubt that we can combat problems with our own puny measures. But we can. Individual action is the basis of change. I believe it is each one of us who drives change as much as governments and businesses. Consumer decisions influence markets and demonstrate that shoppers don't like freeze-wrapped coconuts. Meanwhile, individual support for green behaviour puts pressure on governments to make changes (why else would politicians be competing for green credentials?). And, most importantly, small actions taken by many snowball – especially once you start holding forth to your friends about the joy of home-grown vegetables and taking the slow train to Spain.

The other thing to realize is that one small action, such as recycling, sets in motion a way of thinking about others. You'll hear people scoff: 'It all goes to China, anyway . . . It ends up landfill . . . It takes more energy to recycle than to make from new.' Believe me, I've heard them all before, but what this fails to account for is the fact that once you become a devoted recycler, your purchasing habits change too. You'll be steering clear of overpackaged items and avoiding plastic bags. You'll soon be wondering whether you really need to make that purchase at all.

Before we begin, I would like to introduce my cast. First, there is an assortment of friends and family members who have walk-on parts, offering up their expertise in subjects as varied as cocktails, baking and cold-frame making. Many of them are as passionate about the environment as I am and their exploits have regularly sparked off my own.

This is no truer than of my friend Patrizia. She's a bit like me, but greener. Whether growing vegetables, learning about permaculture or climbing hills, she exudes such enthusiasm that I quickly soak it up and want to play too. Together we have baked bread, gone WWOOFing, climbed in Sardinia, trekked around the Lake District, gardened, cooked fabulous food and sunk an awful lot of beer.

Another significant role is played by all those who have written to me in response to my column or blog. Your stories and helpful tips feature through-out the book – not least, to show that it is not just me obsessing about making chutney and learning to crochet. There is a web community out there that is truly knowledgeable and equally joyful about going green and how much richer and more pleasurable it makes life.

Then there is a long-suffering boyfriend, Gervase, who plays leading man. Often referred to as the eco-sceptic boyfriend (a title I bestow lovingly, his reticence being part of his charm), he helps me to gauge when my eco-mania has tipped too far.

Gervase says his attitude to the environment is pretty standard. Mild concern that flares up once in a while, balanced out with a tendency to leave lights on and overfill the kettle. Nothing too devastating. Needless to say, I shouldn't hassle him about his bad habits, but we've been together so long he has grown accustomed to a degree of green bullying.

Over the chapters that follow, there will be plenty of occasions when you will do better than me, I'm sure of it. Not only at domestic diplomacy. If this book is nothing more than a starting point, to encourage you to think about what makes you happy, what makes the environment happy and where the two meet, my job is done.

JANUARY

DECLUTTERING AND
SLIMMING YOUR WASTE

LEEDS COLLEGE OF BUILDING
LIBRARY

I T HAS TAKEN ME MOST OF MY ADULT LIFE TO REALIZE THAT I HAVE BEEN BARKING UP the wrong tree. That my quest to become a fitter, slimmer and more sober individual in early January is utterly misguided. Apart from the obvious fact that, like everyone else, I am always reeling from the double impact of over-indulgence and what my Granny used to call 'burst balloon feeling' – to describe the comedown after Christmas – there is something else amiss about New Year pledges. They are, when I think about it, always the same old recipes for self-improvement. Worse still, they are pathetically half-hearted. Or mine are, anyway.

'I'm going to drink a bit less,' I'll mumble to a friend, over a glass of wine. 'I'll jog round the park every morning before breakfast,' I'll swear to my boyfriend Gervase, after an evening polishing off the Christmas cake on the sofa. He'll raise an eyebrow. He knows, of course, that I won't. The regime will fall apart before I've even sorted myself out with a tracksuit. The alfalfa sprouts will go brown in the fridge and the yoga mat will stay curled up in the corner of the living room. It's as predictable as the thumping hangover that greets me on the first day of January.

With this in mind, last year I vowed to leave my wobbly bits alone and implement some green improvements instead. I reckoned my time would be better spent using the New Year to spark broader environmental good. You never know, maybe a commitment to my bike and sorting out the garden would get me in better shape, and it would be easier to sustain than ending my relationship with the biscuit tin.

To work out where to begin, I had only to glance around the flat I share with Gervase. My first challenge was laid out in front of me. Over the holiday period, piles of objects had started multiplying around the flat like mushrooms on a boggy autumn day. Crawling up walls and filling cupboards, Christmas gifts mixed with dusty boxes of homeless items that I'd meant to take to a charity shop months ago. It was less a question of where did it all come from, and more a question of where should it go?

Facing such a task, I am grateful to have descended from a long line of thrifty women who have all, in their day, taken reusing, recycling and rehoming seriously. I should probably add that the remaining green commandment, reducing – the most worthy of all – has been more of a struggle. The only good thing I can say about an inherited reluctance to throw anything out is that it prevents you from becoming an enthusiastic bin user. In a display of dubious resourcefulness, I tend to use the corners of my home as a handy alternative to landfill.

I'd use the cupboards if they weren't already crammed. In fact, it is a large white one that forms my first memory of recycling – a dizzyingly tall affair (or so it seemed to me aged five or six) that ruled over my mother's bedroom, and had a strange hold over me. Out of its cavernous interior all sorts of treasures would emerge come birthdays and Christmases.

With the arrival of January, the magic cupboard would reverse its function, swallowing up shiny packages that rustled with unknown promise. Like Mary Poppins' carpetbag, it could hide large objects of enormous interest to small children. Sometimes my sister and I would peep into my mother's bedroom when she was tucking something away on one of the upper shelves, just to listen to the crinkly sounds and check that she didn't disappear completely, gobbled by the mysterious cupboard.

As I grew older and bolder, I'd tiptoe into the room and reach up to have a rummage myself. Always a mistake. I'd often unearth something that had been intended as a present for me. Realizing instantly what I had discovered, the magic of the surprise would drain away, leaving me feeling foolish and flat.

Other times, I'd find familiar objects – colourful scarves, the odd piece of jewellery and boxes of biscuits – that I couldn't quite place, but I knew I'd seen before. Mystified, I'd bundle them back into the cupboard's jaws, and, quiet as a mouse, disappear from the room before anyone could hear the squeaky floorboards in the kitchen below.

What I did not know back then was that my mother was practising the ancient art of regifting. By stashing away unwanted presents, she had a constant supply of ready-to-go offerings, should a friend or relative's birthday creep up on her. Not only did this method save her pennies, it also guaranteed that a gift would not be put to waste or left languishing in a drawer. Instead it would be redistributed, and, for all I know, passed on again and again, if other families were as dedicated to the practice as we were.

The funny thing about regifting is that it has yet to come out of the closet. Even in these pea-green times, when being sparing of resources is no longer the preserve of radical environmentalists and recycling has become a national obsession, you still get the feeling that it would be better to drop into dinner party conversation that you use your old undies as dishcloths (not a bad idea, come to think of it) than admit that you're giving something to someone that was not bought first-hand.

For some reason, the idea persists that it is cheating; that you can only really show someone you care if you've sweated blood and tears in Habitat to find just the right glazed vase. Of course, that's balls. A good present is one that makes the recipient happy, whether it is a passed-on necklace or a jar of homemade chutney.

In the States, where people are more forthright about these things, there is a website, *www.regiftable.com*. You can share your 'regifting stories'; unload the burden of the musical socks doing the rounds, carefully wrapped up in recycled tissue paper and sent on their way to someone who might appreciate the Rudolf the Red-Nosed Reindeer tune. There are also tips on etiquette.

Never regift handmade items, it warns, and always spruce up a regifted object with a new card or gift tag. Watch out for signs of the festive season, too. Holly gift tags and mince pie crumbs caught in the sellotape will serve as incriminating evidence if found on a gift given in April.

The ultimate sin with this regifting lark, as I'm sure you can imagine, is to give a present back to its original owner, thus eliciting an awkward moment when the recipient recognizes your gift and you recognize that they recognize it and an icy silence descends, during which you wonder whether to come clean. So far, it hasn't happened to me. If it did, I suspect the only way through would be by laughing and confessing all. The fear of it holds back the regifting movement, I'm sure of it. Which is a shame because all you need to do is stick Post-It notes to presents destined for regifting that identify who they came from. Easy.

Understandably, not everyone has the time or inclination to wait for the right gift to pass on. For my birthday present for the last few years, I've had 'doing' presents from my father. He has offered his services as an odd-job man, turning up in a builder's hat with a packed lunch for both of us. A day's worth of putting up shelves and giving our home appliances the once-over is a thousand times more useful than any bought gift, as well as meaning that we spend the day together. Albeit with me standing next to him, forbidden from moving, while he, surgeon-like, belts out the usual instructions: 'Screwdriver! Spirit level! Where do you think you're going?'

Regifting as a means of decluttering, I hasten to add, is only the beginning. I don't know about you but the sort of stuff that comes to light when I explore the uncharted territory under my bed is rarely improved with colourful wrapping paper and a recycled ribbon. As my mother would say: 'It doesn't pass the present test.' (I've never understood the exact perimeters of this test but I have learnt to recognize what is sub-standard. Palm a ten-year-old toaster and a pile of Tina Turner CDs off on a friend and you might not be invited to next year's birthday party.)

That you cannot regift something does not mean you won't find a willing member of the public to relieve you of it. That's step two in my New Year plan: rehoming, a means of finding items a second home where they'll be cherished all over again, rather than given a lonely, lengthy sentence rotting in landfill.

My first port of call? Local charity shops, exchange forums and community swap shops. Increasingly, they operate online (for a list see back of book) so you can negotiate a future for an unwanted armchair without having to get up out of it. Freecycle is my decluttering saviour. It is an online message board (*www.freecycle.org*), where you can give away stuff you don't need and find what you do. As such, it is the grand master of transforming one person's trash into another's treasure, creating a 'free cycle' of giving which aims to keep stuff out of overcrowded landfill sites.

Once you're in the Freecycle club, you can post up messages to say what you're offering, or looking for. One of the benefits is that people come to you to pick up the stuff you're getting rid of, so you don't have to stress about how you're going to heave a sofabed out of your home.

Not everyone takes to it. Gervase remains unconvinced by Freecycle, reminding me that I haven't yet acquired anything vaguely desirable. The shelves I picked up didn't fit the alcove in our walls; the bulky radio was soon trumped by one I was given as a present, and the rug was, quite frankly, hideous. He has a point, but I don't think this should be a reason to hold back. Even if its services as an alternative shopping method are in doubt, it triumphs as a means of getting rid of stuff.

No matter how miserable my offerings, nothing has been rejected by my local forum. I am amazed by what gets snapped up. When I post up a message to say that I have a broken Hoover in the cupboard and does anyone want it, several people email to say they would take it off my hands, and it's gone by that evening. How could a clapped-out domestic appliance that you could buy new for twenty quid from Currys appeal to anyone? It restores my faith that a 'make do and mend' culture lives on.

The best thing about Freecycle is that it takes no more time, and possibly less effort, than stuffing belongings into a black bag and sending them to landfill – and you feel much better for it.

The downside is that you won't make a quick buck, since no money changes hands. For that, you'd be better off with eBay. But I've never got round to selling anything on the world's biggest online marketplace. Put off by the effort of taking flattering pictures of my tatty belongings and the prospect of trips to the Post Office to send off packages, with only a cheque for a fiver or so as an incentive, I'd rather pursue speedier solutions.

One such is the 'Put it on the Pavement with a Note' method, which rarely gets the attention it deserves. As implied, you haul things on to the street and leave them with a sign perched on top to encourage passers-by to scoop them up. Obviously, if they are rejected, you have to think again; lug them back inside and maybe sign up for a space at your local car-boot sale. A muddy field dotted with cars and makeshift tables on which broken teapots and bobbly jumpers are laid out is in many ways the end of the line for domestic clutter. Don't think I'm not keen; I love a car-boot sale. Towards the end of the day, the ones I've been to have transformed into a free-for-all, with sellers keen to shift leftovers, whether or not they are paid for. 'Go on, take it, I'm not lugging it home,' a kindly woman once told me, as I toyed with splashing out 50p on a tatty laundry basket.

With my own stuff, I never reach the car-boot-sale stage. Where I live, nothing stays on the pavement for long. I've even managed to offload a muddy pile of flowerpots by piling them into a cardboard box and balancing them on the wall outside our flat. Please take me, I wrote on the note. And someone did.

Naturally, the idea is not to get rid of anything that you can find a use for in your own home. I'm all for growing beetroot in old kettles (just remember to drill holes in the bottom) and making a bird-scaring device from unwanted CDs (although when I tried this, it looked so ugly that even the neighbourhood cats stopped popping by for a roll in the flowerbeds – which is probably the idea). Yes, you might look as though you've employed Stig of the Dump as your interior designer, but at least your home won't resemble an Ikea catalogue.

When my editor at *The Times* asked me what she should do with a grubby shower curtain, I could scarcely contain myself. I love playing 'What can you do with this?' What about a tablecloth for picnics; a protective layer in your car boot; a BBQ cover for the winter months, or even a lining for a garden pond? It can be all this and more, I insist, sounding like a *Blue Peter* presenter after a double espresso. If it's mouldy, cut the best bits out and use them as mats under pet bowls or to protect the carpet from muddy wellies.

Given this attitude, you will understand that it was out of character when I succumbed to a shameful bout of panic binning last year. You know, when you shove stuff in a bin at great speed before anyone can stop you or your conscience has time to put in a bid for eco-correctness? My only defence is that it was during a moving-house episode. Nonetheless, I committed more green sins in the space of a few stressful weeks than I would normally in several months. Under pressure to shift all my belongings from one place to another, the bin and I indulged in a secret relationship, an affair that was ridden with guilt and an overriding sense of shame.

Piles of unwanted DVDs that usually go to a recycling organization, along with all sorts of odds and ends, from unwanted kitchen appliances to fashion throwbacks that are normally distributed among friends and family or, as a final resort, sent to a charity shop, disappeared into its plastic embrace. I did not feel good about it. The only sign of what I'd done was the uncommonly large number of black bin bags outside our house – and the guilty look I wore as I crept around the streets half expecting a ticking off from a neighbour.

Gervase remarked wryly that if I a) acquired less 'junk' in the first place, b) didn't insist on keeping stuff for so long, I wouldn't end up in this mess. In other words, if I edited my possessions more rigorously as I went along, all would be well. But what he fails to grasp is that you never know when piles of too-tight jeans and clapped-out sewing machines salvaged from the street could come in handy.

Anyway, that wasn't the problem. Looking back, I can see that it was more that I didn't leave enough time to do everything. I should have started my packing and pile-making sooner. As with many aspects of green living, a little planning goes a long way. To atone for my sins, I promised that I would set up a mind-bogglingly efficient recycling system in the new flat to restore my rubbish reputation.

A combination of guilt and an efficient council made this possible. As with most city councils, Hackney operates a door-to-door weekly collection system. I can fill my green box with shoes, textiles, household and car batteries, as well as the more commonly recycled materials, such as glass, PET plastic, paper and aluminium. It even sends round friendly recycling officers to see how residents are getting on and to give out plastic liners for the blue bins that we can fill with our kitchen waste, making cleaning out the bin a slightly less mucky job.

Should I happen to move outside of the city, I'm aware that I might be less fortunate. My rustic moles – no, not furry ones, friends living in the countryside who report on life off the Tube – tell me they have to drive miles to their nearest bottle bank and spend hours on the phone trying to find out what kind of plastic can be recycled. I tell them to look up their council's facilities on *www.recyclenow.com*.

But the phoning approach, while tedious, is a good one. I'm often on the blower to Hackney council. Given that it's the best way to make sure that you're doing the right thing with your rubbish, I'm surprised people don't do it more. Only the waste and recycling department knows exactly what is picked up from your door and where it goes in all the glorious detail you might, or might not, crave. Hackney council enlightened me about the companies that deal with the sorting and transport of my waste, and explained exactly what my baked-bean cans and newspapers turn into (see page 36).

All this should come with a warning: once you start breaking down your rubbish, dividing it up into different piles and working out exactly what you've created, expect it to become something of an addiction. In the spirit of reconnecting with my rubbish, in recent months I've taken to poking around in my kitchen bin on an almost daily basis. Not everyone's cup of tea, I'll give you that, but I enjoy it. It's like spending time in your walk-in wardrobe except a bit soggier and you end up looking less glamorous.

I find myself less squeamish about it too. There is nothing in any of my bins that repulses me. When rubbish is all mixed up in one bin, leftover food with cardboard, leaky wine bottles and meat packaging, it does get pretty nasty. But divide it up and you'll see there is no reason for it to be an embarrassment.

Looking in the bin enables me to identify my main waste culprits – in other words, items that have escaped my dual system of composting and recycling, and so will be sent off to landfill where they will rot, releasing methane, a potent greenhouse gas, and other pollutants. To give you a taster, this morning's assessment yielded yoghurt pots, several plastic milk-bottle lids and the wrapping from a block of cheddar.

Having worked out what's bulking out my bin, I can alter my purchasing habits accordingly, or that's the idea: to roam shop aisles thinking of my rubbish system and choosing scantily clad items over those swathed in plastic. I do my best to go for safe options: loose, fresh veggies, and meat and cheeses from the deli counters (see page 38 on how to avoid packaging).

Suits me fine, as I like to graze while I'm shopping and you can ask for tasters at the counters. Slivers of salami and crumbled lumps of cheddar are passed over as you work out which to buy. I also try to support products that have been relaunched with lighter, more eco-friendly packaging that can be recycled or reused. This might be an attempt by a food company to gain green credentials, but if it has the knock-on effect of encouraging other companies to rethink packaging, it's worth supporting.

Of course, it is better to produce less rubbish than to produce an environmentally friendly variety; better not to bother with avocados that are sitting in plastic moulds than to buy ones that are resting on recyclable plastic. No packaging is better than recyclable packaging. Consuming less, in other words, reducing – the queen bee of green commandments – is a tough challenge. It's harder to quantify and brings fewer obvious rewards than recycling. There is none of the satisfaction of heaving out your green bin on a freezing January day, warmed only by a virtuous glow from within and admiring glances from neighbours. I'm sure I'm not the only one who takes curious pleasure in watching the council truck pull away, packed with items deemed worthy of a second life.

In the long term, decluttering is about 'buying less'. And yet, though I try to exorcise my consumer instinct, to march past shops sticking my chin in the air and saying, 'Nope, sorry, feel nothing . . . not interested,' sometimes, mostly at weekends, after five long days of work, I give in. I coo over a John Lewis catalogue or part with hard cash for soft furnishing. Not of the sofa and absurdly expensive furniture variety; more likely salad bowls and tea trays and pointless trinkets to make our home look pretty – second-hand mostly, but sometimes brand spanking new.

I've worked hard to rationalize this instinct, asking myself how long the buzz of buying something actually lasts and how happy it really makes me, but the answer, when I spot something irresistible, cannot be trusted. Under the influence of consumer lust, woozy with desire to acquire, I can convince myself of anything – usually, that what I have found will improve my life beyond belief.

Infuriatingly, Gervase is much better than me. He is a natural resister. Somehow he doesn't want things so much as I do. More easily content, he is less likely to swoon over anything found in a shop.

Come on, Anna, you don't need that, he says. And he's right. I don't. But my nest-building instinct to gather things around me that reflect my taste and make me feel like me is hard to resist.

More than once, having got within an inch of buying something and then managed to resist, the desired object – or something very like it – has turned up in a skip a few weeks later anyway, as if to reward me for abstaining. Scattered around our flat we now have several chairs, a fold-up table, a palm tree, some shelves and a basket that used to be for carrying cats (and smells accordingly), all acquired for free, courtesy of skips or the street. Something for nothing – I love it. But I overdid it once and heaved a pane of broken glass inside to construct a cold frame to germinate seeds. Gervase put his foot down. Enough from skips, he said. Our flat is full. For now, we are closed to salvageable items.

When I interviewed Josephine Fairley, who co-founded Green & Black's chocolate company with her husband Craig Sams, for *The Times*, she told me about a mantra that she developed to stop herself over-consuming. It has lodged in my mind ever since. She asks herself three questions before she buys anything: Do I really need it? Will it last? Is there an alternative?

It is to this that I aspire, give or take the odd delicious thing to lift me out of the winter blues. Should I discover when I get home that I didn't need it and there was an alternative, it can always go in the present drawer. A humble, slimmed-down, but equally magical version of my mother's cupboard.

WHAT'S IN IT FOR THE PLANET?

By regifting, rehoming and reusing . . . you are bringing less new stuff into your life and making the most of what you already have. This helps to cut out the energy required to manufacture and transport new products. Most importantly, you will be packing less off to landfill. Landfill sites produce methane, a powerful greenhouse gas that is contributing to climate change. They also create water pollution, as liquid leaks into our water system, and can lead to land contamination. Plus, we're running out of landfill space. More rubbish is emptied into our ground than any country on the continent. We dump twice as much waste as Germany, which has a bigger population. The Local Government Association estimated in 2007 that our remaining landfill capacity would last between six and nine years unless we start finding alternatives to dumping in the ground.

By recycling . . . you are saving energy and easing the burden on landfill sites. By recycling an aluminium can, 95 per cent of the energy needed to make one from raw materials is saved. For paper, this is between 25 and 50 per cent (see the Waste and Resources Action Programme, *www.wrap.org.uk*).

By reducing . . . you are doing all of the above. Up to 60 per cent of what's in our household bin is packaging, according to Friends of the Earth. By buying less and avoiding overpackaged products, we should be able to halve this.

Freecycle: The Etiquette of Online Swapping

Here's how it works

Sign up to your local Freecycle group online (visit *www.freecycle.org* and go to 'find a group near you') and you gain access to a forum that allows you to read and post up messages. Of these, there are two kinds: wanted and offered. You can also reply to members who are offering something you want. I saw some shelves up for grabs a few months ago, so I emailed the poster to ask if I could have them. He said yes and gave me his address. It turned out he was only a few streets away, so I was home with the shelves in minutes. Shame they didn't fit.

Playing by the rules

• The crucial thing is that no money exchanges hands. Asking for payment is shockingly bad form in Freecycle circles. Expect to be ostracized by your community.

• It's up to you who receives the item you're offering. If you receive hundreds of emails from people wanting it, you'll have to find your own way of choosing the lucky new owner. Most worthy? Most speedy to collect? Many Freecyclers go with whoever responds first, but if you wait a day or so, you might hear from someone who you would particularly like to have your belongings.

- You're supposed to wait one month before re-posting your message. If no one replies to say they want Granny's tablecloth after two postings, I'm afraid you're just going to have to keep it. Or even better, regift it.

- Watch out for Freecycle freeloaders. It has been reported that some people simply sell items on eBay that they have received through Freecycle. If they can be bothered, good luck to them. In green terms, at least the stuff is not going to landfill, although if you come across your Freecycled fridge on eBay, you have every right to demand a share of the profit.

- It is not a solution to your short-lived hamster love. Most groups won't allow you to use Freecycle to get rid of pets, although I did once see some Giant African Land Snails up for grabs on my forum. There were several interested parties, including my friend Sophie who wanted to know if she'd be able to ride one to work.

- Be friendly with your fellow Freecyclers. Not so pally that it looks like you haven't got any proper friends and you're trying to make them by offering up an armchair, obviously. But one of the best things about Freecycle is that it encourages a sense of community. I've been offered countless cups of tea on my travels around Hackney. That's about as far as I'd take it, although it would be rude to refuse a slice of cake.

- Take a friend with you if you feel uneasy about going to someone's house to pick something up. I've never had a problem, but better safe than sorry.

Giving to Charity Shops

Choose your charity shop wisely

Give to reputable charities you know and trust and make sure you ask what is going to happen to the items you donate. Will they stay in the shop, or get sent back to a central office to be sold to textile traders? Overburdened charity shops often sell excess stock to the rag market, in which case garments may wind their way to markets in the developing world. While there may be a need for cheap clothing, there is also concern that dumping our rejects disrupts local economies and (according to the UN) has contributed to the collapse of textile industries in countries such as Zambia. Happily, not all charities hop into bed with rag traders. To cut out the middlemen, Oxfam has its own recycling plant, Wastesaver, in Huddersfield, for textiles it cannot sell in its shops. Another pioneering charity shop, Traid, uses donated textiles that it can't sell to create one-off pieces for its own-label fashion range.

Reuse rather than replace

One problem with bundling stuff off to a charity shop is that everyone else has the same idea. A surge of unwanted belongings, dumped outside doorways, often in the dead of night when no one is around to witness these embarrassing displays, is flooding charity shops. They have become ethical dustbins, allowing us to make more room in our homes to acquire new stuff, thereby compounding the problem. This had led to shops becoming fussy about what they accept. You may find your bag of old CDs and leggings being spurned by the nice lady in Help the Aged. In the long run, this might be a good thing. You'll have to come up with a more inventive second life for them – leggings can be ripped up and turned into dusters; CDs can be sent to one of the companies listed on *www.recyclenow.com*.

Be wary of kerbside collections

If a leaflet flutters through your door asking for your clothes for charity, raise an ethical eyebrow before you start trawling through your wardrobe. Plenty of unscrupulous individuals are more than willing to relieve you of belongings, which they will sell to make money. True, your clothes will be getting further use, but if you care about supporting charity, this is not the route to take. Of course, some leaflets are genuine. The collectors will be local volunteers with charitable tendencies and robust consciences, unlikely to pilfer the best items. To be sure, look for the charity logo and a registered charity number on the flyer. Or, for more info, go to *www.charityshops.org.uk* or *www.charitycommission.org.uk*. If there's no website and no charity details given, tut loudly and recycle the flyer.

Think twice about using textile banks

You'll probably have seen them in supermarket car parks or at pavement recycling centres. More worryingly, you may have seen groups of kids posting their crisp packets and half-finished milkshakes into them. Textile banks would not be my first choice when it comes to clothes recycling. What generally happens is this: after you shove in your clothes, they are picked up by a private contractor, who sells them on to a textile trader. A portion of the profit will go back to the charity advertised on the outside of the bank (according to Sophie Parkin, writing in the *Daily Mail*, sometimes as little as 20 per cent). Environmentally, this is no bad thing. What matters is that your clothes are not going to landfill, where woollen garments will produce methane, contributing to global warming, and synthetic products won't decompose at all. Ethically, however, there are complications. As explained above, most of the UK's textile waste ends up being sold to developing countries. I have mixed feelings about this. I'm uneasy about my old blouses entering the international textile trade. Then again, all recycling becomes a commodity once you've offered it up to the green-bin men. Like everything else, it is driven by market forces, not charitable ones. And this is what ultimately will sustain the recycling process.

Try it in January . . .

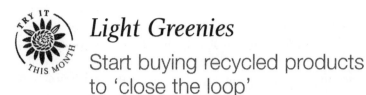

Light Greenies
Start buying recycled products to 'close the loop'

Filling your green bin is only half the story. Creating a demand for its content, by buying the products made from it, is just as important. Otherwise it'll clock up a merry carbon footprint travelling the world to somewhere where there is a better market for it. China relieves us of much of our plastic recycling, before selling it back to us in its various new incarnations. When I visited a recycled-loo-paper factory in Lancashire – a surprisingly absorbing trip, before you smirk – I learnt that the recycled-paper waste we create far outstrips the demand for the products that are made from it. While we are very good at filling our recycling boxes with waste, we are less good at buying the products it turns into. So, if you don't mind, please abandon your affection for perfumed Andrex and take to the recycled products on the market. There'll be no complaints from sensitive derrieres, I promise. Recycled loo paper is neither prickly nor a disturbing muddy colour. It's actually rather soft and silky, no different from your average square of bathroom tissue.

Loo accessories aside, spread the word to friends about champagne flutes made from recycled glass, picnic blankets made from scrap textiles and light shades and other interior design pieces, all from *www.recycledproducts.org.uk*.

Dark Greenies

Bring in an eco-auditor

Like a personal trainer called in to get you off the sofa, an eco-auditor will whip your carbon footprint into shape. There are a number of green inspectors available who will visit your home to conduct a home audit, telling you how you could improve your commitment to the planet (see back of book for info). After nosing around in your cupboards and gasping at your planet-trashing habits, a plan of action will be suggested, tailored to your lifestyle and concerns. The best thing about the service is that it provides someone to report back to and inspire you. In other words, someone to impress with your efforts to improve. Anyway, once your dirty habits have been exposed, you'll probably feel humbled into altering them.

The only drawback is that it doesn't come cheap (usually about £200 for the first visit and assessment). Although it will save you money in the long run, it's not one to do if you're struggling to buy the next pint of organic milk.

Eco-Cheats

• Solve the January food glut by inviting your hungriest friends around for a Feast of Eat Everything. As well as sparing you from a compulsion to chomp through every last Quality Street, it will cut the risk of food that is flagging in the fridge being binned.

• Plant your Christmas tree outside, instead of adding it to the tree graveyard out on the streets – a sad sight to behold in the early weeks of January. Obviously this only works if you've got one with roots – harden it off against frosty temperatures by leaving it in a shed or by a back door for a few days first. If it's a chopped tree, your council may be able to recycle it. Find out on *recyclenow.co.uk*.

• Instead of giving old shoes the boot, try planting flowers in them. Winter pansies and cyclamen would work at this time of year. All you have to do is make some drainage holes, put some soil and the plants inside and hope that they won't mind their unusual – and potentially smelly – environment.

Is It Really Going to be Recycled?

We've all done it. Watched the recycling lorry pull away and doubted whether our sticky soup cans and plastic milk bottles are really destined for a rosy future. Reservations creep in – however much your council reassures you and posts flyers through the door flagging up its recycling success rates. TV exposés of illegal dumping in developing countries and bad practice at recycling sorting centres don't help.

Back when I was living in Camden, I was even suspicious of the collection process. I'd watch as the recycling men piled the whole contents of our green bin into the back of the lorry. Who's going to sort through that mess, I'd wonder. To set my mind at rest, I began grilling council officials to find out about the journey my rubbish would take.

What I discovered was that there are two kinds of collection. The first, co-mingled, involves tossing everything from junk mail to wine bottles in a lorry and whisking it away to a sorting centre, where a clever machine divides it up. At the Materials Recycling Facility in

Greenwich, southwest London, which looks after much of the city's waste, materials are separated with the help of a 12-metre-long rotating machine called the 'trommel' (which, incidentally, is German for 'drum'). It rotates twelve times per minute, like a giant washing machine. Paper and cardboard, the lightest, are the first things to drop down holes in the middle, while a magnetic belt attracts metal such as aluminium cans and drinks cans. Finally, glass is crushed and separated from plastic using a giant sieve called a disc screen.

The other system, doorstep dividing, is superior, according to Friends of the Earth. The waste immediately becomes a commodity, minimizing the risk of it ending up in the wrong place. It is also easier to trust. You see your compost waste going into one lorry; your paper and cardboard into another and you have faith in the value of the separate materials.

From the sorting centre, lorries carry off the different materials to reprocessing plants across the country. My cans, made from recyclable steel, head to Birmingham, to the AMG metal plant where they are cleaned, melted down and turned into pellets. They are bought by Ford Motor Company Ltd, so they stand a chance of whizzing around on wheels next time round.

Most plastics, such as milk cartons, have a more tiresome journey ahead, in the cargo hold of a ship bound for China, or possibly Singapore – my London council is vague on this point. Here, they will be processed into flakes and pellets, which in turn will be sold to a packaging company of some kind, and probably shipped back over here. It's the same story for most of our plastic recycling, given the UK's limited means of reprocessing it on home soil. While this is still preferable to sending it to landfill in the UK, it might make you less inclined to buy that plastic bottle of mineral water next time.

The Trouble with Plastic and Packaging

Five reasons to make plastic your enemy

• It is an emblem of our throwaway lifestyles and a by-product of the petroleum industry: in other words, it comes from oil, which means it is non-sustainable. Plastic production uses 8 per cent of the world's oil production (according to Friends of the Earth).

• It is a tricky customer when it comes to recycling, made up of complex polymers that are difficult to separate. Many of the hybrid forms of plastic used in packaging cannot be recycled. Even with plastic that can be recycled, it is often cheaper for companies to make fresh stuff.

• The majority of our plastic waste that is collected for recycling ends up abroad because we have limited facilities for reprocessing it in the UK. There have been several scandals about the illegal dumping of British waste intended for recycling in Asia.

• If you burn it, it releases nasty things called dioxins, which you don't want to hang around with, for health reasons. This makes it a bad idea to incinerate plastic.

• Quite frankly, there's too much of it about. In the UK, we produce 3 million tonnes of it every year. According to FOE, 56 per cent of all plastic waste is packaging, and three-quarters of it (see *www.wasteonline.org.uk*) comes from household bins.

Take control of packaging

1 Don't buy products you feel are overpackaged. This sends out the message to manufacturers that items swathed in plastic are unpopular with consumers.

2 Buy from deli counters in supermarkets. Generally speaking, your meat and cheese will come with less packaging. It will not be freeze-packed nor rest on a polystyrene tray. It's often cheaper, too, and you can have a chat with the person working on the counter instead of limiting your shopping interaction to the trolley.

3 Buy fruit and vegetables loose wherever possible. Avoid packets of pre-chopped vegetables and ready meals that invariably require more packaging to keep them fresh. They don't taste as good either.

4 Support companies that are changing their packaging for the better. Two years ago, Heinz introduced a lighter baked beans can that required less steel, and Innocent was the first company to put its smoothies in bottles made up of 100 per cent recycled plastic. It's easy to find out about this stuff. Companies rarely miss an opportunity to explain what green steps they've taken, either in adverts or emblazoned on the products themselves.

5 Don't try to decipher what kind of plastic to recycle by looking at the symbol, unless your council tells you to. Broadly speaking, the grade of plastic is represented by a number: one being for high-grade plastic that is easily recyclable; six for yoghurt pots and plastic cups that many councils won't collect at all. But *wasteonline.org.uk* says this is a tricky way to work out what to do with materials. Many products feature symbols from abroad that we are unfamiliar with. You are better off phoning your council and acting on the information they give you – each region has access to different plastic reprocessing facilities anyway.

6 Biodegradable plastic cannot be recycled; it clogs up plastic reprocessing machines. Several pioneering sandwich companies have started to use it in the past few years and you may also come across carrier bags and bin bags that are biodegradable. Usually made from cornstarch, which on the plus side is a renewable resource, it is hotly debated how much they help. The material will biodegrade quickly (within roughly 12 weeks) when it ends its life in a compost bin, thanks to the hard work of micro-organisms (bacteria). However, buried in landfill, conditions will be less than perfect and it will take up to a year to decompose. Biodegradable carriers should be reused until they start to come apart and then ideally composted, or, as a last resort, put in the bin.

7 Don't be wooed by the term degradable – it is not the same as biodegradable and it's nothing to get too excited about. Unlike biodegradable plastic, which is made from plant-based materials, degradable plastic is made from oil, like normal plastic, and when it breaks down it doesn't disappear, it forms tiny particles of plastic. Everything degrades eventually, it is a question of how long the process takes and the environmental impact it has. Don't let supermarkets impress you with that one.

8 Look in your bin more often. Go on, open it up. What's going on in there? What are its main components? Once you've worked this out, try to alter your purchasing habits so that there are fewer of them.

9 If you're still fired up with anti-packaging rage, write to the companies responsible for overpackaged goods that offend you. Demand that they take a more sustainable approach.

Go cold turkey on plastic bags

Of all the obstacles to thwart our path to a greener life, the plastic bag takes prime position. Made from oil, a non-renewable, polluting material (according to the Worldwatch Institute, it takes 430,000 gallons of oil to produce 100 million plastic bags), an average person in the UK gets through about 167 a year – that's 10 billion a year across the whole country. They take 500 years to degrade, spouting that methane – a key contributor to climate change – and causing death and injury to marine animals and wildlife. (Check out the Plastic Ain't My Bag campaign on *www.wearewhatwedo.org.*)

Here's how to wean yourself away from them:

1 Designate an area in the kitchen for storing plastic bags for reuse. The more prominent, the more likely it is to jog your memory to grab one when you're leaving the house. Or equip yourself with a plastic-bag dispenser. Material ones look pretty dangling from a hook in the kitchen, cheerfully broadcasting their good intentions.

2 Get in the habit of stuffing a bag in your pocket or in your handbag when you leave the house. I keep a couple lurking in my cavernous handbags at all times. You never know when you're going to end up in a shop.

3 Explore other ways to put the plastic bags you have to good use. Line your bin with them, pack your sandwiches in them, use them for freezer bags or, for the undignified end they deserve – once they've served as shopping bags several times – turn them into pooper-scoopers.

4 Better still, secure a sturdier carrying vehicle. Plastic, after all, is an unstylish accessory. Then you can announce smugly to shop assistants that you don't want a bag; you have your own, thank you very much. Don't be put off by the Anya Hindmarch affair in which ethical consumers revealed their dark side by trampling on each other for the £5 bag sold in Sainsbury's; there are plenty of equally stylish shopping bags out there. I'm pleased as Punch with my Crazy Carpet Bag from Hatti Trading, and I've also got a tote bag from Superdrug which folds down to the size of a handkerchief.

5 Ignore any comments suggesting you are becoming a bag lady. You may have a pocket full of plastic and fabric bags slung over each shoulder, but you'll be feeling good about it.

Seasonal Food

With all those potatoes and leeks around the place, it's a good time to make warming **soups** – a relief after last month's meaty feasts. I like Nigel Slater's tip of floating old parmesan rinds in leek soup when you get to the 'adding stock' stage. Before you blend the mixture, don't forget to remove them, but only after scraping out every last smudge of cheesy yumminess.

Beetroot is also in season. Try it boiled, skinned, sliced and then drizzled in homemade chilli oil and a sprinkle of salt. Serve it hot or cold, with feta crumbled on top if you like, as a starter to nibble on or as a side dish.

A bottle of **homemade chilli oil** looks domestic goddessy on the table; does a wonderful job of spicing up pasta, pizza and winter veg, and only takes seconds to make. You need a bottle with an airtight top or cork – I save up pretty wine bottles for the job. Pour in the olive oil, followed by a couple of sprigs of rosemary and several chillies sliced down the middle. The seeds will spill out into the oil. Don't put too many chillies in at the beginning; you can always add more later if the oil doesn't have enough of a kick. Don't remove the cork at all for the first two weeks while it brews, then afterwards keep it in as much as possible to reduce the chance of any chillies that are exposed to the air going mouldy.

FEBRUARY

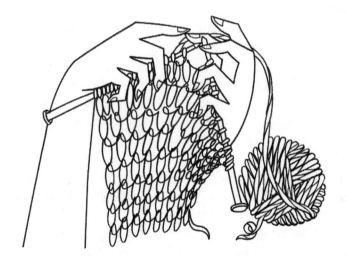

DRESSING IN A HALO

WHEN YOU HAVEN'T HAD FRESH BLOOD IN YOUR WARDROBE FOR SEVERAL MONTHS, the joy of stumbling upon a forgotten jumper or long-neglected dress is not to be underestimated. So when I recently pulled out a yellow crochet cardigan bought second-hand years ago, I could barely contain my excitement. It had been wedged between winter coats and I'd clean forgotten I owned it.

Yanking it from its hiding place, within seconds I was teaming it up with dozens of other outfits – and I've barely taken it off since.

It hasn't always been like this. There was a time when this sort of discovery would have inspired nothing more than a nonchalant shrug, a groan perhaps, not another cardie to find space for. That was before the days of my Wardrobe Challenge. In February, when all I wanted to do was wave my credit card at stylish garments that would take my mind off winter weather, I did the opposite. I vowed to stop buying new clothes for a year. Sick of filling my drawers with badly made, ethically dubious items that looked identical to everyone else's, I would survive on what I already had.

The idea came from a blog called Wardrobe Refashion that encouraged crafty chic and suggested that people renovate and reinvent their existing clothes. How hard could a fashion fast be, anyway, I thought. You simply tighten your purse strings and off you go.

Except that for the first months, I didn't go anywhere. To avoid temptation, I stayed at home, vigorously baking cakes as shopping replacement therapy and writing about the Challenge on my Eco-Worrier blog to see if I could rope anyone else into joining me. Before long, I could make a mean lemon drizzle, but I knew I had to get out more.

In truth, the challenge was not as extreme as it sounds. Let me explain the rules. While during the challenge I could not buy anything new, I could – and on rare and desperate occasions I did – take advantage of stuff already in circulation by shopping at charity shops and other second-hand stores.

The etiquette with gifts from friends was that if it was a cast-off, I accepted it; if brand new, I did my best to decline tactfully. As you will see, I was not too hard on myself. Otherwise, like a crash diet that is impressive to tell people about but totally unsustainable, the whole exercise falls apart.

The day before I officially began the challenge, I snatched a couple of hours on Oxford Street to pick up some essentials. It was my last chance to top up my tights drawer. This hadn't originally been a priority, but Gervase had looked appalled. 'What about underwear for the next year?' he'd said. 'Don't you think you should stock up?'

After seven happy years together, it was a bit of a blow. Was he having the same thought every night? 'Not that greying old bra again . . . and when will she jazz up her pants collection?' The thought was mortifying. If my ancient under-wear wasn't good enough for him, I'd have to get down to Marks and Spencer.

It was a filthy wet afternoon when I arrived and the shops were packed with the final post-Christmas sales crowds. It was the kind of day when you can see why a splurge on the high street might seem a reasonable way to lift spirits. But no one looked as though they were having fun. A light drizzle forced people low into their winter coats, avoiding eye contact. I saw stead-fast expressions on their faces that suggested they might not be enjoying it now, but their efforts would be worth it in the long run. I wasn't so sure.

I queued for my 'six for the price of five' packs of pants and bras and headed out into the rain. I reached the swinging doors as an undignified scrum started to gather around the sales racks. A lady rushed past me, letting the doors slam in my face. She was probably rushing to buy the last lacy bra,

I reasoned; maybe her partner had sent her. But still, I'd had enough of this.

There was a time when shopping felt like a treat, a pleasure to be indulged on a Saturday. As a teenager, I'd go to Cambridge. It was as much about the café you sat in and who you might bump into as what you'd bring home at the end of it – which would often be nothing. It's an old joke in my family that my sister only has to smell a shop and she'll want to stop for a coffee. But with only a Starbucks or another high-street chain to choose between and little chance of running into an old friend in a five-floored emporium, it's not quite the same.

For me it's not, anyway. Not because I'm a hardcore hippy who is as comfortable in a shapeless oatmeal smock as a slinky designer number. The fact is I liked to dash into Topshop on my lunch hour as much as the next girl. I always found the thrill of the new to be seductive and I confess to having had a terrible weakness for the 'nipping in when no one's looking' sort of shopping. And yet, while clothes remain an important part of my identity – you'll find plenty of high-street labels, along with charity shop bargains and hand-me-downs salvaged from the family dressing-up box, hanging in my cluttered wardrobe – high street shopping had already lost its panache. After a 'nipping in' purchase, generally I wore my trophy once, maybe twice, and then it lay around making me feel guilty.

Once I'd given it up, I felt happier, richer, and more like me. And I had masses of time on my hands. I found myself twiddling my thumbs when I got back from work, wondering what there was to do when you're not darting off to Hennes. I discovered that buying less enables you to do more.

Obviously you might not spend all those extra Saturday afternoons feeding your brain down the local library, but there's hope. I squandered it in the intellectually stimulating environment of my garden, tending to the wormery or fiddling around in the beds, trying to turn my fingers green.

While it might not work for everyone, I was also liberated from a lifelong habit of flicking through the fashion sections of newspapers. I don't mind admitting that I used to pore over them, prior to reading, say, the meaty foreign news pages. I always told myself it was because Gervase had nicked the serious bits, but I'm not sure if there was any truth in that. Instead I have a horrible feeling that I am hardwired to plump for pretty pictures over text-heavy articles. A shocking admission for a journalist. The fact is I liked the light relief of colourful girly magazines. But something changed. I no longer enjoyed eyeing up gladrags I couldn't afford. I have high hopes that I am becoming simultaneously greener and wiser.

And I can vouch for this as bliss. It's a chance to establish yourself outside of your consumer choices. To stop thinking that if only you could find the perfect summer jacket, your wardrobe would be complete. It's a common trap. You look for one item, convinced that it will put an end to your search and make you a satisfied individual, only to realize when you find it that you need just one more. The new garment itself gives rise to new needs, so you keep on looking – and buying.

As for how I looked, it's hard to tell. I didn't feel any worse for it. Friends probably knew my favourite outfits backwards, but I received no fewer compliments. To imagine that it is always your new top that makes you feel and look good is misguided. Most often, it is your mood. I've noticed that people remark that they like my clothes when I'm feeling happy and exuding confidence. It's nothing to do with what I'm wearing. Of the many sources of happiness, I've found that the sort that comes from what you've just bought is the least permanent.

And I'm not the only one to feel this. What surprised me is how many people got in touch to say that they are on some form of Wardrobe Challenge, and that it has altered the way they consume not just clothes but everything. Some of them have been at it for years. Far from doing something radical, I realized that I was a newcomer in a well-established network of resisters.

'My family cope quite well on second-hand clothes,' wrote Hannah. 'Every now and again the sewing gets started and we revamp what we have. Then we recycle what we don't want and buy some more from charity shops. Most of the presents I give my two boys come from car-boot sales or Freecycle. It works; do not be afraid.'

Nowhere is this network of consumer resistance better established than in San Francisco, where a group of friends decided to stop buying anything new, except 'health and safety items', food and underwear, three years ago. The movement is called the Compact and so-called compacters survive on eBay, Freecycle, donations and other sources of second-hand stuff, charting their progress on a blog (*http://sfcompact.blogspot.com*).

The same virtues of thrift and restraint were called upon by Judith Levine in her year of consumer resistance, as described in her book *Not Buying It: My Year Without Shopping*. As the title suggests, she bought nothing but health-care and food essentials for a year. The book looks at why we buy and what we get out of it; the same questions that Adbusters, a global network of activists, has encouraged people to consider for over a decade by holding a Buy Nothing Day every November (see *www.adbusters.org/bnd*). Buy less, do more, it advises, by locking up your purse for 24 hours and spending time with family and friends.

Saying no is becoming popular. When I explain to people my year of fashion rationing, they often ask if it was in this same spirit of anti-consumerism, or whether I expected to make a difference to the notoriously unethical fashion industry.

I'm quite happy to admit that I did it as much for my benefit as anyone else's. Like the compacters, I wanted to prove to myself that buying clothes does not define me; that I could take them or leave them. And while I expected to splash out on replacement jeans and frivolous frocks the moment the year was up, I found to my surprise that my appetite had shrunk. Like when you give up booze in January and the following month you discover that you only need a small glass of wine and you're slurring.

That is not to say that the thorny issue of cheap labour did not play an important part. In many ways, it was the clinching factor. When a report came out at the end of 2006 claiming that women in Bangladesh were working eighty hours a week for just 5p an hour to produce cheap clothes for the UK's high-street retailers, I made the decision to boycott these shops. The report, called *Fashion Victims* and published by the anti-poverty charity War on Want, based its findings on research among employees of six Bangladeshi factories. The cheapness of the clothes is the giveaway. Buy a T-shirt for £1.99 and somewhere along the line, probably all the way along, the people producing it will have been paid, and possibly treated, badly.

It's hard to pinpoint which retailers are the worst. That some have not come under fire from human rights campaigners is as likely to result from their having been lucky enough to duck the searchlight as from their ethical commitments.

I realized that it was quick-fix, low-cost and high-turnover fashion – let's call it 'fast fashion' – that I wanted to give the slip. The admirable opposite is 'slow fashion', a concept launched with a catwalk parade of ethical labels at the Soil Association's annual conference in 2007.

If slow food works on the concept that making time to eat, rather than succumbing to a quick fix, rewards you with satisfying nosh, slow fashion works on similar principles. Instead of a 'grab it, and a few months down the line dump it' approach, you buy less and of better quality. Now that I am post-Wardrobe Challenge, I am introducing myself to 'slow' retailers I feel I can trust, with the aim of buying clothes with a longer shelf-life. In other words, I buy less and buy better.

It helps to think about clothes in terms of 'wears per buy'. If you spend a tenner on a top from Primark and only wear it a couple of times before it goes out of shape or you get bored of it, that's five pounds per wear. A more expensive dress that you wear dozens of times can end up being better value.

I cannot say the year was always easy. I experienced a seven-month itch when my clothes were starting to look about as interesting as Gervase's sock drawer. Caught off-guard on a practical trip to the bank, I found myself heading, zombie-like, to a rail of dresses in Monsoon. Not even sure how I got there, all of a sudden I was fingering the price tag and the pristine fabric. A fog of desire descended and it took an enormous summoning of willpower to steer myself out of the shop. The funny thing was, once out in the street, I was relieved. The spell had been broken. I knew almost instantly that I didn't need another floral dress. What had I been thinking?

But would I manage to resist the next time? Would I last the year? To my rescue came wardrobe sorter and thrift connoisseur Kira Jolliffe. Best known for setting up *Cheap Date*, the cult fashion magazine that mocked mainstream trends and challenged consumer habits, co-edited by stylist Bay Garnett, Kira has now established herself as a wardrobe therapist, untangling the knots in people's cupboards.

Oddly for an ex-stylist and self-confessed clothes addict, she doesn't like shopping. She's very cynical about the high street, she told me as she peered into my wardrobe: 'I don't like being a cog in a wheel that I don't understand. The only thing I know is that the whole process is about making me part with my money.'

The best thing about having Kira over was that she was full of enthusiasm for my clothes. She had the knack of pulling out neglected dresses and saying: 'Have you tried wearing this with this top?' Genius: another outfit in the bag.

Being a wardrobe therapist, Kira says, is mostly common sense. It's about encouraging people to spend time thinking about their individual style and the clothes they enjoy wearing. Most people only wear a tiny proportion of what they have. (In my case, the ones that were scattered on the floor of my bedroom, giving me easy access.) If you have a lot of clothes, but still feel as though you have nothing to wear, you have to work out what is going wrong, Kira says. What habits you have developed that are encouraging you to shop in an inefficient way.

We sifted through everything, working out why I had stopped wearing certain outfits and how I could reinstate them. She suggested altering some professionally, not something I would normally think of. I would be more inclined to put a heap of them on the arm of the sofa, in the hope that the urge to sew might overwhelm me at some point in the next decade. To help me get through the year, she also proposed that I hide a couple of my favourite pieces, to whip out when I'm really losing the will to dress.

Talking this through was oddly revealing. It occurred to me that the internal monologue we have when we decide what to wear in the morning is deeply intimate and gets to the bottom of all sorts of feelings about our appearance. We choose clothes that hide our perceived faults and stop wearing certain clothes if we think they draw attention to them. This must be the therapy bit. I had to try to resist opening up to Kira about my childhood fashion traumas, most of which involved Clothkits and an enthusiastic seamstress for a mother.

The next day, for the first time in months, I was spoilt for choice. I realized I had enough in my cupboards to keep me in business for years. Once the crumpled balls at the back of a drawer and the piles under my bed had been unravelled and hung up in an orderly fashion, the possibilities were endless.

And should I get sick of my own supplies, there was always my sister's. Followed by the extensive collections of friends – some of whom tossed a frock or two my way in sympathy.

This sort of clothes swapping is nothing new, long practised by women who eye up each other's garments and wonder if they might look better in them. Traditionally done on a small scale, through people you know, maybe over tea and cake at someone's house, it's a brilliant way of breathing new life into your wardrobe.

But now a formal version of the clothes-swapping party, nicknamed 'swishing' by London-based sustainability company Futerra, is growing in popularity.

Similar to a jumble sale, it's a sort of Oxfam shop meets Women's Institute affair. Garments are brought along by a large number of party-goers and piled on to rails before being expertly pilfered through and redistributed, with no money changing hands. Punch and nibbles are generally provided to loosen inhibitions (otherwise who would take home the lime-green jumpsuit?). At one I visited – before embarking on my fashion fast – I left in a completely new outfit. A fabulous pink miniskirt and a linen blouse.

And did I mention how much money the Wardrobe Challenge saved me over the year? An estimated £900, to splurge on, ahem, eco-friendly products like water butts. I worked out that normally I spend roughly £80 a month on new clothes. Over the twelve months of the challenge, I spent a meagre £60 (on a second-hand dress, a T-shirt and a skirt).

The risk was that I would shift my consumer appetite straight on to other things, like nesting materials for our flat. Deprived of new clothes, I might develop a soft-furnishings habit or start spending ridiculous sums at the garden centre. To some extent, this did happen. Not with cushions or compost bins but with food. Delis became my new Hennes. Marinated artichokes began to unleash the same yearning that empire-line dresses once did. On the rare times I braved a shopping trip with friends, they beelined for Topshop; I whiled away the time browsing delis.

Food apart, though, I became acutely conscious of anything I bought and I am now more questioning about whether I really want to hand over my money for something. Do I want to line the pocket of this company? This is encouraging me to shop from responsible fashion labels. It is a pleasure to browse sassy labels such as Edun, set up by Bono's wife Ali Hewson (*www.edunonline.com*), and Brighton-based Enamore (*www.enamore.co.uk*) with its silky kimono tops and vintage-print bolero jackets, and so convenient to have an online ethical emporium such as Adili (*www.adili.com*).

Having done a good job of shaking off its sandals reputation, ethical fashion – generally considered to involve garments that are made adhering to fair trade and environmental principles – is making progress. It is more pricey, yes, but the important thing is that while the money is properly distributed, the clothing itself is standing up in the style stakes. Where once we might have supported ethical retailers as our good deed of the day, now we can lust over handwoven tea-dresses from People Tree and pink satin heels from vegan shoe company Beyond Skin. (Note: leather, despite being a natural material, consumes considerable amounts of energy, water and chemical solvents during its production.)

But my concern with ethical fashion – and ethical consumerism in general – is that it becomes about buying differently rather than less. I'm all for companies being more accountable and I certainly don't want to rain on the eco-fashion parade – especially now it has become such a fetching one – but I worry that an ethical stamp becomes an excuse to splash out. It's our way of wriggling out of environmental problems. Shop with Bono's American Express Red card, we are told, and because you're raising money for fighting Aids in Africa, your consumerist sins will be forgiven.

But you cannot buy your way to being green. If you could, I agree, it would be an easier message to spread. An afternoon spent in Selfridges hunting down organic Levi's is significantly more fun than staying at home and mending the holes in your old ones. But it will not repair the damage we are doing to our planet. For that we need to become judicious shoppers, consuming less and living within our limits to allow others their fair share of the earth's resources.

I can safely say that consuming less, instead of differently, doesn't need to be the dreary option. I have found new ways to reward myself after a long day in the office. A stiff gin and tonic with a girlfriend, a long walk ending with pints in the pub, or a lovingly prepared meal for me and Gervase. As a forbidden treat, I can always flick through a fashion magazine to gaze at the clothes that I now know I don't really need. Life doesn't get more satisfying than that.

WHAT'S IN IT FOR THE PLANET?

Buy less . . . and you will reduce your contribution to the 900,000 tonnes of textile waste we create in the UK every year. When clothes go to landfill, synthetic material doesn't decompose at all, while woollen garments produce methane, contributing to global warming. There are also the resources required to manufacture textiles to consider. The processes involve irrigation, fertilizers, bleaching and dyeing, all of which require considerable energy and water.

Buy organic . . . and you will reduce the amount of pesticides that are being used across the world to treat cotton crops. Mass-produced cotton accounts for more than 22 per cent of the world's insecticides and 10 per cent of the world's chemical fertilizers. The WHO (World Health Organization) has linked this to an estimated three million instances of pesticide poisoning among farmers every year.

Buy quality . . . and you will reduce the chance that your clothes have been produced in sweatshops in the developing world where workers get low wages to work long hours with few labour rights. By getting in the habit of asking your favourite retailers how and where their clothes are produced and whether they have signed up to the Ethical Trading Initiative, the message will sink in that consumers want them to take responsibility for the way clothes are made.

Myths About Being an Ethical Fashionista

The clothes are ugly and unstylish

That sort of assumption is out of date. Have you checked out the Adili website recently (*www.adili.com*)? Or admired designs by ethical T-shirt company Tonic T-shirts (*www.tonictshirts.com*), which include vintage images of David Hasselhoff and *EastEnders*' Dot Cotton, among other cultural icons? And how can anyone live without American Apparel's leggings? As far as I can see, this US-based company spends most of its energies promoting workers' rights and creating sexy adverts. Its shamelessly bright clothes, mostly cotton basics and undies, are irresistible.

You don't get fine fabrics

This couldn't be further from the truth. More care is taken in the production of ethical garments; the process is often audited and the companies selling the clothes are likely to be involved in each step, from raw material to garment hanging on the rail. The quality of the fabric is generally higher. According to Safia Minney, People Tree's founder, it is usually after customers have tried on an organic cotton wrap dress or a handspun silk skirt that they are converted to eco-fashion. Unlike with fast fashion, where the focus is on creating something as quickly and cheaply as possible, the best of ethical fashion involves making imaginative use of handwoven fabrics and natural, breathable fibres, such as merino wool.

It's too expensive

You have a point. Your purse doesn't always thank you for doing the right thing. You might feel better about buying a T-shirt certified by the Fairtrade Foundation or an organic pair of jeans, but it can be slightly more expensive. With Fairtrade fashion, you pay a little bit more to guarantee that the producer has been given a fixed and decent price, regardless of fluctuating world market prices – just like with a Fairtrade cappuccino. But it's only too expensive if you insist on shopping for new clothes every week. Shop less, buy better clothes and you will still save money.

You can't shop on the high street any more

By all means shop on the high street, if it suits your taste and budget, but make sure you ask questions while you're there. Be an active consumer. Find out if your favourite retailer has signed up to the Ethical Trading Initiative. If not, why not? Can the manager tell you where the clothes have come from? By visiting the resources page on *www.labourbehindthelabel.org*, you can arm yourself with ethical ammunition.

Then there's the debate about whether to trust multinational companies that play the green card. I suggest developing a highly tuned 'greenwash detector' to uncover companies that are flexing their eco-muscles to little effect. Do this by paying special attention to the depth of their commitment and the details of how and when they are going to put it into practice. Find out if they have followed up on their promises. That I am giving the high street the cold shoulder does not mean that progress isn't being made. Sometimes it is worth reassessing long-held grudges.

I won't be able to wear vintage fur

This one's up to you. Most vegans, vegetarians and dark-green hardliners would be appalled at any kind of fur-wearing since it sends out the message not only that it is acceptable to kill animals and wear their skins but also that it looks good. Vintage or modern-day, it is difficult to know exactly where your fur came from and whether the animal was killed humanely. And yet there are those who count themselves as eco-aware individuals who still slip into something warm and furry on a frosty February night. I admit that the skeleton in my closet is a fox-trim winter coat that belonged to my mother. As well as playing the family-heirloom card, I weakly defend wearing it for cold weather emergencies with the argument that I'm not perpetuating the fur trade. My granny kindly did that for me by buying the coat for my mother. Nor am I adding to textile waste by dumping it. My belief is that it's better to recycle vintage fur than bundle it into a cupboard for the moths to feast on. The honourable thing to do would be to donate it to a homeless charity or make a pet an extremely cosy basket-lining with it.

I'll start wearing socks and sandals and munching muesli

Socks with sandals would be wrong, that much I agree, but muesli is delicious. Munching it for breakfast is highly recommended for health and taste. Make your own by piling porridge oats, nuts and seeds (of your choice) on a baking tray and toasting for 20 minutes in a hot oven. Then mix them up with some raisins and chopped apricots or other dried fruit; add some extra untoasted porridge oats if you want to bulk it out, and store in an airtight storage jar. As for sandals, I can't live without my Birkenstocks in the summer. Sandals marched away from their stodgy rambling associations years ago, so what exactly are you worrying about?

Washing Clothes the Green Way

Fill the machine

Go on, pile 'em in. Not just the meagre lump of clothes you think will fill the drum: the whole lot. As well as cutting back on water and energy, this will mean the bother of putting on a wash will come around less often too. Machines usually take about 5kg (11lb) of clothes and, while the drum may look too full to clean them properly, once the water floods in, they will shrink, leaving more space. Only when the combined forces of your household can't shut the door, or you have forgotten to account for a heavy bedspread that will take up more room, have you gone too far.

Wash on a low temperature

Times have changed since a scalding wash was the only way to clean your clothes. Modern washing detergents work just as well at low temperatures. By using a 40-degree wash cycle instead of 60, you will use a third less electricity. Reduce it to 30 degrees and you'll cut it in half. And no compromise on cleanliness, I promise.

Try an eco-friendly detergent

We all get fixed in domestic routines, choosing one washing powder (or liquid) over another because of its familiar smell or special-offer status. But it's important to shake things up now and again. Go for a phosphate-free detergent because phosphates are fertilizers that stimulate algae growth when they end up in our water system. Algae use up the oxygen in the water, suffocating fish and other aquatic life. Give Ecover's washing detergent a whirl; as well as being phosphate-free, it is made from renewable, plant-based ingredients that break down easily in our waterways. (For more about Ecover, see page 73.)

Hang out to dry

One of the most energy-gobbling appliances in the home is the tumble-drier. By reducing the number of times you use it by just one load a week, you will reduce your carbon dioxide emissions by 91kg a year. Even better, cut it out of your life completely and turn to the glorious outside where you can dry your clothes in the breeze. There's nothing like it: wicker laundry basket balanced on hip; boyfriend's socks flapping in the wind. Not everyone's idea of heaven but I have taught myself to enjoy the shameless domesticity of hanging out washing. It's the sort of thing that leads to apron-wearing and cake-baking – which might or might not be considered a good thing. Watch out for rain, which ruins the whole thing. It forces you to pursue indoor drying techniques, the success of which depends on space and equipment. Rather than draping bed linen over doors, where it picks up enough dirt and dust to merit another cycle in the machine, consider investing in a collapsible free-standing drying rack or a nifty airer that hangs off radiators, reducing the need for ironing.

Avoid dry cleaning

Blame a chemical called perc (perchloroethylene) for causing so much trouble. It does a good job of cleaning, but it's also carcinogenic and a polluter of air and water supplies. Then there are the swathes of plastic your clothes are dressed in when they are returned to you and those pointless safety pins and extra clothes hangers. All of which suggests this is a process that should be avoided whenever possible. Think twice before buying garments that are dry-clean only; for those clothes that must be dry-cleaned, their only salvation is the march of the green cleaners. Perc-free and coming to a high street near you. The Johnson Services Group, which owns Sketchleys, uses a process called GreenEarth, which uses a less polluting silicon-based solvent to clean clothes.

The sniff test

Everyone in my family uses this reliable method to decide what
needs to be washed without delay and what can be worn again.
Sometimes an outdoor airing is all clothing needs not a full-blown
spin in the machine. I'm not endorsing Swampy standards – a return
to the time when being green was associated with slightly whiffy
road protestors who lived up trees – but it is worth checking that
you're not tossing clothes in the laundry pile just to avoid hanging
them up. I'm speaking from experience.

Try it in February . . .

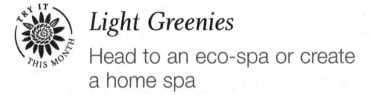

Light Greenies
Head to an eco-spa or create
a home spa

A month like February, one must scatter with as many treats as possible,
otherwise the combination of bad weather, lack of light and distance from
summer holidays can get you down. So it makes sense that many of us book
in for a soak and a scrub at a spa. But before you curl up on one of the countless fluffy, freshly laundered towels, I'm afraid it is my duty to alert you to the
fact that spas are resource-gobblers.

They rely on water and heat, along with truckloads of pool chemicals and overpackaged beauty products. Behind the scenes, an army of appliances – from dishwashers and washing machines to vehicles delivering just the right blend of alfalfa sprouts and fresh salmon for your lunch – work to ensure that your body and mind are rebalanced.

Unless, that is, you visit the UK's one truly halo-worthy eco-spa. Set in a converted mill in Huddersfield, Titanic Spa has its own water borehole – the original water source for the mill – which provides drinking water as well as water for the swimming pool and showers. No chlorine is used, or other water chemicals. Electricity comes from photovoltaic roof tiles and heating from a biomass generator that burns chippings from industrial waste.

Can't manage a trip to Huddersfield? Then create a home spa. Stock up on soya wax candles to place around the bath – these are made from a sustainable resource, unlike paraffin wax, and last longer – and use up all the half-finished oils and cosmetics that litter the bathroom cupboards (unless they are more than two years old, in which case there's not much to do but chuck them out, especially if the consistency has changed or there is any discolouring). You'll also need some fancy herb teas and, ideally, the house to yourself, so banish any significant other for the evening. Should they refuse to take the hint, at least put them to good use by employing them as a masseur.

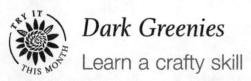

Dark Greenies
Learn a crafty skill

For life's natural knitters and crochet queens, as well as the seamstresses among us, buying fewer clothes and all the thriftiness that goes with it must be a piece of cake. A few evenings on the sofa with a bag of wool and the *24* box set and they've whipped up a new outfit without the worry of cheap labour and inflated price tags. But the rest of us should not be disheartened.

Even if you can barely attach a button to a shirt, it is never too late to pick up a needle and thread, or, for that matter, a knitting needle. Ideally, get an old hand to teach you. Or you might find that your nearest department store offers lessons.

Over the past few years, old-fashioned crafts have flourished. Knit Chick networks and public knit-ins, as well as the brilliantly named and American-led Stitch and Bitch network, have cropped up all over the country. If knitting isn't your cup of tea, try crochet. Even the word sounds somehow more exotic. It's got that 1970s vibe: a little bit cooler, the stitches are looser, you even drop the needles and use a hook, so none of that clackety, clackety, watch-out-or-I'll-poke-your-eye-out thing that you get with knitting.

My only word of advice is that you try it out before promising shawls to friends and booties to unborn babies. Despite my own efforts being supported by a session with a crochet guru in the haberdashery department of John Lewis, I only managed a small yellow square, at which point I forgot how to turn corners and promptly gave up. The perfect beer mat, pronounced Gervase, kindly.

But don't let that put you off. Even if the product of your labour is not a masterpiece, the process is immensely satisfying. It exercises a completely different part of your brain and it's just the trick for fidgets who can't relax or fingers that are missing a cigarette.

Eco-Cheats

• Once you know that a mobile phone charger uses up energy whether or not it has a phone attached to the end of it, it's harder to leave them switched on at the wall. To encourage other less energy-savvy members of your home to follow suit, put sticky labels on the chargers saying Turn Me Off, Please. It worked for me.

• Spend an evening every few months going through all your clothes, pulling everything out of the cupboard and reminding yourself what you've got. After you've tried on a million different combinations, you'll probably realize that you don't need a trip to the shops after all. Instead, you can spend the day clearing up the mess you've made of the bedroom.

• Find alternative uses for clothes you don't wear any more. Turn a much-loved but past-it skirt into lining for a chest of drawers. Cut it into rectangles using pinking shears; the scraps you could use as dusters.

Sprucing Up Your Wardrobe

Ten tips from wardrobe therapist Kira Jolliffe

- Neatness is the way forward. Be tidy and organized to make the most of the clothes you already have.

- Weed out what you never wear. It's a waste of space.

- Hang your clothes in order so you can easily see what you've got. All the skirts together; all the trousers together. It might sound a bit OCD, but you'll know where to look in the morning when you're half dressed.

- Time is crucial. Spend lots of it with your wardrobe, trying out different combinations and getting to the bottom of exactly what you've got to work with.

- Make sure you have good lighting and a decent mirror.

- Iron out any knots in your cupboard. Do you have lots of tight jeans but find them uncomfortable? Are you unable to let go of clothes you can't fit into? It's better to have a slimmed-down wardrobe full of stuff you wear than a huge one of stuff you don't.

- Get in the habit of repairing your clothes. Either by sewing up little rips yourself or, if you can't face a DIY job, finding a local alterations specialist.

- And nurture a good relationship with your specialist. Then you can extend the life of the clothes you love when they start looking tatty. And, if you like the fabric of something but you no longer like the garment as it is, it can be turned into something else.

- Remember what you like. It sounds obvious, but with so many things crowding in for our attention, retaining an individual sense of style can be a challenge. Think about which combinations you like best and why, and then see if you can create more of them.

- Don't throw any clothes away at the end of it. Think about which of your friends might like certain items, give them to charity shops or give them to Kira – she thrives on hand-me-downs.

How to Host a Clothes-swapping Party

- Season change is a good time for a clothes swap. Hold off until the end of February or October if you can, when spring/winter is around the corner and people are wondering what to do with all their winter woollies/summer dresses.

- Choose a date and a place. It could be your living room, a pub garden or a town hall. Real parties require invitations; email is fine, it saves paper.

- State on the invite that each clothes swapper should bring at least one good quality, clean item of clothing to gain access. Ideally, they should bring bags full of them.

- Prepare some food and nibbles. Even if it's only a few plates of Twiglets and a rum-laced fruit punch.

- You'll need as many rails and full-length mirrors and as much changing space as possible. Chairs and ladders can also be used for displaying clothes creatively.

- Encourage people to participate in any way they would like. Lucky Dips are always popular. Use a laundry basket filled with ripped-up newspaper and scatter Fairtrade chocolate bars and organic soap within. Charge people 50p a go, which you can either give to charity or use to cover the cost of the party.

- Say you invite people for 7pm, don't officially start the clothes swapping until 8pm. Otherwise the early birds will get all the good stuff and latecomers will moan.

How to Spice Up Your Undies Drawer
(or the Virtues of Dyeing)

Not totally won over by either the eco-friendliness or the aesthetic merits of home-dyeing clothes, I was tempted not to include it at all. Then I looked fondly upon my pea-green pants and remembered the fun I had concocting a potion of Dylon dye, salt and greying undies. If it revives tired clothes and prolongs the life of what's in your drawers, what the hell, it's worth a mention. It's not hard to do, either. You simply heap the clothes you want to transform into your machine with the dye (instead of washing powder), a large amount of salt and on the second cycle some detergent to fasten the dye.

Here are some things to remember:

- Don't try to dye synthetic items. Natural fabrics, such as cotton and linen, are ideal dyeing materials. As my reminder of why not to bother with synthetics, I now have a jacket shrunk to dwarf proportions.

- Often the dye will work only on parts of the garment depending on the different fabrics. While this could lead to a pretty two-tone effect – I am perfectly happy with my pile of apple-green pants with their original purple trim – it could also lead to disaster, if, for instance, the idea was to mask the garment's original colour.

- Use the colour advertised on the dye packet as only a vague indication of what your clothes might look like. It might be my own pathetic failure to follow instructions, but each of my items took to the dye differently and came out a slightly different shade.

- Expect to feel guilty about the amount of water and energy required. The process involves three 40-degree washing cycles – roughly 195 litres of water each time. The first introduces the dye to your clothes; the second binds it with detergent; the third cleans your drum so you're not responsible for turning your husband's shirts a light shade of lime. Dyeing is not necessarily the greenest way to approach fashion, but as a means of updating your clothes, it should be weighed up against the alternative. Shopping for new items involves packaging, raw materials being used and transport to get you to and from the shops.

How to darn a sock

It might not be for everyone, but I find an episode of darning worn or moth-munched socks and jumpers every month or so to be a pleasant way to spend some time. Especially if you're sitting in front of a roaring fire with a decent film on the telly and a mug of hot chocolate by your side. I'm not very good at it, mind. My mum gave me a lesson a few years ago, but I promptly forgot most of it and now I make it up as I go.

It's pretty obvious what you're trying to do: fill a hole with darn. Should you fail miserably, you can do what generations of women have done before you and nick your boyfriend/husband's socks. There's an unspoken rule about this: once sock is on foot, you have ownership rights.

Here's what you will need:

• One mushroom – a wooden version, that is – over which to rest your holey item.

• Some wool or darn, sometimes called mending thread.

• One wool needle – different from a normal needle by being blunter, with a bigger eye.

• One mug of good quality hot chocolate, ideally made by someone else.

Here's what my mum recommends:

• Don't wait for the hole to develop. Darn a sock, jumper sleeve or whatever, as soon as it wears thin.

• First go around the hole to stop it from fraying, picking up any loose threads and making the circumference of the hole neater.

• Then with your needle and thread, pick up a loop of wool from the edge of the hole and take your thread across, picking up another loop of wool on the other side. Come back across the underside, slightly further along the hole. Keep going, picking up loops in the circumference and making stripes across the hole.

• Then once you've done this, you can start weaving, taking your needle over and under the stripes from left to right, working from top to bottom – or bottom to top! What you're doing here is weaving a bit of extra sock across the hole.

• By the end, you'll be able to freestyle, weaving in and out of any bit that needs extra support. Finish off neatly.

• Admire your sock. If it's a disaster, cry: 'Darned sock!' and go and nick your boyfriend's, citing sock rule (above).

Seasonal Food

Cabbage gets a tough time from most people but to wrinkle your nose at its mere mention is unfair. Time to consign school dinners to the past, OK? Packed with vitamins, it goes beautifully in a beany broth or sliced thin as part of a pasta bake. I like the red variety during the cold months, bubbling on the stove for at least an hour with brown sugar, a couple of cloves, a glug of cider vinegar and a few slices of apple. Served with your butcher's best sausages and maybe a smattering of lentils, it brightens up a winter supper.

MARCH

THE TYRANNY OF CLEAN

WHEN DID WE BECOME SO CLEAN? THAT IS WHAT I WONDER AS I CRUISE SHOP AISLES in early spring taking in the dizzying number of products dedicated to banishing filth. I'm not talking personal hygiene here – any advances on that front can only be a good thing – but in our homes. At what point did we start yearning for floors so spotless that you could eat your morning bowl of muesli off them, and bathrooms blitzed with an army of bacteria-killing sprays?

You may think this is hardly something to worry about: if our lives are fresh as a daisy, so be it. But I'm suspicious, always have been, of superior levels of hygiene. Maybe it's because I've never been able to achieve them myself. Or maybe it's the result of being brought up in a house that was often less than gleaming. But I can't help wondering what horrors people hope to hide by sloshing bleach around like a cabin boy cleaning the decks.

The fact is that cleanliness is always going to be an uphill struggle. Life in its natural state is grubby around the edges. Take your eye off the game for more than a few moments and a layer of grime will have built up under the sofa and behind your ears. Everyone has their own way of keeping on top of this – an attempt to preserve order among chaos. My own is based around denial for most of the year, with a touch of obsessive devotion thrown in now and again.

It is when spring unfolds and the first watery sun warms the window panes (showing up all the dirt) that I am most inclined to pull on the Marigolds, don some kind of flowery headband and hop to it, with great swoops of the mop and dramatic wipes of my brow. The work is hardly inspiring, but I enjoy the occasion of it. After all, the concept of a spring clean makes sense. It is at this time of year that you feel perky enough to pull yourself out of a groggy winter stupor and prepare your home for the brighter, warmer months. In the right mood, on the right day, when the desire to create a new gleaming start to the season takes you, it's really not that bad.

As for method and required artillery, all of that changed when I visited a factory in Belgium that makes the UK's best-selling eco-friendly cleaning products. On an industrial estate outside Antwerp, Ecover HQ churns out 130,000 halo-worthy household cleaning products every day.

The factory alone is a vision of a better world. Made from several tonnes of sustainable wood and recycled bricks, its crowning glory is a 5,600-square-metre sedum roof: a living, breathing meadow of vegetation. This, combined with south-facing positioning and a ceiling studded with skylights, allows the building to run without central heating or air-conditioning, and with little artificial light.

Inside, cardboard boxes and plastic packaging are recycled and there's a water purification system that enables waste water to be used again. There's even a low-energy robot, called Bruno, who busily boxes up products with minimum movements. I stop to admire him, wondering if Ecover would lend him to me when I move house.

It is on this trip that I am reminded why it matters what chemicals go down our sink. Like everyone else, I learnt at school about how our waterways have to cope with the dirty water we slosh down the drain, but I suppose I'd stopped thinking about it. One of the luxuries of life in a developed country like Britain is that the unpleasant aspects of daily life are discreetly removed – usually flushed down the pan – and promptly forgotten about.

Ecover's managing director, Mick Bremans, patiently explains to me how the petroleum-based ingredients that form the basis of conventional cleaning products do not easily break down, instead accumulating in our water system. When they do degrade, many release toxic compounds that harm fish and other wildlife.

Phosphates, he says, are a good example. They encourage algae to grow and therefore suffocate aquatic life.

To combat this, a number of green cleaning products have been developed, made from plant- and mineral-based substances that biodegrade quickly and without toxic repercussions. You can buy the bigger ranges, such as Ecover, in supermarkets, and the smaller ones in health-food and organic shops.

An added advantage is their health benefits, what Mick calls 'skin compatibility'. Plant-based products are popular with people who have sensitive skin or respiratory problems such as asthma, since the complex chemicals in other products have been linked to a range of health problems from diarrhoea and earache in children to headaches and depression in adults.

This is a subject plagued with controversy. Scientists say that when chemicals are said to be 'linked' to illnesses, this normally means that there is not enough scientific evidence to prove that the substances actually cause the problem; in other words, the jury is still out. Environmental groups such as Friends of the Earth respond by pointing out that there has not been enough long-term research into the effect of many chemicals used in household cleaners on human health to prove either way.

When I leave Belgium (by Eurostar, not plane, of course), I have a new perspective on the contents of the cupboard under my kitchen sink. I return with renewed commitment to respect the water system. I imagine I'll have to rid myself of myriad cleaning products that are sure to wipe out generations of aquatic life every time I give my loo the once-over. But, in fact, my cupboards are puzzlingly bare.

A couple of bottles of ancient multipurpose spray donated by concerned family members, some vinegar for unblocking the sink and de-limescaling the showerhead, and that's about it. I already have green cleaning instincts, you see, sometimes known as non-cleaning.

But before I stock up on biodegradable supplies from companies such as Ecover, what should be done with the old stuff? It seems wrong to chuck it, especially since it will only leak into landfill sites and seep into our water system anyway. Surely pouring it down the sink in one go would be even worse, and, if I keep it, I risk being led astray and reverting to it in my moment of need.

This is just the sort of dilemma that environmentalist Donnachadh McCarthy likes to get his teeth into. As an eco-auditor, he visits homes answering similar queries and giving advice on how households can lessen their impact on the environment. I ring him to say that I am considering boxing up some products and giving them to the bin men. He says I'd be better off palming them off on friends who buy conventional cleaning products anyway. At least then they won't be buying new stuff.

So the next time people come for supper, instead of an after-dinner chocolate, I offer round my multipurpose cleaners. No one's keen. It's hard to do a sales job on something that you don't want darkening your own kitchen cupboards. They're bad for the planet and possibly give you asthma, but anyone want one of these? It's not a tempting proposition. As a green cleaning conversion tactic, it works a treat, but I'm left with my sinful supply and some rather bewildered dinner guests. In the end, they loiter menacingly in the kitchen, until I do the dirty and chuck them out (the products that is, not my guests).

Donnachadh's other advice on green cleaning is that a bit of elbow grease goes a long way. Before I get hooked on the latest range of green cleaning products – that don't always come cheap, by the way – he suggests I try my hands at traditional methods using an assortment of good-value household products such as vinegar and bicarbonate of soda. You can buy these in bulk on the internet from companies such as Summer Naturals (*www.summernaturals.co.uk*).

Some of them, I already put to good use. Vinegar has always been chucked down my loo instead of bleach (see recipes, page 89), mainly because I'm more likely to have it to hand, and I rely on bicarbonate of soda to remove tea stains off mugs. But I've never managed to clean a window with vinegar – in fact, I've never managed to clean a window at all, only smear it and get cross that I've made it look worse than it did in the first place. Nor have I been able to get a sink sparkling with lemon juice. And, quite frankly, I don't imagine it'll be easy.

So begins Operation Green Clean. With recipes gleaned from Friends of the Earth, I set about the front window. It suggests cleaning windows first with soapy water, followed by a solution of one part vinegar to four parts water and finally using crumpled newspaper to dry-shine the glass.

It's tough on my upper arms, acting as an evening gym session at the very least, but amazingly it works and I have more success than I did last time, when I used a lurid blue window-cleaning product that was probably about as eco-friendly as an oil spill. As my confidence grows, I invent my own recipes, including a lemon and vinegar mixture to scrub the bath, adding half a cup full of salt at the last minute for exfoliation purposes.

I'd love to flash a dazzling smile at this point and insist that all this makes cleaning less of a bore, but I don't think you'd buy it. What I can honestly say is that the dreary process is brightened by the potion-making element of green cleaning. It's a bit like cooking, mixing up these peculiar concoctions. Except you don't have to worry about taste or presentation, just slap it on and see what happens.

It's ideal for a professional procrastinator like me, as I pootle around the house trying to find distractions from writing. If time is at a premium, I would recommend combining the homemade approach with some reliable green cleaning products. At least then your vinegar use won't leave the whole house smelling like a fish and chip shop.

As with all aspects of greening up, it's not all or nothing. You can pick and choose which parts of your cleaning duties you do with green products and for which you prefer to stick with your old supplies. I have plenty of friends who are more than happy to use Ecover washing-up liquid but still prefer a splash of something stronger inside the toilet. I'm not saying that I don't try to thrust bottles of vinegar in their hands every time they visit the bathroom, but I don't blame them for taking one green-cleaning step at a time.

Whatever happens, don't be a sucker for the smell of conventional cleaning products. The biodegradable products I use, including a floor polish that contains linseed oil, give off a gentle, often lemony odour. They don't immediately alert you to the fact that your home has been cleaned. There is no talk of pine forests and lilac fields on the bottle, which if you ask me is a good thing. The sweet sickly odour of many cleaning products are supposed to be reminiscent of the natural world, but if a lilac field smelt anything like the toilet product I once came across with the same name, our planet really would be in trouble.

The problem is that we have come to associate fake smells and gleaming furniture with cleanliness, even though the reality is that we are being won over by smelly, shiny residues and artificial musks. This means that committing to a green spring clean requires a shift in expectations. You have to realize that your home is still clean even if it doesn't smell like your great aunt's favourite bowl of pot-pourri.

You won't be surprised to hear this suits me fine. I'd rather my home smelt of the fresh flowers I picked for the kitchen table, or even of the burnt toast leftover from breakfast, than an odour called 'pine' that has never even seen a forest. These are life smells, not fake smells. I'd go further and say that I prefer my home not to be scrubbed to perfection every week.

That's why I'm backing a return to life that is grubby around the edges. The only problem is that you have to make sure that whoever you live with is on-message. I can't say I've ever had to wrestle Gervase to the floor to stop him bleaching the bathroom, but he isn't naturally inclined to favour green cleaning strategies. While he is up for many aspects of eco-living, particularly if it involves drinking local ale (to support our indigenous booze habits, he claims), anything that makes the job of cleaning longer or harder will not easily win his vote.

There have been a few clashes on this matter, including one, a few years ago, in which he wielded a terrifyingly toxic oven cleaner, an item laden with such a catalogue of unpronounceable and corrosive chemicals that I was convinced he should handle it only once he was togged up in a nuclear mask and overalls. Given that our oven hadn't been properly cleaned for two years (I did warn you about my non-cleaning habits), even committed eco-enthusiasts may have been forced to lay down their homemade vinegar spray and give in to the heavyweights. Only this, I was forced to admit at the time, would guarantee the deposit back on our rented flat.

That's the thing about green cleaning. If you're using products that are made from natural, biodegradable materials, often plant extracts, they are going to be less powerful. Don't expect to kick back on the sofa to the sound of fizzing and flying sparks. It follows that you have to clean more regularly to keep on top of the grime. Neglecting an oven for two years, I hasten to add, turns out not only to be unhygienic but also ungreen. Such an eco-sin can be forgiven once, but I've vowed to mend my ways.

But enough of my slovenly habits, back to domestic tensions. If it was only ovens and how to clean them that sparked me and Gervase off, ours would be an easy life. Instead it has gradually dawned on me that we have a new arena in which to conduct our squabbles. Like everything else, they have gone green.

How to run your home, who makes purchasing decisions and whether to pay more for green products are just some of the subjects that can descend  into sharp words and conflicting views. This, I'm afraid to say, is the territory of the eco-argument. Instead of traditional rowing subjects that have rattled couples for generations – who does the washing-up and why the shared bank account is overdrawn – raised voices now belt out words such as Fairtrade, food miles and flight restrictions. Accusations of carbon criminality have become daily occurrences in some families, along with less articulate insults.

For us it all started with a kettle. A full one, I should add. Too full, I said, for tea for two. 'Think of the wasted energy when you boil all that water! Is this what happens when you make the morning tea?' Breakfast was ruined. Once it lay in tatters, what was the point in holding back. My beloved told me that I was a green bully. Worse than that, he tried to blame the row on what he infuriatingly calls 'my controlling tendencies'.

To prove my point, I demonstrated how seven cups of tea could be made with the water he had boiled (perhaps this was overdoing it). He said if I cared so much why didn't I run off with Swampy. Anyway, it escalated, as these things do, and before we knew it, we were in the grip of our first fully fledged eco-domestic.

Sometimes, I am ashamed to say, they come thick and fast. There was the time I nipped back to the flat for my packed lunch. Lo and behold, my planet-trashing other half was in the bedroom with the electric blow heater on full blast and the window wide open. What better way to abuse electricity. If I hadn't had to rush off to work, it could have turned nasty. Switching lights off is another well-trodden battlefield. Five minutes is the amount of time you need to be out of the bedroom to make it worth switching off the light, I say, quoting the Energy Saving Trust. 'But I was about to go back upstairs,' he mumbles, slumped in front of *Prison Break*.

While I like to think that virtue is always on the side of the green and it goes without saying that I parade the moral high ground – uttering a heartfelt 'think of our grandchildren' if I think it'll sway the argument in my favour – I can imagine why you might be on Gervase's side. My friends often are. When I regale tales of pea-green domestic disruptions, I can tell they are silently sympathizing with him. Imagine living with someone who has a go at you before you've had your morning tea, they're probably thinking. The traitors.

Indeed, I begin to wonder myself, as I punch the TV standby button off for the umpteenth time, if I am the only one saving the planet at the expense of my relationship. Will I end up a lonely old biddy hanging out used teabags for my next cuppa and polishing the windows with a drop of diluted vinegar?

A post on the blog, asking others to air their eco-arguments, suggests not. Tracy Stokes, a 35-year-old fellow green blogger, who set up *www.ecostreet.com*, reels off her complaints. 'Why does he take so long in the shower? Why won't he press the eco-button to save water while he's in there? And why does he have to drive over the speed limit on the motorway, creating more carbon dioxide emissions than necessary?' she writes.

The subject of heating is what sparks off Anna Robinson, 34. 'I prefer a cold bedroom and to turn off the heating when we're out,' she says. 'He likes a tropical environment and maintains that my method is more wasteful because the heating has to work harder when it comes on.'

Next I catch up with my friend Livvy, whom I have convinced to install a wormery after having great success with mine (see April). Her boyfriend, Xav, is appalled; he calls them 'the filthy worms' and won't go near the thing, or even discuss it. Worse than that, she is sure he is looking for a way to pay her back by doing something she hates. I tell her to stay firm and repeat the mantra: 'Love me, love my worms.' This is what I did when I set up my own bin, along with setting the ground rule that Gervase would at least have to feign enthusiasm for my pet wrigglies.

The fact that Livvy's worms are sluggish sickly creatures doesn't help (for more on this see page 101). Even she won't get too close to them; instead she uses several poking sticks kept nearby to check they are still alive. Really, considering their treatment it's no wonder the worms don't do a good job on the household's kitchen scraps. But Livvy won't give up. She ignores Xav's moans of disgust and continues to cajole her subjects into eating carrot peel.

In relationship-counselling speak, what we are seeing here is conflicting core values. I know this because I spoke to Penny Mansfield, the director of One Plus One Marriage and Partnership Research, about the rise of the eco-argument. 'Like where to send your children to school, whether to go to church or your political alignment, our views on environmental conduct have become something that we want our partner to share,' she tells me.

'The rows become about who you are and how you see the world.'

When you consider the sparks that fly when the terrible trio of politics, religion and private education are dissected around the kitchen table, it is little wonder that we're getting rattled about going green, often referred to as a 21st-century religion.

But what I want to know is how doomed a couple are if they can't even agree on whose turn it is to take out the recycling. Penny is reassuring. 'Many people would die of boredom if their views were never questioned in a relationship,' she says. 'As long as your partner respects your values, he doesn't have to share them, or echo your world views at all times. It is the difference in people that often attracts them.'

I bear this in mind next time I return home to find the lights on and the laptop running. I force myself to imagine what it would be like if I lived with a green saint. He would be hot on my tail on the days that I decide not to cycle to work or when I forget to take a plastic bag with me to the shops. Come to think of it, he'd probably make me clean the oven with vinegar and lemon juice on a daily basis. It would be hell, and I don't think I'd take kindly to the competition. One eco-worrier per household is probably enough.

WHAT'S IN IT FOR THE PLANET?

Buy plant-based eco-friendly cleaning products . . . and you know you are not contaminating our waterways and damaging aquatic life. The fewer complex chemicals you flush down the loo, the less of a burden you are putting on the sewerage system, where 90 per cent of the water we use ends up. The problem with many conventional cleaning products is that they are 'persistent polluters'; in other words, they persist in the environment after they've gone down the drain, increasing their concentration and combining with other chemicals.

Avoid products made from petroleum . . . and you are slimming the carbon footprint of your cleaning endeavours. You are also making a sustainable choice. Manufacturing petrochemicals harms the environment, and oil is non-renewable – it's not going to be around for ever.

Make your own cleaning concoctions . . . and you will avoid the plastic packaging that comes with buying cleaning products in shops. You can fill your old spray bottles with your new homemade products (see page 89 for recipes). By considering what goes down your drains, you will also become more aware of wider environmental issues and your place within them.

Yes, Your Home Will Survive Without . . .

Disposable wipes

Cruise the cleaning aisle of supermarkets and you will notice that every household surface has its own special bottle. Gone are the days when you used one cleaning product everywhere. But aren't they all the same thing, just in different forms? Take the rise of disposable wipes, surely one of the most absurd cleaning trends. There are now garden furniture wipes, along with those for houseplants, bathtubs and even different parts of your body. I say use one wipe for all, and make that a recycled rag wipe, not a disposable one. Use a fresh one for your face, on second thoughts.

Kitchen towels

You can understand why nifty squares of absorbent paper are favoured over a sticky cloth that has been festering in the sink. But they cannot be recycled as they are classified as contaminated waste so unless you buy kitchen towels that have been made from recycled paper, you are ploughing through virgin fibres, fresh from forests, for a one-use-only product. Much better to use washable cloths as much as possible; when you need to, buy recycled kitchen paper.

Air fresheners

Most contain a toxic blend of artificial musks and *parfum* (for more on *parfum*, see page 235) – none of which manages to make them smell very nice. They are also the household product linked most often with allergies and respiratory problems. Research has showed that women who use them frequently, and therefore have higher levels of VOCs (volatile organic compounds, not nice things, don't be fooled by the O word) in their homes, are more likely to suffer from headaches. In terms of planetary impact, some products have even been made to carry warnings to say they may have long-term adverse effects on the aquatic environment. The plug-in variety are obviously the worst, draining electricity while filling your home with a fake smell that might give you a sore head. Open the windows or make a homemade spray with essential oil. For bad smells in the fridge or bathroom, I sprinkle bicarbonate of soda into a ramekin or open jam jar, and leave it to absorb the odours. You need to change it every few months.

Products that contain triclosan

Used widely for its antibacterial properties, this is an unnecessarily strong chemical to use in your home – unless you do something deeply mucky behind closed doors. There has been concern in the UK that a build-up of triclosan in our water supply is threatening to create strains of bacteria – namely, superbugs – which are strongly resistant to disinfectants. Meanwhile, in the States, it has been registered as a pesticide by the United States Environmental Protection Agency, such is the concern raised over its eco- and human-health implications. Effects of long-term exposure are unknown, so I avoid it like the plague.

Laundry detergent with phosphates

As mentioned, although phosphates are natural minerals and they are not toxic like many of the worst ingredients used in cleaning products, they work as a fertilizer in our waterways for certain types of algae, therefore suffocating aquatic life and creating an unbalanced ecosystem.

Towers of foam in your washing-up bowl

As evidence that washing-up liquid is doing its job properly, we have come to expect lashings of bubbles in which to submerge our dirty crockery. Consequently, stuff made by green cleaning companies can be a disappointment. It is short on chemicals and also short on bubbles as it skips the artificial foam boosters used in conventional washing-up liquids. Is it still cleaning? Yes, and you won't have to spend twice the time, and water, rinsing off the sticky soap either.

Optical brighteners

Found in laundry detergents, this is a broad term for the many synthetic chemicals that make clothes appear whiter by absorbing ultraviolet light and emitting it back as visible blue light. Put simply, your clothes are no cleaner than they would normally be but the blue light makes them appear to be. The chemicals used in optical brighteners are skin irritants and are also toxic to fish and other animals and plant life. Since they are not effective unless they remain on the fabric after washing, the price you pay for gleaming whites is possible skin allergies. Give in to the gradual greyification of your laundry. What's so good about white anyway?

Try it in March . . .

Light Greenies
Prepare the garden and start sprouting

It being the start of the growing season, you would imagine amateur gardeners everywhere would whoop for joy and throw open the back doors. Problem is, they very often can't open them. Last year's broken barbecue hasn't been cleared out of the way yet and rotting tomato plants in grow bags are backed up against a thick mulch of broken flowerpots. At this time of year, it is quite normal for your patch to resemble a junkyard. It can be a blow for a novice gardener to discover that you have to do things to a garden to make it resemble the ones you knew and loved as a child, the ones that came all pretty and trimmed and full of flowers all year round.

I, for one, was stunned. You mean I have to clear the leaves that are littering the patio? Don't they just rot down in a natural, organicy sort of way? Apparently not. Left to its own devices, nature has an unpleasant habit of running riot as soon as your back is turned. At no point is this more obvious than on your first springtime expedition outdoors. Whether your patch is an urban balcony or a spacious smallholding, it is now that you want to clear some space and think about what you want to grow and where.

In the meantime, get your eye in for the game with some indoor sprouting, something you need neither a garden nor a windowsill to do. You might not realize it but you can sprout almost any seed, from lentils and chickpeas to alfalfa, mustard cress and aduki beans. It's a genius way of growing a superfood stuffed full of health-giving enzymes. Use your home-grown harvest to spruce up salads and stir-fries. My friend Nicole has a multi-layered sprout germinator that she picked up at Fresh&Wild, but you can just as easily rustle up a makeshift version with a jam jar and an old pair of (clean) tights. Soak a handful of dry beans overnight in tepid water in the jam jar and fix a patch of tights material over the jar with an elastic band – it doesn't matter if the beans layer up a little at the bottom of the jar but you don't want it to be too crowded. In the morning, drain the water and leave the seeds to germinate in a warm dark place, rinsing them twice daily to prevent them going mouldy. Don't worry if you don't have an airing cupboard, mine germinate almost anywhere I leave them, although a dark cupboard is another good spot.

 ## *Dark Greenies*
Make a cold frame for seedlings

An inexperienced vegetable grower is often an impatient one. If I'm anything to go by, you will barely have sown tomato seeds in tiny pots and placed them along a sunny windowsill before you'll be longing to get them planted out in the ground. Once they have germinated, poking up their fragile heads triumphantly, you'll think of nothing except where to put them in the garden and what kind of pasta sauce they might eventually become. But it's early days – no one likes seeing their precious seedlings killed off by late frost. If you're serious about your crop of edibles, it helps to create a place for them during the intermediary stage when they are too big for the windowsill and yet still susceptible to frost. This is when a cold frame is an ideal protected space. It's a halfway house for raising seedlings, somewhere between a toasty windowsill (or greenhouse if you're lucky) and being out in the soil. For anyone short on sunny windowsills, who needs somewhere for young plants to benefit from light without experiencing the harsh conditions of rain and wind, a cold frame is just the ticket.

Dozens of gardening companies will offer to sell you cold frames, but they are a doddle to make, even if your previous construction experience was with Lego. All you need is a pile of bricks and a rectangle of glass. I managed to pick a sheet of glass out of a skip but you could also try asking at a picture-framing shop. With the bricks, mark out a rectangle, as big as your space allows and the amount of plants you are growing requires. It needs to be about three or four bricks tall so that you can fit small plants in the middle without their shoots poking out of the top. Lay the glass on top and you've done it. The only thing to look out for is that you don't roast your seedlings on freakishly sunny spring days. Remove the glass lid when it's warm to let your little darlings breathe.

Eco-Cheats

• A few seashells picked up on a beach will keep your kettle limescale-free. Drop them in the bottom and they'll knock about noisily every time you boil water, preventing it from building up. A collection of pretty Norfolk shells has been rattling around in our kettle for over a year now.

• Instead of using air fresheners, open the windows. Let the crisp spring air in and the indoor pollutants out. Or put a couple of drops of your favourite essential oil in a spray bottle with some water and you have a homespun version. You can buy small spray bottles from most chemists, although it would be better to reuse an old one.

• Put dishcloths on top of plates in the dishwasher to take full advantage of its cleaning powers. They'll come out gleaming. The same goes for rags and dusters (made from old clothes, of course). You don't need to wash them separately: put them in the washing machine with the rest of your clothes.

Recipes
for Homemade Cleaning Products

Windows

Half-fill a bucket or washing-up bowl with soapy water (I use a squeeze of Ecover washing-up liquid) and do a quick sloppy clean of the windows with a sponge, not worrying too much about smears. Tip this on the garden and refill the bucket with a solution of one part vinegar to four parts water – it doesn't need to be more than an inch or two deep. After cleaning with this (I wear washing-up gloves as the vinegar stings), scrunch up bits of old newspaper to dry-shine the glass – as you'll discover, this is the bit that'll shift the calories.

Baths and sinks

Mix the juice of one lemon (or more if you've any going spare) with a quarter of a mug of vinegar and two mugs of hot water. If you're trying to get rid of stains, add half a cup of salt – obviously not your best Maldon, cheap table salt will do. Douse the mixture around the bath/sink and leave for 10 minutes. Come back, scrub and then rinse with water.

The loo

As often as you remember, pour an eggcup of vinegar down the loo to prevent limescale. If it builds up, scoop out all the water in the loo with a plastic cup – an acceptable time to use something disposable, I reckon – and then scrub at the limescale with undiluted vinegar. Should this fail to budge it, try a sprinkling of bicarbonate of soda. Such an inglorious task as this should definitely be rewarded with Fairtrade chocolate. (I should mention that I favour green cleaning products for the loo. Never bleach, mind, just Ecover's toilet cleaner.)

Shower curtains

Tea tree oil is a natural disinfectant, so if you're worried about germs – and who wouldn't be after they had slung out their harsh chemicals and reduced their cleaning cupboard to vinegar? – add a few drops of it to any of the above cleaning recipes. It is expensive, but you only need to use a little. It works especially well on mould and mildew. Add a teaspoon to a mug of water, combine in a spray bottle and spray on to mouldy section of the curtain. Leave for at least an hour before you scrub off.

Floors

Another solution of vinegar, lemon juice and water, I'm afraid. Don't overdo the vinegar this time as it is strong smelling; use as much lemon juice as you can afford – you might have noticed that bulk-buying lemons for your potions is a pricey way to clean – and use hot water. So a quarter of a mug of vinegar, diluted with a full kettle of hot water, sprinkled with at least half a lemon. I gather that wood floors come up lovely if you polish them with a mixture of equal amounts of olive oil and lemon juice. To me, it sounds a bit sticky. I'm happy with my linseed oil Ecover floor polish.

The oven

Ahem. Well, actually, can I duck out of my role as eco-adviser for a moment? If truth be told, I have only used noxious chemicals on my grubby oven and it's not something I'm proud of. Where I go wrong is by waiting until it is filthy before tackling it, instead of doing a little scrub now and again with something natural. Don't follow my bad behaviour, try this instead. Sprinkle bicarbonate of soda on the bottom of the oven or on any stained pots and pans; leave it for 10 minutes, then add a splash of boiling water and leave overnight. Scrub away the filth in the morning, or get your other half to take over for the nasty bit.

Clothes cupboards

Anti-moth tactics are not strictly a cleaning subject, but they are important if you want your jumpers to remain intact. Spring is the peak egg-laying season for moths, so at this time of year you may find yourself cursing the 2002 ban of conventional mothballs. Rest assured, we're better off without them. They contain dichlorvos, a chemical that has been linked to damage to the human nervous system. Instead I scatter lumps of cotton wool with drops of lavender and citronella on them in my drawers. Cedar balls and lavender sachets also work well as preventative measures. As moths are material snobs, they'll nestle down in your cashmere but won't go near manmade fabrics, so concentrate on the finer ranks of your wardrobe. If you've already spotted holes in your clothes or seen any sign of these creatures, you'll need to kill the larvae by putting all your clothes in polythene bags, squeezing out the air and freezing them for 72 hours. This is greener than laundering them at high temperatures – the other effective solution.

Tea-stained mugs

Bicarbonate of soda is heralded as a genius alkaline solution that helps to dissolve dirt and grease. If you're ever in doubt about how to spice up a homemade cleaning product, bicarb is a popular answer. Until recently, I cleaned stained mugs with it. And very well it worked too. Then I discovered an even better quicker way to get rid of the brown marks. Yep, you guessed it, vinegar. Our green cleaning saviour. It works brilliantly if you leave it un-diluted soaking in the mug for a few hours and then scrub off the stains with a brush. Beware though, it takes a few washes to get rid of the smell. You'll want to do this before you make yourself a congratulatory cup of tea.

Kitchen surfaces

To make an all-purpose cleaner – again, you'll need to acquire a spray bottle; try high-street chain Muji, for a range of sizes – mix a handful of soap flakes with hot water, lemon juice and a spoonful of bicarbonate of soda. This potion will need to be rinsed off as it leaves a soapy residue. If you're wondering about the soap flakes, you can buy organic ones, made from vegetable oils, inexpensively, from Goodness Direct (*www.goodnessdirect.co.uk*) and you can also use them as a clothes detergent. For homemade ones, attack a bar of soap with a potato peeler.

Tips on Doing Up Your Home

Sometimes a scrub and a polish is not enough and you'll find yourself wanting to do more than clean your home to improve it. But before you sling on the overalls and bulk-buy some Dulux, remember that polluting gases from paint carry on emitting after you've slapped them around your house, so it's worth thinking about what kind you want to use – and, of course, what colour.

Once your walls are gleaming, the chances are you'll start picking holes in the furniture. Repairing, restoring and adapting old furniture is better than buying new. Not just because it brings character to your home, but also because it minimizes your impact on the world's forests. And it's one of those sneaky opportunities to make stylish choices and allow people to think that you were motivated by environmental concerns. If you don't have the patience to scour second-hand shops and you know exactly what you want and where you can get it, at least follow a few guidelines to make sure you are buying sustainable products.

How to choose: paint

• Avoid VOCs – a general term for a couple of hundred compounds that are emitted in gas form from carpets, cleaning fluids and paints. Their fumes have been linked to asthma and they contribute significantly to indoor pollution.

• Go for zero-VOC paint rather than low-VOC, if possible. Friends of the Earth says the new generation of low-VOC paints often use just as many damaging chemicals in their attempts to bypass the compounds and end up emitting equal levels of indoor pollution.

• Look for water-based paints made from plant oils and simple minerals (see index for suppliers). The gong-winner is Ecos Organic Paint, awarded best buy by *Ethical Consumer* magazine and best environmentally friendly paint by *Which?* magazine in 2006 (*ecosorganicpaints.com*).

• Don't buy too much. It is estimated that up to 25 per cent of paint bought will never be used, but instead left to dry out in garden sheds across the country.

- Give spare paint away. Try the UK's paint recycling scheme (*www.communityrepaint.org.uk*).

How to choose: old materials

- It's easy to track down reclaimed timber. Many building suppliers will have it, or you will find dedicated wood yards that sell it. Look in local papers and ask your local council. By using it, your home will have an extra layer of history. When questioned about your wooden floors, you can say with a nonchalant shrug, 'Actually, they're reclaimed pine from an old school gym,' or some similar smug reply.

- Tap into the reserve of second-hand household items. If it's between an Ikea flat-pack bookshelf and an old wooden version found in a charity shop that you can top up with an antique varnish, it should be an easy decision. One will bring colour to your home; the other will make it look like everyone else's. You may have to wait longer to find the non-Ikea version, but this will give you time to work out exactly what you want, anyway.

- Always keep an eye out for a second-hand bargain. I have found that small villages in the middle of nowhere yield the best old furniture markets.

- Borrow stuff from friends and neighbours. Not everybody needs dustsheets, paintbrushes and a 20-foot stepladder for the one occasion they paint their house. More to the point, not everyone has a place to store this stuff when it's time to hang up your overalls.

- Be creative with what you've got. Are you sure you need to chuck your sofa and purchase a new one? What about finding a rug or throw to revamp it, or even having it reupholstered?

How to choose: new materials

- Does it come in bamboo? As far as I can see, you can't go wrong with the favourite fodder of pandas. As a grass that needs no replanting, grows without fertilizers and pesticides and can be harvested every three to five years, it's the ultimate eco-material. To get to the good bit, bamboo stalks must be crushed and pulped, a process which separates the valuable fibres. Light but tough, bamboo is being put to use in many ways, from bowls to bras.

- Avoid supporting illegal logging practices by buying FSC (Forest Stewardship Council) certified wood that comes from legal and sustainable sources. Lovely as it is, teak and mahogany are two of the world's most endangered wood species. Be on your guard when buying them.

- Avoid anything from the world's endangered forests. Rainforests in Brazil, Indonesia and around the Congo basin are the planet's lungs. The trees collect CO_2 and give out oxygen, providing a vital service in helping to keep our climate stable. In the words of Sir Nicholas Stern (of the Stern Review), if we don't stem the current rate of deforestation, destruction of forests in the next four years will pump more CO_2 into the atmosphere than every flight from the beginning of aviation to at least 2025 in the future.

- Support retailers that sell only FSC-certified garden furniture. B&Q and Marks and Spencer have topped Greenpeace's garden furniture league table for the last few years.

You might spot a bit of forced **rhubarb** about this month, a British delicacy that has been on the rocks for the past few years due to the popularity of imported exotic fruits. Traditionally grown in a small area of West Yorkshire, the process of forcing rhubarb involves depriving the plants of light by replanting them inside sheds. Here the stems shoot upwards and produce a delicate, superior taste combined with a vivid colour.

If you come across any, snap it up, ferry it home (the sight of it poking out of my rucksack when I'm cycling always makes people smile) and slice it and bake it with some fresh ginger slices on top, lots of brown sugar and a splash of whatever juice is lurking in the fridge (apple seems to work best). From this sticky mixture you can make **rhubarb fool**. I fight the corner of healthy fool using yoghurt instead of cream, but Gervase says a fool is nothing without whipped double cream, in stiff peaks, folded in, once you've stewed the fruit – after which it needs an hour or so in the fridge to become firm. So we compromise and I do half cream, half Greek yoghurt (actually, I always use lots of yoghurt and a token dollop of cream but don't say a word).

APRIL

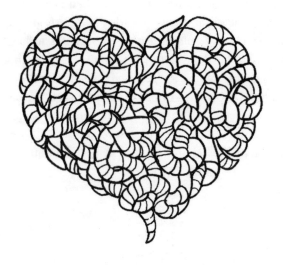

NURTURING NATURE

'WOULD YOU LIKE TO SEE MY WORMS?' POP ROUND TO TEA AT MY PLACE AND I'll probably find an excuse to slot this into the conversation. The fact is that I'm proud of them, the little blighters. You would be too if you saw how hard they worked on my carrot peel and soggy teabags. Two Aprils ago, they arrived – all 1,800 of them – in a wriggling envelope, delivered by a special-delivery postman. He looked bemused; I had that red-cheeked excitement that I used to get before birthday parties as a child – which made sense since this was a birthday present from my mum. 'It's my worms, my worms!' I shrieked to anyone on the street.

But as he handed them over, a sudden rush of squeamishness surged through me. What now? I laid them gingerly on the kitchen table, eyed the instructions for assembling the flat-pack bin – which looked not unlike a small version of a household rubbish bin – and trotted off to find Gervase. Turned out, he was more nervous of the package than me. As soon as it sank in that the contents of the envelope were crucial to successful city composting, and that I would nurture this living bundle, nourishing them on the remnants of my summer salads and winter peelings, I overcame the yuk factor.

At least I'd got the timing right. Several composting websites had suggested getting started in spring. Warm weather helps the contents of both compost bins and wormeries to break down. Worms, I learnt, prefer a temperate climate; they work through waste at a snail's pace during the winter months. You can expect them to grind to a halt completely when temperatures drop below 5 degrees Celsius, although the heat generated by decomposition is sometimes enough to keep them going. Set the thing up in the cold months and the theory is that it is hard to know whether everything is functioning as it should be as the worms are too cold to wriggle around much anyway. Much safer to start up your bin in spring and hope that they'll hop to it faster.

Putting the bin together was easy as pie. If a flat-pack virgin like myself can manage it in 10 minutes flat, it probably doesn't even classify as DIY. Which is a shame, as I felt triumphant once I had knocked all the plastic legs into the right sockets and put the first tray on top. This could be because I bought it from a well-established company called Wiggly Wigglers (a well-chosen name that is always a source of hilarity among those who ask about it). Next I emptied a starter pack of compost on to the bottom of the bin (it comes in the pack), took a deep breath and followed this with the contents of the wriggling envelope. The worms burrowed down into their new home immediately.

Initial squeamishness quickly gave way to fascination, and before long I was plunging my hands into the bin, pulling out worms to watch them wriggle, and fixating on which different materials they liked eating best. My mum gave me a good scare a few weeks after the bin arrived when she announced that I'd get worm eggs under my nails that might end up as intestinal worms. After that, I invested in a pair of Marigolds to hang close by – although her horror story was scientifically impossible, according to my friend Martin the Biologist.

But how does a wormery actually work, you are probably wondering? Well, it converts ordinary kitchen food waste into liquid feed and rich organic compost by exploiting the natural action of tiger worms, or sometimes red worms. Earthworms, by the way, wouldn't be up to the job because they like to burrow back into the earth. Unlike tiger and red worms – wise creatures that they are – earthworms are not content to live within their source of food. By munching through rotting matter, the tiger and red worms enable their owners to harvest what comes out of their back end (yes, there is a front and back end, but don't ask me which one is which), which is a rich organic compost and a liquid fertilizer. In my home, we call the latter worm juice, although it would be more accurate to call it worm pee; either way it's a winning combination of nitrogen, phosphorous and calcium that can be poured on plants once diluted.

The wormery itself – that you'd want to keep outside, or at least in a utilities room, not in the kitchen – consists of a base structure with a tap, from which you drain the worm juice, and several empty plastic trays that you place on top. You start off using one, dropping your scraps and ripped-up paper waste on to it for the worms to tuck into. When it's full – this took almost six months for me – you add No. 2 on top. By putting fresh material on this, the worms will wriggle up through little holes in the bottom of the tray. Meanwhile, the contents of the bottom tray will be well on its way to becoming rich, dark compost. Eventually you remove the bottom tray completely (as the worms will have mostly left it for the scraps above).

As you might have noticed, I'm hooked. What got me going about the wormery right from the moment I deposited my first slither of carrot peel inside the bin is the idea that rubbish that's usually sent to landfill is being transformed. In its place, clumps of compost appear. It reminds me of the first time I grew cress on the windowsill as a child. As the seedlings raised their heads, I had experienced a similar sense of awe.

Sadly, it didn't do it for Gervase. A sorry state of affairs soon developed in which his relationship with the worms worsened as mine grew bolder. Gervase would cruelly blank them, refusing to visit them when he got in from work, feed them or talk about them, while for months I could barely utter a word about anything else. 'Did you see how they devoured those eggshells?' a typical conversation would start up. 'And what do you think about the fruit flies in there, do you reckon we should leave the lid off for a while so they fly away?' it would continue. Silence from Gervase; he didn't want to discuss them. He didn't love them as I did.

For the uninitiated, I suspect it's hard to imagine what kind of person would have their life enhanced by establishing a relationship with worms. It is not what I expected, I can assure you. But it's like when you get a puppy: for weeks you waste hours following it around the house and working out how it functions. It's this incredible living creature with its own set of instincts and needs. Now imagine that you had nearly two thousand of them. And unlike puppies, with worms you can do something useful with their crap.

Owning worms has put me in touch with the cycle of life. It is a biology lesson in action – and a reminder that I didn't pay proper attention the first time round. My worms quietly go about their job of creating a useful, living substance from something dead. In the end, theirs is the most crucial of all jobs.

Aside from that, I like having pets. OK, so they're not cuddly, but still, they are there waiting when you get in from work. You nurture them, learn to consider their needs as well as your own and wonder at their humble, unimaginable lives. Honestly, the pleasure to be had from these gentle companions is incredible. Never mind the undiscovered thrill of worm racing – we'll get on to that later – and the impact these creatures have on your green credibility.

Avocado and banana skins were one of their favourite meals at first. They have since developed a taste for root vegetables. Organic, naturally. To be honest, though, they're not fussy. They get what we get, after we've taken what we want from it. Harder stuff like the ends of carrots and apple cores takes longer to be devoured, but that's just because they can't eat it until it's soft. Worms have no teeth, you see.

Give them too much and it'll rot before they can eat it, which makes the bin smell. Other than that, I have never found the wormery has assaulted my nostrils. Gervase says otherwise, but he's a London boy born and bred. I don't think he's spent enough time in wellies to appreciate the earthy fresh smell of compost. He'll hate me saying that as he says he picked West London blackberries as a tot which means he could easily assume the title 'urban forager'. I tell him he should be braver with the worms and hold one in his palm for a few minutes every day to get used to them. He wrinkles his nose in defiance and slopes off to play hip-hop records.

Believe me, life is richer with a bin full of worms. You'll even make babies, worm babies that is. Lemon-pip-shaped eggs will appear, followed by mini worms, the length of a fingernail. My bin is a vision of health and fertility. The only thing some people might not like is the flies that are attracted to the bin in the summer months. Some are tiny fruit flies, others are just hanging around for the heck of it. They are nothing to worry about, though; all bins have them. The flies don't hurt the worms and all the creatures get along fine, although it's not very nice when you lift off the lid. Worth standing back so they don't fly in your face.

Sometimes I wonder if it gets crowded in there. But, according to wormery websites – which I all too often find myself browsing – unlike humans, a colony of worms regulates its numbers to suit the available resources. Worms are clever like that.

The funny thing about our blossoming relationship is that I've realized the bond is with my own worms rather than the species in general. In the same way that your own baby's vomit is one thing but another's is quite something else, I've discovered that other people's worms turn my stomach. My friend Livvy got a budget bin off the council and it took a lot of work to get going. In fact, it never really did; she suspects she was stung by a bad worm dealer. The creatures were sluggish and uninterested in chomping. She tried all sorts of food combinations but they barely touched it. I was brought round as the closest thing to a worm doctor and instead of willingly plunging my hands into her bin of sickly subjects, as I thought I would, I took one look at them and wanted to do a runner. These foreign, somehow fatter, repugnant-looking things were nothing like my sweet companions. I declared them beyond help and quickly made my excuses. I gather they have since been liberated in West London's suitably named Wormholt Park.

The only other worm tragedy I've come across was a result of drowning them. It's important to give them enough dry stuff to keep the bin from getting waterlogged. That's how my godmother's worms met their end, gasping for air in a sea of soggy teabags and tangerine peel. Wiggly Wigglers suggests one-third dry stuff to two-thirds wet (vegetables and food waste). This means seeing off the inside of toilet rolls and bank statements in style. In these days of identity fraud, what better way to dispose of personal correspondence? The worms won't breathe a word.

They can't be rushed though, these wrigglies. Don't expect them to plough through all last year's accounts. However much you pile on the coffee grounds – which speeds them up just like it does us – they make their way slowly through what you give them. I've found that I can create more vegetable peelings than the worms can get through and I'm not even vegetarian so I collect up the extra for our doorstep food-waste collection scheme.

Should crisis strike, Wiggly Wigglers has a worm hotline. I'm not sure whether they'd like me saying that, as the company is probably sick of people like me phoning up and asking why the worms are off their food; why they've eaten the moisture mat that's supposed to keep them warm, and other such worries. Still, they regularly reassure me down the phone that everything is probably OK. These days, it is. We've settled into a steady twice-weekly feed and I've found an old cardigan that I shrunk in the wash to replace the moisture mat. The taste of it hasn't impressed them so they've left it alone.

Meanwhile, I have embraced my role as worm educator – spreading the word not only to friends and family, but even to unfortunate members of the public who make the mistake of sparking up conversation on the bus. Amazingly, when friends come round, the squeamish are as intrigued by the bin as the insect hardy.

An after-supper trip to see it is a common occurrence. Some people choose to stand at a safe distance peering into the bin. I fish one or two fine specimens out and place them in my palm, feeling like one of those brazen wildlife presenters who pick up snakes. To anyone who is still sceptical I point out my tomato plants. Hard evidence of the merits of keeping worms. I've had double the fruits from them in the years that I've started dousing them with diluted worm juice.

I feed the tomato plants roughly every three weeks once the yellow flowers appear, about as often as you would dole out any kind of plant food. Two years ago, I almost felt sorry for my four plants, overburdened as they were with fruit. At one point, I counted 36 marble-sized green tomatoes on one plant. Last summer, sunshine was in shorter supply and my plants, though wonderfully bushy, were less bountiful – or maybe the worms had stopped trying as hard to please and were creating a less fertile waste product.

Such is my enthusiasm, Gervase says I should be careful not to be a compost bully – or bore, for that matter. It never takes long before I'm holding forth on exactly why everyone should have a wormery and how worms can change your life. I speak with the conviction of the converted, having reached a point where I cannot understand why anyone in possession of a metre square of outdoor space or even a draughty utilities room doesn't get worming.

Despite warnings from Gervase that I shouldn't talk worms at the dinner table, I fear I may have developed a proselytizing tone. It comes not from righteousness but from discovering what fun it is to concoct your own compost. I want everyone to have a go. The problem is, this can come across as eco-one-upmanship. Green living has created a new frontier of etiquette and navigating this territory is not always easy. In this case, tradition does not point the way; we have to make up the rules as we go. Is it acceptable, for instance, to ask where the green bin is at the end of dinner? Or will you publicly humiliate your hosts if they don't have one?

In my experience, you should not expect anyone to share your eco-ideals, any more than you should suppose that they will convert to your religion or sexuality. Friends and family will turn over a green life when they're good and ready, not when you hassle them. A thunderous banging of the drum leads only to deaf ears.

Should you plan to bring up environmental credentials at the table,

I recommend doing it with humour. Whatever you do, avoid the eco-trump –
an opportunity to 'outgreen' someone. As *The Times* columnist Philip Howard,
an expert in modern manners, once told me, this is no better than boasting
about the expensive school your children go to or the five-star hotel where
you spent your summer holidays. It is unacceptably smug.

I do my best to do the right thing, leading by quiet example, but it's not
easy. In early summer, once I've managed to coax a few green shoots out of
the ground in the garden, a song and a dance around the vegetable patch is
almost irresistible. I long to take friends on extensive tours of my tiny garden,
in spite of the glazed look in their eyes when I suggest it. It is a painfully slow
activity, largely because I stop every few centimetres to appreciate miracles of
nature that I have only recently taken notice of myself.

Look at that clever dwarf bean pushing through fruits where white
flowers have been, I'll gasp. Can you believe how far that nasturtium has crept
in search of something to climb? The funny thing is, it is exactly how my
mother behaves when I return home. Before I can get on with doing anything,
I'm dragged around the garden to monitor its progress.

Now it is me who fires a steady stream of horticultural observations at
Gervase when we're out in our small patch: me nosing around in the beds;
him reading the papers. He has developed a cunning trick of pretending to
acknowledge them without his eye wandering from the newsprint.

But the biggest domestic achievement has been the developing relationship between Gervase and the worms. I believe they are growing on him, so
to speak. The other day I caught him feeding them, and I could have sworn I
heard him talking to them. In fact, he was talking to me, complaining that I'd
given them too many banana skins and that they had started to rot before the
worms could get around to eating them. Of course, it was his penchant for
banana cake to blame, but I kept this nugget of wisdom to myself. I don't
mind a little overfeeding as I'm keen to harvest my third tray of compost.

It's nearly ready, just a few more chunks of avocado skin to break down.

Soon I will be able to plunder it, pulling out a pile of dark, rich soil, shining like melted chocolate and probably still dotted with the odd eggshell. This I will mix with normal garden soil and organic compost from the garden centre. Alone, it is too potent; it is soil conditioner rather than suitable potting compost. Some worms will escape their captive life at this point, burrowing down into my flowerbeds when I dig the mixture in, but there are more where they came from. Thousands more. Fat ones, skinny ones, busy ones and listless ones; recently I've noticed some that are translucent and, frankly, pretty ugly.

But you won't hear me say much against my worms. We have a strong and mutually beneficial relationship. I leave them in peace as much as possible; in return they get on with the important job of compost creating. Early in the morning, before Gervase is up, after I've made my first cup of tea, is the time that I can't resist a visit. Chucking them the teabag, I perch on the garden wall and watch them burrowing contentedly in their casts. As I said before, I'm proud of them.

WHAT'S IN IT FOR THE PLANET?

Compost and you will . . .

. . . lighten your household waste by up to 60 per cent and spare the world some methane, a potent greenhouse gas generated by household waste left rotting in landfill sites.

. . . provide a home for food scraps. You can also use a wormery to dispose of Hoover dust, cardboard and personal documents; even some eco-friendly paints can be composted (you have to dry them first).

. . . have an incentive to avoid fruit and vegetables packed in plastic. This infuriatingly dampens the feel-good buzz when you realize how little you would otherwise be putting in your normal bin.

. . . be encouraged to start growing something to eat since you'll have steaming trays full of compost for your pot plants or garden and liquid fertilizer (worm pee) from the tap – a winning but stinky combination of nitrogen, phosphorous and calcium.

Common Wormery Worries

Cold weather. Your worms may become a little lethargic as temperatures drop – don't we all – but they will survive the winter. To make them more productive, put a circle of old carpet or an unwanted jumper on top of the moisture mat. Will the worms freeze solid? Yes, but they survive this trauma, thaw out and carry on working.

What if I go on holiday? Worms will be fine for a couple of weeks; any longer than that and you might want to give your bin to a friend to look after. I did that and Martin the Biologist ended up taxing me by taking a few prize worms to build his own bin.

What if they try to escape? You are probably giving them the wrong balance of food, such as too much acidic fruit. Don't worry if plenty of worms gather in the lid of the bin when it rains. This is normal; it's their instinct to come out of the ground to stop them from drowning.

Will it attract rodents and vermin? In the summer, the bin might attract flies, especially fruit flies, but this won't cause a problem in the house or elsewhere in the garden. The only reason you should worry about rodents is if you have left the lid off. Otherwise, it fits snugly on top, keeping the worms secure.

Will my dog/children eat the worms? They may sample one or two if the mood takes them. My old flatmate Tom ate one once for a £2.75 bet and he lived to tell the tale. He went a bit green though.

What's the point if I don't have a garden? It's not hard to find a home for trays full of rich compost. Should you have more than your houseplants can manage, you can give it to friends with gardens or pile it on local park flowerbeds for a spot of guerrilla gardening.

What if my neighbours complain? They won't. Not if you look after your bin and check that it's not becoming totally overrun by flies and bad smells. If they are still not happy, you can flag up the planet-saving benefits of a wormery, which they will be hard-pushed to argue against.

Wormeries Versus Compost Bins

Wormeries, if you ask me, are just plain cooler.

By harnessing the powers of thousands of living creatures to munch through your veggie remains, you get them broken down faster than a normal compost bin could do. This means less pong and more respect from (human) visitors. And how can anyone deny the joy of having low-maintenance pets thrown into the equation? As with compost bins, you can pile dry materials such as cardboard and household dust on to a wormery, and you have the benefits of 'worm pee' or liquid fertilizer coming out of the tap in the bottom, which might, or might not, be considered a good thing, depending on who you ask: your houseplants or your flatmates.

In defence of **compost bins**, I must, grudgingly, admit that they pulp up some ingredients wormeries do not. You can chuck cooked meat and as many acidic scraps like lemons and onions as you want on a conventional compost pile. It's a simple job of scraping your plate straight into the dedicated collection pot rather than having to think about the tastes and habits of worms. For those with decent-sized gardens, a compost bin is more suitable because you can fill it with the green waste from your weeding, mowing and pruning. It used to be true that for city types who still want to compost but only have a tiny roof terrace or balcony, a wormery was the best option. But now there are compost bins to suit city slickers. A good example is the Bokashi bucket, which was developed in Japan. It is so small and neat you can keep it in the kitchen. When you've dropped your food scraps in it, you sprinkle them with a special kind of bran that contains bacteria, fungi and yeasts necessary to start the whole composting process.

Worm racing

Without a wormery, the delights of worm racing will always remain a mystery to you.

You can spend many happy hours worm racing with friends. It might not carry the speed and adrenalin rush associated with other forms of racing, or indeed the word 'race', but there is something absorbing about watching a couple of worms weaving their way across a table at a leisurely pace. Don't mock it until you've tried it.

First, a note on worm welfare. As far as I know – and there has been little research into this area – you can race without compromising the wellbeing of your worms, so long as you look after the needs of those chosen to race and return them safely to their wormery at the end of the evening. There is nothing to suggest that the worms will suffer from spending a few minutes on the table. Do make sure, however, that between races, your worms rest on a bed of soggy lettuce to minimize that common worm ailment: drying out. It is also advisable that you use a large rectangle of slightly damp cardboard for your racetrack. Mark it with lanes if you wish, although don't expect the worms to take the slightest bit of notice. They will generally ignore them and plough across each other's lanes.

1 Prepare the track. You will need scraps of your worms' favourite food dotted along the way as encouragement. Mark a starting point for each worm and a finishing line. Don't make the race too long. Roughly 30cm is often sufficient, unless you've got all night.

2 Choose your worm. Long is not always best. Short fat worms, in my experience, can be surprising movers.

3 Place your worm at the starting point and wave the flags.

4 Worms that go the wrong way can be gently turned around once or twice. Should they continually fail to head in the direction of the finishing line, however, they should be disqualified and sent back to the wormery in disgrace.

5 Touching your worm during the race, in an attempt to stimulate it into moving faster, is not allowed. Gentle whisperings of encouragement, however, and the waving of food scraps in the right direction are acceptable.

6 Put a time limit on the race. After which point, the owner of the worm closest to the finishing point has won and should be duly rewarded with a month's supply of compost.

Urban Animal Husbandry

Eggs in the city

Karen Patrick lives in Stoke Newington, North London, with her husband, two daughters, two cats, one dog and ten hens. They cohabit without too much trouble, except for the young terrier that has to be shut indoors when the hens are out on the lawn. Throw in some vegetable beds made from old railway sleepers, a wormery and a compost bin and it's an unusually sustainable set-up for the city. It helps that the garden is a decent size and that Karen is an actress who spends a fair amount of time at home. Some people keep hens with a lot less outdoor space, she tells me.

This is in part thanks to the final-year project of four design students from the Royal College of Art who invented a way of making chicken-keeping easy for town-dwellers. Their project culminated in the Eglu, a bright, modern-looking hen house complete with run, feeders and an 'eggport' from where you collect your breakfast. This stylish accommodation for city chickens is where Karen's reside, although her husband has also made them an extended run.

Over glasses of blackcurrant cordial on a sticky August day, she tells me that once she'd started growing vegetables, hens were a natural progression. Her grandmother had kept them during the war and she likes to think it's in the blood. Her home has become greener as a result since food scraps are divided between the compost bin, the hens and Hackney council's doorstep collection;

nothing goes to waste, even the hen droppings are composted and in turn nourish the vegetables.

When I arrive she's just finished cleaning the egg-laying part of the Eglu. She does this every week and it's probably the single biggest task that comes with keeping hens. Other than that, there's feeding them and making sure that they are safely tucked away in their house at night. Of course, it's not all plain sailing. Sometimes they get sick or start pecking each other and she takes them to the local vet, who isn't experienced in these things and has to look it up in a book. When the family go on holiday, a house-sitter is required to care for them. But the biggest problem is prowling urban foxes who prey on them when they're out pecking in the garden. Over three years of keeping hens, she has lost four to foxes.

The ten hens produce roughly seven eggs a day, most of which are sold to friends and neighbours; the rest provide quiches and cakes for the family. Karen can't remember the last time she bought eggs in a shop. By now, her children are pretty blasé about having fresh eggs for breakfast, but it's a source of fascination among their friends. At one birthday party, when Karen offered to cook breakfast with eggs from the hens, a little girl replied: 'But I don't like eggs from hens.' She tells me that city children who visit often have no idea where their food comes from.

When we go out to inspect her brood, they are gently clucking at the bottom of the garden, scratching in the soil and making mud baths to clean their feathers – I notice Karen's rows of vegetables are well protected with chicken wire. Given how jerkily they move, it is surprising how calming they are; and somehow comical too, as though intended to bring humour to the farmyard. I defy anyone to watch a hen for more than a few minutes without breaking into a smile. 'You could watch them for hours, couldn't you?' I say to Karen, transfixed. She smiles and shakes her head, as if these ten shuffling birds have already taken up too much of her time. Yet to see this functional and charming city garden, full of movement, colour and fresh produce, there's no question that it is time well spent.

Try it in April . . .

Light Greenies
Eat less meat

Excessive meat consumption is not only bad for our bodies, it makes for an unhealthy planet. No doubt a vegetarian will have already told you that, while insisting that a tofu curry tastes as good as a lamb chop. Whether or not you believe it, veggie defenders are right about one thing. The more meat we chomp through, the more grain, soya and other foodstuffs are required to rear animals, and it is grown on land that could otherwise be providing food we could eat first-hand. Did you know, for example, that an acre of arable crops could feed twenty times as many people as an acre dedicated to cows? The flaw in the argument, say farmers, is that grazing cattle is a vital part of creating healthy soil. It's a tricky dilemma. A clinching factor on the side of veggies and vegans is flatulent animals. Though hard to discuss without a smirk, the problem of windy livestock is a serious one. They are responsible for 14 per cent of global methane emissions. To give you some idea of the potency of the problem, a single dairy cow produces roughly 400 litres (88 gallons) of gas a day. Not only from its rear end; the majority of bovine emissions come from belching. Some farmers have already started to look at ways the methane from slurry could be harnessed and used as energy on the farm; others are investigating different feeds that reduce wind.

My answer to the meat question is to proclaim yourself a flexitarian – someone who is perfectly happy being vegetarian, but welcomes a good quality pork chop or plateful of shepherd's pie now and again. At this time of year, meat has an important role to play as there's not much growing in the garden. But your meals can be made more ethically acceptable by choosing good quality meat, reared as locally as possible, and by getting stuck into the nose-to-tail, waste-not, want-not approach, pioneered by the chef Fergus Henderson. Try as many different parts of the animal as you can bring yourself to and your meat consumption will be more sustainable. Chewing on chitterlings and lunching on liver might not be everyone's rump steak, but at least you are making the most of the animal and it means less methane per meat meal.

Experiment with different cuts

There's more to life than chicken breast and stewing steak, but before you experiment with unusual cuts of meat, it's helpful to establish a good relationship with your butcher – or, if you can't kick your supermarket habit, a friendly manner with the man behind the meat counter. Be bold. Admit that you've never handled lamb's neck or brisket steak and that you are not sure how much of either you will need. My experience is that you'll come away with recipe ideas, cooking tips and information on quantities for next time.

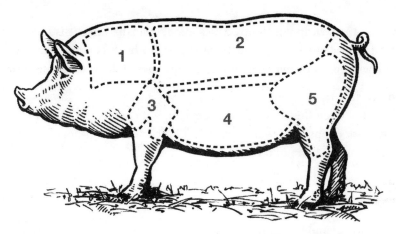

1. **Neck end & Shoulder**
2. **Loin (Pork Chops)**
3. **Hand (Hock)**
4. **Belly (Spare Ribs)**
5. **Leg**

Pig

Spare ribs A barbecue favourite. Marinade in a sweet and sour mix of honey, ketchup, cider vinegar and a sprinkling of cayenne pepper for spice. Or, in winter, fry garlic and an onion, add chunks of spare rib, then some red wine and a can of tomatoes for a meaty stew.

Leg With this you can't go far wrong; it's the best pork joint available. Cook slowly with cider, or use diced in stir-fries.

Neck end A rarely used cheap cut. It is slightly fatty but perfect for flavouring a broad bean stew. You could even do away with the neck after cooking: give it to the dog, once you've stolen its flavour.

Shoulder A cheap cut with a rich flavour. Bit tough to fry, but perfect for a casserole.

Hock Another cheap cut that requires a long cooking time. It is the recommended ingredient in many pea soups. Smoked hock is very tasty – you'll sometimes find it sold in jars. Raymond Blanc cooks his hock with green lentils.

Loin A prime roasting joint that will give you plenty of crackling. Ask your butcher to loosen the bone, without detaching it completely, so that carving is easy. Pork chops also come from the loin; perfect for grilling after being rubbed with a mixture of olive oil, salt and herbs.

Cow

Brisket You wouldn't call it a naturally tender cut of beef, but after a long slow cook, it's delicious. There's much to be said for cooking brisket in beer – Guinness, ideally. Half-drunk cans hanging around the kitchen are perfect for the job.

Neck Quite fatty so lots of flavour but it needs to be cooked for a long time. Because it's cheap and butchers will sometimes be almost giving it away, you can make up for it with a decent selection of seasonal vegetables to throw in the pot.

Chuck or blade Sold as braising steak but it's surprisingly tender. It will only take an hour or so to cook in a casserole.

Oxtail Originally, this was the tail of the ox – as you might expect – but now it refers to the tails of all kinds of beef. It is not to everyone's taste, but oxtail gives rich flavour to soups and stews. Some people use it for stock and take it out once it has released its flavour.

Topside A lovely cut to chop into thin steaks for frying or grilling. Very lean so you could also use it cut into cubes in a stir-fry with black beans and soy sauce.

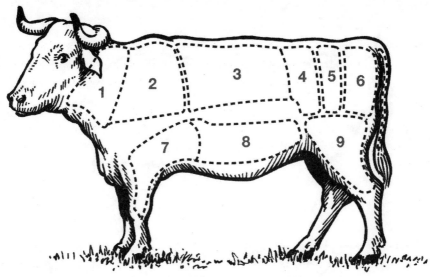

1. Neck
2. Chuck or Blade
   (Rib-Eye steak)
3. Sirloin & fillet

4. Rump
5. Silverside
6. Topside

7. Brisket
8. Flank
9. Leg

Lamb

Saddle of lamb Can be used for a classic roast lamb to feed a good number of people, but you'll have to visit a butcher because you won't find this cut in a supermarket. Chef Heston Blumenthal recommends that you ask your butcher to trim the saddle so it looks like a T-bone in cross section, with the fat still across the top and the chine bone trimmed off so the base sits as flat as possible in a pan. This means the meat is protected by bone on one side, fat on the other.

Scrag A cheap cut from the upper part of the neck that is good for stews as it's quite fatty and there is rarely enough meat to cook it as a roast. On the upside, the bones impart a meaty flavour to any liquid they are cooked in and the vegetables will taste delicious after bubbling alongside the meat.

1.	Scrag	4.	Shoulder	6.	Breast
2.	Neck	5.	Loin	7.	Fillet
3.	Rib (Cutlets)		(Saddle of Lamb)	8.	Knuckle

Loin A more expensive cut, from which you get cutlets, chops and noisettes – small lamb steaks. You can also buy it from most butchers boned, rolled and ready to roast, although this will be more expensive. The two loins form the saddle.

Cutlets Easy to cook and always popular, they are ideal for grilling or frying. Cutlets – or lamb chops – have a long bone and a circle of succulent lean meat.

Breast Another cheaper cut that can be roasted on the bone, or boned by a butcher and stuffed with something delicious, such as a rosemary and garlic stuffing. You might also see it in butchers' shops sold in strips for barbecuing, or as cubes to make kebabs, or mince to make burgers.

Dark Greenies

Bake your own bread

It is a source of great anguish to me that when I have taken my own advice, attempting to bake a loaf of bread so crustily rustic anyone would think I was born in a barn, I have failed, miserably. The fruits of my labour have more in common with baked bricks than a surface for butter and jam. More than once, I have seen my dough rise, then fall, before it has entered the safety of a hot oven. More often than I care to remember, I have glumly fed the birds with the resulting leaden lump. And yet, I soldier on, wasting more time, flour and muscle power (kneading dough is not for puny-wrists). Until one day it occurred to me that I have a secret weapon: my friend Patrizia. I've seen her dough-handling skills and I know her no-nonsense attitude to baking anxiety. Who better to come to the rescue? Patrizia agreed to spend an afternoon giving me a bread masterclass. In return, I plied her with baklava from the Turkish bakery round the corner.

While Patrizia is an instinctive cook, rarely to be found hovering over scales, she is firm about the importance of following recipes when you're making bread. She says that unless you bake it on a regular basis, it's easy to lose the knack and forget what you did that worked. In which case, return at once to the recipe. She uses Eric Treuille and Ursula Ferrigno's book *Bread*.

For a gentle, confidence-building exercise, we decide to make the simple wholemeal loaf on the first page.

Here's what we do:

We deal with the dried yeast the long way round because Patrizia says this is best, and she's Italian, so I believe her. Instead of adding it dry to the flour, we mix two teaspoons of it with 100ml of water (at body temperature, no warmer) and a teaspoon of brown sugar.

While that begins to froth, we measure out the flour – half brown, half white – plus a teaspoon of salt. Patrizia finds some spelt flour in the cupboard which gets thrown in for good measure, but any combination of flour is fine as long as it weighs in at 500g in total.

At this point, Patrizia adds the yeast to the flour by making a well in the centre and then pouring it in slowly, all the while beating the well with a fork as if she was beating an egg, gradually taking in more flour. The centre of the bowl ends up containing a porridgy sludge. We leave this for 10 minutes and have a cup of tea.

With the same egg-beating method, we add another 250ml of water at body temperature, slowly gathering up the flour from around the well. By now we have dough ready to bring out of the bowl and start kneading.

I long to add handfuls of flour to stop the dough sticking to everything but Patrizia says no, it's important to keep the dough as sticky as possible – she learnt that from a professional baker. Instead she shows me how to work the dough quickly; kneading, stretching and turning it simultaneously. Add some seeds, if you like; we added sunflower seeds. (For more kneading tips, I recommend Delia Smith's *Complete Works* book.)

When our dough was springy and light, after about 5 minutes of kneading, it was ready to go back into the lightly floured bowl, with a tea towel on top, and to be left in a warm place, such as an airing cupboard or next to the boiler, to rise for one and a half hours.

Meanwhile, Patrizia and I took a nap.

The second knead sounds like an awful bother, but actually it's more about knocking the air out of it than actually kneading. It doesn't take long. Then we put the dough on a greased, floured baking sheet, although you could put it in a proper loaf tin. We let it rise for another hour, before transferring it quickly into a hot oven (200°C) where it cooked for 40 minutes, until its bottom sounded hard and hollow.

It was delicious, the perfect surface for butter and jam. Now I'm ready to go it alone.

Eco-Cheats

• This is the time for fair-weather cyclists to get back in the saddle. Safe from the sleet and hail of winter, you can ride elegantly through blossom-filled streets, listening out for the signs of spring. No longer any need to bother with raincoats and bulky gloves to stop your fingers falling off, you should now be able to arrive in style – vintage-outfit intact, give or take a touch of spoke damage. The fact that your bike has been hiding in the shed since last October and your cycling season is shorter than most need not be mentioned.

• Everybody grows herbs and flowers in terracotta flowerpots. Who wants to be like everybody? Why not improvise with redundant household items, from old kettles (with holes drilled in the bottom) to tyres donated from a nearby garage and sturdy food packaging. I use old fruit punnets to start off salad seedlings and cut off sections of mineral water bottles to protect young plants from slugs and snails.

• Don't ask me why, but cat pee in the garden is more of a problem at this time of year. If the neighbourhood moggies are turning your veg bed into a toilet, construct an off-putting cotton maze. Find a dozen or so sticks – I use barbecue sticks – dot them around the plagued patch and then wind some cotton thread round them. Weave in and out in different patterns. It works best when plants are still small as you wouldn't want the maze restricting plant growth. If that fails, invest in a water pistol.

Keeping Bees in the City

Anyone who keeps bees deserves extra greenie points given their current plight. These hardworking creatures – which pollinate our crops and in turn provide us with food – are under threat from Colony Collapse Disorder. At the time of writing, the cause is unknown but a variety of factors from GM crops to pesticides have been blamed for declining bee populations across the world.

Thirty-six-year-old Toby Mason lives in Bloomsbury, central London, and looks after eighteen beehives in Regent's Park. As well as providing him with respite from the hustle and bustle of city life, it is a contrast to his work running a marketing training business. To keep one or two hives in your garden or even on your roof is a tiny commitment, he says; you only need to spend half an hour a week on them. In return you get to slather homemade honey on your morning toast. Here, he gives the low-down on keeping bees in a small space.

How to get started? As well as hunting down someone who already keeps bees and picking their brains about how it all works, look for your local beekeeping association. It might run an evening class or some kind of training. Toby was lucky because the North London Beekeepers' Association runs an Adopt-a-Hive scheme that lets you look after a hive with a friend. Every other Sunday, he would go to the apiary to learn bee-management skills.

Don't bees prefer life in the country? Far from it. Suburbia is the best place for bees, says Toby, because people grow plants that flower all year round so there is a constant source of pollen and nectar. In the countryside, the reduction of wildflowers and increase of herbicide and pesticide use on agricultural land has not found favour with the bee population.

Don't you need a big garden? Any sized garden will do, or even a roof terrace. Bees fly up to three miles looking for nectar and pollen so you don't have to have a food feast on their doorstep. If you have no outdoor space, speak to local churches about using a graveyard or find out if your local allotment association has a spot that you could use. Or follow in Toby's footsteps and ask if you can keep bees in a nearby park.

What about the neighbours? They will probably be happy to have an abundance of bees to pollinate their plants. The only problem you may have is with bee poo. Tiny streaks of brown found on freshly laundered clothes hung out near a hive could cause tensions – Toby's car is covered in the stuff. Best not mention it to your neighbours.

What happens over the winter? Everything goes quiet so you can have a break from bee maintenance. Between autumn and spring, the bees stop venturing out of the hive so much; the colony dies down and so does the job of the beekeeper.

Are you able to go on holiday? It's no problem to go away for a couple of weeks in the summer, although you may wish to find a bee-friendly individual to check on your hives. Toby stays in the UK during the summer as it's by far the best time to be in the park with the bees. He goes away in February when the bees are sleepy and the weather's grim.

How do you get the honey out? For this important job, you need a special steel tank, a bit like a tumble-drier lying on its side. You put the frames from your hive inside and it spins, throwing the honey against the side of the tank. From there it drips down and you collect it. If you only have a small number of hives, it's probably worth renting the tank off a beekeepers' association rather than buying one.

Problems to look out for? In spring, bees like to swarm. A colony will hatch a new queen and then if left to its own devices, half of the colony will go out with the old queen looking for a new home. In the countryside, this is less of a problem, but in urban areas, it should be avoided by removing any queen cells before they hatch.

Will I get honeyed-out? Not unless you are really greedy. The only problem Toby has is that sometimes he licks his fingers too often and starts to feel a bit sick.

Where are the bee's knees? Although bees have legs with joints like any insect, they do not have kneecaps, therefore they do not officially have knees. Perhaps it is their absence that has made them desirable.

Greening Up Your Pets

Of all the topics I have dangled in front of my blog readers, the unspectacular subject of cat litter trays was a surprise hit. I should have guessed it, really. We all love our moggies. If further proof were needed that the British are a nation of animal lovers, look at the way we keep some animals for no good reason at all. A goat in the garden providing milk and cheese is one thing, as is a chicken or two to help with breakfast omelettes and scrambled eggs, but a doleful mutt that demands to be walked and fed, and in return contributes nothing more than a spadeful of foul muck every morning? What were we thinking? Of course, I'm in no position to judge anyone for their choice of domestic pet, having spent most of this chapter arguing that worms make decent companions. I'm also partial to eager-eyed spaniels – a firm favourite in our family – along with all members of the feline family. So I don't go with the line that if you were truly green you wouldn't have a pet at all. There must be indirect, albeit slightly questionable, eco-benefits. Don't pets bring with them an interest in wildlife and the natural world? One thing is for sure. If you have a dog, you'll get out more. You'll spend evenings in the park being dragged along by your energetic escort. Here, your carbon footprint is safe; the only energy you burn is your own. Unless, of course, you've driven there in your SUV.

Tiddles' toilet

When it first launched, the scoopable cat litter tray was a bit of a coup in the cat world. Its advantage was that the clay ingredient, sodium bentonite, clumped together when wet, making it easier to remove the soiled bit without replacing the whole tray. But it didn't take long before dust in the clay was found to be carcinogenic and the claws came out. No clinical trial has confirmed that it is a risk to human health, but we must think of the poor furry creatures that squat on this stuff every day. Such is our focus on allergies that cats cause in us, it is easy to forget that we also contribute to their ill-health. Feline asthma is on the rise, caused in part by cats inhaling silica dust and other chemicals from their litter trays. They also ingest the clay while cleaning their feet; it forms a solid lump in their intestines and can cause dehydration and urinary tract problems.

On the blog, Dee wrote a warning to cat lovers to stay away from any product that has deodorizers or added fragrance. 'Our two cats were constantly chewing their claws and washing their paws,' she writes. 'Finally, a vet worked out what was wrong. The skin on their pads and around their nail cuticles had been irritated by the perfume and fine dust of their cat litter. We switched to a fragrance-free and dust-free cat litter and it has stopped.'

There are several biodegradable products on the market but the one that many blog readers mentioned is World's Best Cat Litter (that's straight-up marketing for you).

While it is more expensive, several people wrote in to say that you make the money back because you have to change the tray less often, which also means a reduction in cat litter waste.

Such was the vigorous endorsement by people on the blog, I became suspicious. I began to wonder if the comments were left by World's Best Cat Litter staff writing under pseudonyms. Then I found that Lisa who had raved about the product really was a cattery manager for the RSPCA in Leicester and I felt better.

Scoop the poop

In so many cases, the green thing to do is also the easiest, cheapest and most natural. But when we're dealing with what is jettisoned out of the backside of your precious pet, probably the biggest environmental negative about animal ownership, it's a different story. Leaving it in its organic state, steaming on the pavement, is not recommended. Not on my road, anyway. It's not a bad idea to use old supermarket bags for the pick-up job, but remember that these take hundreds of years to break down in landfill. Better to arm yourself with a 'biobag' made from cornstarch and vegetable oil. Sold by *www.ecoutlet.co.uk* and also by several supermarkets, biobags break down in a matter of months. In a compost bin or wormery, they disappear even faster, but composting pet waste is controversial. The consensus is don't try it as it is riddled with pathogens (disease-causing organisms) that don't break down fast enough. For the same reasons, you should not bury it in the garden if you have any intention of eating anything from the same outdoor space. You can, however, buy a dog-waste converter, devoted to breaking down the bowel emissions of your canine buddy with a system of worms and trays. The final product is used on flowerbeds, but not on the veg patch. Having seen one in action at the height of summer last year, I can testify that the stench is nothing like as bad as you might imagine.

Pet food

The amount of aluminium cans destined for your recycling pile inevitably goes up if your beloved little bit of fluff is a gobbler. This isn't necessarily an eco-atrocity, since recycling aluminium is one of the most successful examples of recycling – especially if you crush your cans with one of the nifty devices you can buy online so that they take up less room in the recycling lorry, reducing transport emissions. Aluminium recycling saves up to 95 per cent of the energy needed to make the raw material. But lessening the amount your pet eats – without pushing size zero among the animal world obviously – is no bad thing. A mixture of dried food that is packed in cardboard boxes and meat in tins would be healthier anyway, given that 25 per cent of dogs and cats in the developed world are said to be obese. As we love our animals, so we overfeed them, which is neither kind nor green. Come to think of it, fat cats, both of the human and feline variety, take up more than their fair share of the earth's resources. If you are cutting back, why should Tiddles escape?

The White Stuff
Learn to Milk a Cow

The path to greener living can lead you to peculiar places. It took me under the heaving udder of a Friesian cow in the Peak District, from where I learnt to milk the animal that provides me with my favourite breakfast accompaniment. It is learning a skill such as this, I was told by the farmer's wife, which puts you back in touch with your food, making you more likely to search for quality, ethical produce. Should you ever find yourself in a similarly sticky – and come to think of it stinky – situation, or should you simply want to bluff your way in farming circles and bag a James Herriot-style chap, here is the bare minimum you should know.

• Do not decline any offers of overalls, gloves and wellies, whatever you think you might look like once you are togged up in them. You will be grateful for any barrier between you and the business end of your chosen herd of heifers.

• To hand-milk a cow, you need to gently squeeze the top of the teat between your thumb and forefinger. One by one, squeeze each of your fingers around the teat, forcing the milk out in a stream. The technique is a bit like playing scales on the flute or recorder, but thankfully you don't have to use your mouth.

• Be calm and gentle. Imagine how you would feel if an inexperienced stranger started fiddling with your bits.

• Before the udders can be milked with an automatic milking machine, each teat needs to be plunged in a disinfectant solution, often iodine, and then wiped clean. This is repeated, with a different solution, at the end of milking.

• To extract the milk, you have to apply the four suction caps to the appropriate udders. For a novice, this can be a fiddly process. A word of advice: try to spend as little time as possible with your head directly under the cow – for obvious reasons.

• If you haven't done this before, you are more likely to make a cow nervous and then she is more likely to crap. A lot. And probably on your head. See this as a form of punishment for not being more in touch with rural ways.

• Good reflexes will help you dodge the cowpats, otherwise resign yourself to dollops of something warm in your hair. Imagine it is conditioner.

• It's not only milking that takes time. Half the work is rinsing the parlour down and keeping it clean (this is also the least fun bit). And all this is only the bookends of a farmer's day. In between milking, there is the farm to run.

• Don't expect anyone to come too close to you afterwards. You might not be able to smell yourself, but trust me, you stink.

Seasonal Food

While going easy on your meat quota, you shouldn't feel obliged to miss out on **Easter lamb chops**, so long as they are British. They make a scrumptious, simple supper, sizzling in a frying pan with a chunk of onion and a splash of wine at the end to make gravy. Serve with any greens you can lay your hands on – I've usually managed to coax a few leaves of spinach into existence by now – and mashed sweet potato combined with anything else that needs using up. I fear I've picked up my mother's habit of getting carried away on the mashing front. She throws in other vegetable remnants; sometimes carrots, leeks and parsnips, all pulverized together.

For those with vegetable beds, you might have managed a row of **radishes** about now. Not being mad keen on their peppery taste has never stopped me from growing them – probably because they look so cheerful with their bright pink bottoms balancing on the soil. Fortunately I've discovered that if you dunk them in enough hummus or a cheese and chive dip, they don't taste half bad.

MAY

GRAZING IN THE GARDEN

TAKE ME TO A GARDEN THAT IS EXPLODING WITH VIVID FLOWERS AND WELL-PLACED shrubs and I'll agree that it looks fabulous. Secretly, though, I'll be eyeing up the beds, imagining how many courgette plants I could squeeze in and wondering where to put a row of radishes. I like to be able to graze in a garden, you see. I like to wander round in my nightie, stopping now and again to chew on things – and you can't do that with most herbaceous borders.

Because I love eating and I love kitchens, a space outside that serves as an extension of these two things is always going to win my affections. Especially at this time of year. Being outside in May is a pleasure, a gentle reminder of the long days, picnics and suntanned feet to come over the following months. Obviously if there are broad beans around to pluck from their leathery jackets and peppery rocket to chew, all the better, but I would hang around virtually any green space just to witness the surge of activity in the soil and to recharge my own pasty batteries with some sunlight.

It hasn't always been like this. For most of my life, I have been oblivious to soil-based goings on. Like many people, I didn't see the point in paying attention until its fruits had landed on my plate. Change came three summers ago when my friend Patrizia sorted herself out with an allotment. She insisted on taking me to see it when I visited her. 'There's a café close by with tea and homemade cakes,' she told me, as she knows me well.

When we found her humble piece of ground, marked out with rows of onions, carrots and salad greens, I was not an instant convert. I hovered uncomfortably, trying not to tread on anything important, while she darted

LEEDS COLLEGE OF BUILDING
LIBRARY

around tearing off leaves for me to taste and insisting that I thrust my hands into the ground to look for carrots.

Sure enough, I found one, which seemed a miracle at the time and remains a benchmark moment in my relationship with the soil. Fancy there being one of these familiar things all the way down here, I thought. It seemed like a very odd place to find a carrot, which is a disturbing insight into what life in the city does to you. I tugged it out of the ground and held it in my palms for a few moments, tenderly, as if carrying a newborn baby. My next instinct was to gobble it, only a thick layer of Yorkshire mud put me off (let's hope that doesn't happen with my firstborn).

That evening, we returned home as the sun was setting, carrying a hand-ful of spring onions, carrots and an assortment of salad leaves. Complemented by a bottle of rosé, they made up the most delicious salad of my life. Whether this was because I'd been outside all day, because I'd plucked the vegetables with my very own hands or simply because I'd drunk too much wine and had started fantasizing about wearing floaty dresses and carrying wicker baskets full of home-grown bounty, I have no idea; but it was at that point that I realized this was something I wanted more of in my life.

Crunch time came some weeks later when Patrizia sweetly sent me a package containing all sorts of vegetable seeds from curly kale to boltardy beetroot. She enclosed instructions on each packet about how deep to sow the seeds and what conditions the plants preferred.

At that point, I only had a small balcony in a Kentish Town flat that I rented with friends, but in the spirit of experiment as much as anything else, I gathered some flowerpots left behind by previous occupants and almost broke Gervase's back by getting him to heave home a giant bag of organic compost from the garden centre.

All for a good cause, I assured him. Two weeks later, I had lettuce, beetroot, tomatoes, dwarf beans and rocket seedlings, all poking their noses out of the soil and reaching up towards the light. I started them off inside on our sunny kitchen windowsill and then when they grew bigger I transplanted them into separate pots and put them outside on the balcony.

To be honest, I had no idea what I was doing. I didn't even know how – and if – my plants would produce fruits. When people asked about them, I tried to sound like someone who had done this before, using words like 'thinning out' and 'bolting', but the reality was that each stage of the growing process was a wonder to me.

There is no doubt that getting started is the trickiest bit. Once you're up and running, and you've acquired some skills and blown several weekends and all your lunch hours browsing 'grow your own' internet forums, everything starts fitting into place. But it's a daunting process if you've never plucked a home-grown sprig of rosemary.

Sadly, affordable horticultural courses for beginners are few and far between. Meanwhile, books, which you would think would be an obvious starting place, I've found to be the opposite. They never explain the really easy stuff. Bring me a beginner's guide to gardening and I'll show you a dozen assumptions that readers will know how to prepare a seed bed, transplant seedlings and thin out young shoots. For the authors – veteran owners of green fingers – barely a second goes by when their conversation is not sprinkled with words like mulch and horse manure, so it's hard for them to realize how little most people know.

I suspect some of those already in the gardening club want to keep newcomers out; perhaps there's only a certain number of pak choi seedlings to go round. But don't let it put you off. Gardening should not be left to the professionals. For thousands of years we have cultivated food, long before we were could recite Alan Titchmarsh (or his organic counterpart Bob Flowerdew).

The internet was my lifeline. The Royal Horticultural Society's Grow Your Own Veg forum became a familiar haunt (*www.rhs.org.uk/vegetables*). And I'm sure I spent more time than was entirely necessary Googling my plants' ailments. Quite aside from the amount of conflicting advice you get on the web, there's a special sort of paranoia that sets in when you realize what you thought was a straight bit of mould on your spinach could be the dreaded *Peronospora effuse* fungus. Or that's what John on the forum says. Like turning to the internet to diagnose your own health problems, it can lead to horticultural hypochondria.

What I learnt on my North London balcony was the importance of the 'give it a go' school of gardening. Poke a couple of seeds into a flowerpot, water them, top up the hole with rich soil and see what happens. You might mess things up but there are always a few foolproof, hardy crops like rocket and mint that won't let you down.

During that first summer of growing, the mini bounty I produced would scarcely have filled a wicker basket, but it brought disproportionate pleasure. 'It's all home-grown' is one of the most delightful sentences imaginable. If you don't believe me, try it. See how smugly it trips off the tongue and conjures images of rural idylls and glowing women in aprons.

But enough of my Ma Larkin fantasies. The unedited truth is that the beetroots during that first year never grew larger than ping-pong balls (but grated in salad they were divine); I often had to nip to the shop to bulk out my salad leaves with an iceberg (but no one noticed), and the four of us living there probably ended up with roughly two beans each (this dish is tapas-style, I insisted). Mind you, I managed to coax enough tomatoes off my four plants to make spicy tomato chutney (see recipe page 214) so I must have been doing something right.

Some things didn't work at all. I gave up on the potatoes, realizing how much space they would need, and my chard inexplicably shrivelled and died after making sterling progress for several weeks. At the time, I blamed any failure on growing in pots. It was the perfect excuse for shortcomings in my harvest. 'What these plants really need is to be out in the ground,' I would announce to people. 'There, they'd really flourish.'

It was only when I moved to Hackney the following year that I realized that container growing is, in many ways, the easy bit. As well as having total soil control (I shipped in quality compost from a garden centre), you can vary plants' positioning and you have a better handle on pests. What I discovered in my new – albeit small and mostly paved – garden is that there are many things beyond your control when you have a living, breathing ecosystem outside the back door. Squirrels answer to no one, they will insist on digging up your seeds; cats will pee on your herbs; dry stone walls harbour armies of snails, and weeds never, ever give up and die.

That second year of growing, I pulled up the neglected shrubs left behind by the previous owners and dedicated half of the flowerbeds – the sunniest half, as edibles love sun – to veggie growing. The closest section to the house was for easy-to-grab salad crops; the rest for beans, aubergines, courgettes, cucumbers and tomatoes. To find out what kind of soil I was dealing with, I followed instructions on the internet to take a handful of it and form it into a ball. If it falls apart in your hand, you have light sandy soil, which drains fast and is considered easy to work with. If your ball holds its shape, like mine did, you have heavy clay soil, which is the worst, likely to become waterlogged in winter and hard as a rock in summer. For worse misfortune, you will find, as I did, that the local drunks have been chucking wine bottles into your garden and you'll spend half your time removing chunks of glass from the soil.

Fortunately there is a solution to all soil deficiencies. It is advice that organic gardeners never tire of giving out. Add organic matter. All vegetables like rich, nutritious soil. It enables plants to better survive attack from pests. Should you not be the sort to brew your own compost (what? even after the previous chapter?), you can buy bags of organic compost or even horse manure at gardening centres.

It's the easy option, a cure-all remedy, but it keeps vegetable growing nice and easy. There's more to it, of course. Brassicas, for instance – the cabbage family – like rich, firmly compacted soil, whereas peas and beans prefer lighter, well-drained soil. But once you start on this territory, learning about how different crops need different types of soil, you risk being put off the task ahead. If you're anything like me, you'll end up tempted to hang up your spade and head inside for a nap.

I decided that ignorance was the best policy. Right from the start, my lot had to lump it and deal with the soil they were given, this being the clay soil I had inherited in the garden, with some compost from the wormery and some from the garden centre, which Gervase dutifully dug into the beds. This you're supposed to do at the start of the growing season and again at the end.

But I'm in no position to hand out nuggets of wisdom. My first sowing session ended in disaster. It coincided with a house-warming party. As friends drunkenly spilled from the patio on to the flowerbeds, rows of beetroot and bean seedlings were trampled. When I found them, or their pitiful remains, the next day, I might have cried if I hadn't been so hungover.

Second time round, I stuck BBQ sticks around the young plants, to punish trespassing ankles and discourage cats from peeing in the beds.

A month later, I brought in a bunch of brightly coloured radishes: my first victory. Or so I thought, until they wilted on the kitchen table. Neither of us much liked radish (until we discovered dipping them in hummus), which taught me an important lesson: only growing what you like eating.

The salad bed probably gave me the most pleasure, enabling me to scoff at supermarkets and their vacuum-packed, £2 bags of lettuce and rocket. It yielded generous quantities of greens from May until December, although towards the end of the year they became bitter, best suited to being cooked. As well as five types of lettuce – the frilly slug-resistant varieties being the most likely to make it into adulthood – I grew spinach, chard, rocket and a chilli plant that became a surprise hit in late October.

I was also thrilled with the broad beans (undemanding to grow and so tasty); the courgettes (worth it for their dazzling yellow and edible flowers) and the French beans, which after a faulty start – several plants disappeared entirely with only a slimy slug trail as evidence – recovered enough to produce fruits up until September.

To my astonishment, after giving up on two aubergine plants and letting the snails have their wicked way with the leaves, I spotted four sausage-sized fruits weighing them down in August. They never grew much bigger but we scoffed them all the same. Some say, a degree of snail damage can encourage a plant to grow even more vigorously, though they probably whisper it, not wanting to speak well of the enemy.

All this sounds impressive, but the fact is these are easy-peasy crops. I haven't even tried serious ones like carrots, onions and cabbages. Nor have I mentioned the failure of our cucumbers – lack of sun, I gather, you need a greenhouse for this kind of thing – and the fact that the birds were quicker than us to appreciate our six gleaming strawberries, or the countless lettuce leaves and bean shoots that I lost to slugs.

By now you've probably got the idea. Not just that it's simple to set up a basic edible garden, but that it's easy to become a grow-your-own bore. I'm there already and I'm only a few years into the game. At certain points in the summer, there is only one subject that I feel equipped to discuss at the dinner table and it revolves around what's growing. Gervase copes valiantly, finding ways to use this to his advantage. He knows, for instance, that he can humour me out of virtually any grump by enquiring after the wellbeing of my oriental greens.

The thing is, once you start growing, even if it's a tray of rocket on your windowsill, it becomes obsessive. You look anew at what is going on outside. On verges, railway embankments, in parks and in open spaces, everywhere you look, there's a thriving parallel world out there that you never knew existed.

A train journey becomes an opportunity to peep into gardens that back on to tracks and to catch flash glimpses of allotments. I find myself peering into people's green spaces at any opportunity. Look! A nasturtium growing up a sunflower stalk, now there's a good idea – and I'll make a mental note to do the same. However many times embarrassed friends drag me away from strangers' front gardens while I take notes on companion planting, I stand firm by my belief that this is the best way to learn. I recommend roaming around other people's gardens – something that is less awkward if you know the owners.

Whereas some people can't resist a nose around the inside of people's homes, I'd rather be out inspecting the soil. Every veg patch I have seen has taught me about how to do things on my own. I honestly don't know how else you would learn. It's all very well reading gardening columns, but you need to see things in practice. You need to look closely at a wigwam structure held together with twine and made from sticks; you need to watch expert hands pushing in calendula flowers and pinching out shoots on a tomato plant to understand how it's done.

For this, some people say a couple of hours spent shadowing a gardener who has come to work in your own garden is invaluable. Expensive, maybe, but a good way to kick-start your relationship with the soil. I haven't tried it myself, though I probably ought to, as I can imagine that it would teach me some crucial skills.

In lieu of this, I wander around with my friend Martin in his garden. Not only does he have a polytunnel in his extensive Hackney patch, but he has the added advantage of being a biologist. He can tell stories about fungal diseases that affect leafy greens and the lifecycle of red spider mites. I know we're on unequal footing, but his thriving salad bed still brings out wholesome green rivalry in me. I wonder if mine will ever look so bountiful. That I would ever claim the upper hand, with my half-shady, half-paved garden, with its poor soil and inexperienced manager, is laughable. During early summer, his patch heaves with suppertime favourites. When he and his brother, Will, come for supper, they bring round spuds, several lettuces and armfuls of radishes. If I reciprocated, that would be half my crop gone.

Therein lies a problem with growing on a small scale in your tiny back garden. Sometimes you wonder if it's worth the effort. All that uncomfortable hovering over the soil, weeding, watering and whispering encouraging words, for one or two dishes of broad beans. I can tell that is what Gervase is thinking when I proudly serve up a miniature amount of produce. It helps that it tastes delicious, but I don't think he believes me when I tell him it's the process and what I've learnt along the way that matters too.

I may have started out compelled by my stomach, but I have come to love the childish curiosity that growing things breeds. The questions that are raised every time you step out the back door. Why are all those hoverflies descending on that flower? Will it matter if the courgette plant spreads its green leafy wings over the beetroots? What shall I do with these bright blue borage flowers?

Even if I try to keep a trip into the garden short and snappy, to bring some washing in off the line, say, I get drawn into the drama. Hours later, I'll stumble back into the house, dust the dead leaves off my shoulders, pick a few money spiders from my hair and get back to what I was doing. So much going on out there, I'll mutter to Gervase. He'll nod politely without looking up from his laptop or realizing the deranged woman I have become.

My favourite time to go out is at night with a head-torch. This peculiar ritual first came about when I was at war with the snails. An hour or so after it got dark, they would troop down the side of the wall, slurping and sucking their way to the salad bed where tender young lettuces awaited, like lambs to the slaughter. If I intervened at the right moment, I could collect dozens, tossing them into a flowerpot or plastic bag to empty in the park later.

Obviously this had implications for my social life. I could not very well relax in the pub knowing that any second the appalling mission would begin. I'd rush back, often to find several of the beasts already clamped on to my favourite young plants. Under the glow of my head-torch, I'd see nothing at first. All would appear normal. But they're devious, these snails. I could well imagine them shushing each other and staying still as statues when they spotted me. After a double-take, a dark shadow on a stem would catch my eye and then I'd start to notice them, leached on to the helpless leaves, munching my lovingly nurtured babies. Like witnessing a murder, the horror of this scene is indescribable.

For these criminals, the park drop-off method of disposal I often deemed too good. I would crush them there and then. Did I feel remorse? None whatsoever. Though I did always regret the slimy squelch that stamping on them left behind on the patio.

After a traumatic few months, trialling various methods of getting rid of them, including piling them into a bucket and pouring boiling water over them, I vowed to stick with the park trips. Never mind that it was more humane for them, it was less harrowing for me. The boiling water approach, recommended by an organic gardening guide, I tried only when I was at my wits' ends, having lost my two handsomest courgette plants, and several marigolds that were attracting bees and hoverflies, therefore keeping greenfly at bay. Barely a stalk remained and I wanted revenge.

But have you ever tried pouring boiling water over a bowl of live, crawling animals? It is not for the faint-hearted, I can tell you that, and it leaves you with the question of what to do with the grey lumpy soup left behind. The same problem comes from setting 'slug pubs', sunken plastic cups filled with beer that the creatures have a taste for and drown themselves in. This may be the organic gardener's favourite trick, but what do you do with the mounds of gelatinous slug you're left with after only a few days? Someone on the blog suggested leaving them out for the birds, but the feathery population of my part of town are far too fussy to tuck in. They have set their sights higher, hanging around near the wormery hoping I'll leave the lid off.

There were times when I was sorely tempted to abandon my organic aspirations and blitz them with chemical pellets, but in the end I held off.

What's the point in going to the trouble of growing things organically, enriching your soil and attracting wildlife to your garden if you're going to ruin the ecosystem with a poisonous chemical, as likely to be imbibed by predators as pests?

The only time my humane dispersal method let me down was one morning when I forgot to empty a plastic bag full of slugs and snails in the park, instead cycling happily to work with it in my handbag, hung over the handlebars. Until mid-afternoon when I detected a crinkling noise coming from under my computer, I was oblivious to my lapse of memory. They were trying to make a bid for freedom, out of their plastic prison and on to the virgin territory of my chequebook and mobile phone. Fortunately, the plastic bag was knotted so there were no escapees, and I quickly released them into *The Times*' outdoor courtyard, where they were condemned to a miserable life among the forgotten pot plants and cigarette butts.

After this incident, I took a step back from my slaying missions. I'd had enough. The creatures were taking over my life; snail trails led paths through my dreams. I'd wake up expecting to see one perambulating across the bedroom ceiling. Fortunately, I had dented the local population by then – except for in the park, which could probably have been reclassified as a snail and slug visitors' centre. It also helped that my lettuces had grown big enough to withstand the odd nibble.

You may have noticed by now that gardening hardens you to nature's ugly side. I think nothing of picking up fat, rust-coloured slugs with my bare hands. I crush as many greenfly as I can find between forefinger and thumb and stamp on unsuspecting ants in my flip-flops. Most disturbingly, I am able to squash baby snails with my fingers. Squeamishness has been replaced by dead-eyed brutality. It might not sound like a planet-friendly attitude to creatures great and small, but when it comes to sparing your supper, it's a vicious business and few gardeners will say otherwise.

Come a certain time in the evening, somewhere between supper and bed, I still instinctively reach for my head-torch and wander out into the garden. There are fewer pests to worry about so instead I admire the earthworms hauling themselves across the soil and I watch spiders dancing in between the branches of my tomato plants. These things would have made me shiver once, but the garden has made sense of them. I'm in awe of the soil, the way it comes alive at night and its ability to transform tiny seeds into plants that we can eat – whether or not you remember to dig in immense quantities of organic matter.

Flowers for All Seasons

What's in bloom in Britain throughout the year

January, February
violets • pussy willow

March, April, May
delphiniums • daffodils • lilies • tulips • lily of the valley

June, July, August
alstroemeria • gladioli • agapanthus • hydrangeas

September, October
michaelmas daisies • white chrysanthemums • sunflowers

November, December
red amaryllis • scented narcissi • nerines

WHAT'S IN IT FOR
THE PLANET?

By eating food from your garden . . . you will be feasting on truly local food. Cheap and nutritious, eating from the garden or allotment also means less packaging in your bin; no unknown chemicals in your supper and virtually no food miles. When you sink your teeth into your first home-grown trophy, you can add to that the superior taste.

By avoiding chemicals . . . you won't be encouraging the evolution of pests that are resistant to chemicals, which leads to even stronger ones being developed. These kill off predators (the good guys) as well as pests (the bad guys). By putting down super-strength slug pellets, remember that you not only rid your garden of slimy pests but of the toads and birds that are poisoned when they eat them. Chemicals used on the soil also end up in our waterways and eventually in our own bodies. In 2003, 80 garden products were banned because EU scientists either had data proving they were unsafe or not enough information for them to be cleared, according to Friends of the Earth. This lack of knowledge about the long-term impact of many garden pesticides is as worrying as what we do know.

By encouraging wildlife . . . you will maintain a healthy biodiversity in the place where you live. Organic principles are based around the belief that a sudden influx of one pest will be checked by the arrival of its predator. You may lose a few lettuces while this natural cycle takes place, but the idea is that wildlife helps to keep pests under control naturally so you don't have to use chemicals. A city garden maintained organically can be home to a more diverse range of wildlife than farmers' fields where chemical sprays are used. It is also by attracting bees and other insects to your garden to fertilize and pollinate your plants that you will be able to grow a healthy harvest.

Starting Off
Growing in a small space

Don't aim too high. Once you've tried the easiest things – herbs, salad leaves and tomatoes – you can graduate to broad beans, courgettes and other suppertime favourites the following year. By that time, your soil will have improved too.

Make a plan. Don't rush and sow seeds before working out which plants would be suited to different parts of your patch. How can you maximize space? What might benefit from being close to a wall? What do you want to have closest to the house? It is said that you shouldn't make drastic alterations to your garden until you've had it for a year and seen how it functions through all the seasons.

Watch out for space-greedy plants. Asparagus are so snooty about being near others that they won't grow properly unless they have a weed-free bed to themselves. Courgettes will also dominate everything around but you only need one or two plants to get a healthy harvest.

Watch out for vegetables that require complicated supports. I was all for a row of raspberry canes until I heard about the posts and wire supports that I'd have to build. It shouldn't put you off, but it is something to think about.

You don't have to choose between a garden full of edibles or decorative plants. You can successfully combine the two: sunflowers will shoot up over a lettuce bed without depriving it of light and marigolds can be dotted all over the place to attract aphid-eating insects. And who's to say that when your runner beans are in flower they're not decorative anyway?

Expect failure – how else will you learn? Seeds will disappear without a trace, others will refuse to germinate and your favourite plants will be trampled by visiting dogs and children. Anything that makes it to your plate is worth celebrating.

Don't persist with failing crops. When your spinach gives up for the third time, try some chard instead. Concentrate on what grows easily and you'll have less work and more satisfaction from your garden.

Try it in May . . .

Light Greenies
Learn the flower seasons

For a fragrant introduction into the world of flowers and their seasons, I recommend a trip to a flower market. There are lots around the UK, and none that a Google search or a scan of local newspapers won't bring up. I explored the New Covent Garden's flower market in Vauxhall, South London, early one summer morning. Like any expedition to a morning market, it's the experience that counts as much as whether you buy anything. I resisted, having been warned that the salesmen can spot a non-industry insider a mile off and hike up prices accordingly. Instead, I gathered a gorgeous bunch of lilies from the gutter outside. Stock considered past its best is dumped out in the streets for anyone to salvage.

My visit started at seven in the morning in the traders' café nearby, full of men and banter. I sat quietly with a mug of sweet tea and a bacon roll and marvelled at the macho side of floristry. 'Eh, Bob, you got them orchids in yet?' 'Nah, mate, try me next week.' These snippets painted a picture a long way away from ladies doing flower-arranging before church.

Within the market itself, I visited C.H. Pratleys and Co., a wholesaler specializing in UK-grown flowers. The manager told me his customers are less likely now than ever before to know the British flower seasons. While the range of blooms available has never been better, there are complications for ethically minded flower fans. They may have clocked up a heavy carbon footprint from being flown across the world in refrigerated planes. Or they may have been grown in energy-greedy heated greenhouses in Europe (which is often worse in terms of emissions). The simplest way to avoid such problems is to support our own diverse flora and fauna and learn to appreciate its seasonal differences. Only 20 per cent of the cut flowers bought in Britain come from here. From Kenya, however, we imported 18,000 tonnes in 2005, nearly twice the number imported in 2001. Some argue that this makes money for poor countries keen to trade with the developed world; others, including the new economics foundation, say a monoculture crop, such as roses, is not a sustainable way to provide income in Africa. It makes producers vulnerable. It would be better if countries like Kenya were growing a diverse range of crops, whether or not they were headed for UK supermarkets.

According to Moyses Flowers, an ethical flower company that is trying to revive the UK flower industry, our own varieties are far more inspiring than people imagine. Unusual varieties of hydrangeas, dahlias and sunflowers, among many others, have stopped being grown because we have turned to other countries' flowers. Like British-grown fruit and veg, our indigenous produce has been sidelined by the exotic. Florists, in part, are to blame. They have become used to having a vast array of materials at their fingertips, most of which come from Holland and have been bred to last longer than British flowers. Why should they risk a fall in sales by bothering with seasonal restrictions, unless consumers stop wanting flowers that can only be delivered at a high environmental cost? This might mean forgoing yellow roses on your wedding day if you happen to be getting married in December, but you could replace them with scented narcissi from the Scilly Islands or red amaryllis.

Dark Greenies

Offer your services to an organic farm

To bump yourself up the ladder of gardening knowledge, sometimes you need to have a break from your own garden. Let the weeds grow, turn your back on the slugs and struggling salad leaves (so what if a few die?) and go and mess around in someone else's patch.

WWOOFing is perfect for this. It stands for Willing Workers on Organic Farms and it is an international exchange movement that has been running since 1971. You join – in the UK this costs £15 a year – to browse the list of organic host farms both in the UK and abroad that welcome volunteers, and find one that suits you. It works especially well for city-based growers who want to experience farm life and see things done on a larger scale.

With no money exchanging hands, in return for bed, board and practical experience, you work on the farm. The idea is that your labour will help the farm and enable you to learn first-hand about organic growing techniques. It's up to you to negotiate with the hosts what kind of work you would prefer and the duration of your stay. Accommodation can range from spare rooms to tents in the garden. When I stayed on a farm in North Yorkshire, a gypsy-style caravan made from coppiced willow was my home. The day started early with porridge and the allocation of the day's activities. I spent the morning planting marigolds in the veg beds and mulching courgettes with newspaper and straw. After a late lunch, the time was my own, but I still spent most of it hanging around the runner beans, half weeding them, half chatting to my hosts. I left with the impression that I had gained more than they had from the exchange. I ate fantastically well, drank their wine, slept like a log and picked up a wealth of information about organic growing.

Another benefit is that you find yourself surrounded by people who are happy to spend the day discussing the many different ways to self-pollinate courgette flowers and how to flavour vinegar with nasturtium leaves.

• An empty jam jar is not fit for the bin, even the recycling sort; it has so many potential futures. Mix up your own cleaning product in it, use it to store vinaigrette, keep herbs and spices in it, or make it a pot for pens by the phone, or a receptacle for pickled vegetables and chutney. For its prettiest incarnation, make a lantern for the garden. An old honey pot will transform into the perfect tea-light holder with the help of some garden twine. Wind it around the neck of the jar and then make a loop over the top. Hang it on a branch to cast a romantic glow on your evening beer in the garden.

• The job of clearing a bed of weeds or preparing a veg patch can seem huge, but not if you rope in a friend. It'll take half the time and you can punctuate it with tea breaks and treats. Find someone who needs a similar task doing in their own home – it doesn't have to be garden-based, it could be a wall to paint or a spare room to clear – and do a swap. One Saturday afternoon at yours; another at theirs.

• Drop edible flowers into ice trays filled with water, freeze and you'll have pretty cubes for Pimm's and summer drinks. This works a treat with the vivid blue flowers from borage as well as nasturtium petals. I know it's only a small step away from starting up a flower-pressing book and other disturbingly grannyish behaviour, but take comfort from the fact that it is a classic double-bluff. It says: I may be doing something old-fashioned but I'm stylish enough to pull it off, so pass the custard creams.

Growing with no Garden

Don't despair. You are in a unique position. You are able to be passionately pro-greenery without having to do much about it. A few pots of easy-to-grow herbs on a sunny windowsill, is enough to indicate membership of the gardening classes. It sends out the message that if this is what you can achieve with no garden, imagine what you would be producing if you had one.

Plenty of easy greens can be grown from seed inside your home. That includes rocket, chives and salad leaves. You could cheat with slightly trickier customers, such as chilli and strawberry plants, by buying them as ready-grown plants.

Make sure pots have drainage holes, ideally more than one. Then throw a few stones in the bottom to stop the soil getting waterlogged.

Join your local guerrilla gardening group. This loose network of horticultural activists undertakes covert missions to 'liberate' public spaces by planting them with shrubs and flowers. The movement is cropping up across the world but it is most active in large cities where it provides a chance for town dwellers, starved of their own gardening opportunities, to come together and exercise frustrated green fingers. So-called 'digs' take place at night, mainly because members work in the day, and involve weeding and planting chunks of neglected, litter-strewn ground for the benefit of the public. Find your local group (*www.guerrillagardening.org*) and join the next dig.

Get on your local allotment waiting list. It is true that in some parts of London, the wait is ten years long, but in other parts of the country new land is being made available. You might end up with your own piece of Eden sooner than you think (*www.nsalg.org.uk*).

Recipes
for Garden Guzzlers

Such is my impatience and general greediness, I lose no time between picking and eating what I've grown. For produce to make it into the house at all is a feat. Apparently, this is good for my health, too, because fresh produce loses nutrients and vitamins fast. Here are some recipes that help keep down the time between grabbing goodies from the garden and gobbling them.

Broad beans tapas-style

Rush the pods inside, fast as you can, and plunge them into boiling water for a few minutes. If the pods are young and still quite small, I don't even bother taking out the beans within, that's how impatient I am. I eat the whole thing, jacket and all. Once I've drained them, dolloped some olive oil on top, along with a pinch of salt and a grinding of pepper, I throw on some grated parmesan and wolf down immediately.

Rocket pesto

For this recipe, I am indebted to Patrizia. It was first published in the Body&Soul section of *The Times* when we ran an article about preserving. At the time, there was concern about her lack of precision. Exactly how much rocket is a handful, my editor wanted to know, and how much oil does she use? The fact is, having made pesto several times now, it doesn't matter. It tastes good whatever – just look at the ingredients! Be Italian about it (like Patrizia) and just throw in what you've got.

First bash a handful of cashews and a handful of pine nuts with a rolling pin until they are reduced to a crumbly powder. Mix with a big bunch of rocket, enough to fill your hands (you can deplete a bed quite substantially and it'll grow back), having chopped it as finely as you can be bothered to. I sometimes add a little home-grown spinach to the mix. Add a couple of chopped cloves of garlic and lashings of olive oil and grind with a pestle. If you have a big enough mortar you could do the whole thing in it, rather than using a rolling pin to break up the nuts. Instead, I use a mixing bowl, pestle and rolling pin combination to do the grinding. Then add as much parmesan as you can afford (if only it were cheaper, that stuff, I'd use more) and salt and pepper to taste. Spoon into jam jars and finish with a final splash of olive oil before sealing the jars. Unopened, it will keep for several months if stored in the fridge or in a cool place.

Grilled courgettes

I do my best to wait for my courgettes to become a decent size, but sometimes I reach breaking point and cut them off when they resemble a small green carrot. I'm told this will encourage others to grow so I don't feel too bad about it. The first few on a plant seem to rot from the flower end anyway, and I have to do an emergency harvesting job and slice off the rotten bit. They still taste delicious, sliced lengthways into three or four pieces, brushed with oil, sprinkled with salt and thyme from the garden and grilled. It's nice to crumble some feta on top once they're cooked and then put them back under the grill for a few moments.

Borage dip

It's an odd herb, borage, but I've become fond of its unusual, cucumberish flavour. A bit like that Body Shop cleanser that used to be popular, my friend Nicole decided, but not in a bad way. Bees go mad for borage, too, so it's ideal if you're trying to encourage pollination in your patch.

Pull off as many leaves as you can spare (from the bottom of the plant so the shoots at the top will keep forming), chop them roughly and mix with some cream cheese, olive oil and chopped black olives (the salty, wrinkly ones if possible). I usually add some plain yoghurt at this stage to make the dip more runny, and season with salt and a liberal grinding of black pepper. For a hostess with the mostess touch, don't forget to decorate with the tiny blue borage leaves.

Is My Garden 'Organic'?

If it weren't enough of a boost to one's green credentials to be poking about in the soil at all, the debate that rages in gardening circles is whether to do it organically. There is no defining line at which point you can say, my garden is now officially organic – and I like to think no one will be trying to catch you out. Only if you were growing for commercial reasons would there be rigorous regulations to follow. For instance, not all my seeds are organic, but I raise them in an organic way. I call this organic gardening, but if I was selling my spuds to the Soil Association, it would think otherwise. Should you want to do things properly, here are the fundamental principles of organic gardening, laid out by Garden Organic (*www.gardenorganic.org.uk*):

- Boost the natural health of soil to help plants resist pests and disease.

- Do not use chemicals, such as herbicides for controlling weeds and pellets to kill off slugs.

- Choose appropriate plant varieties for your garden's conditions.

- Make your patch wildlife-friendly to encourage natural predators.

- Use organically grown seeds as far as possible, and don't use genetically modified varieties.

- Collect rainwater; compost and reduce your use of finite resources in the garden.

- Don't think you can have one part of your garden organic and douse other parts in chemicals. That won't work.

It's a Jungle Out There
How to lure wildlife to your garden

There's an old saying among organic gardeners that if your lettuces are being munched by slugs, your problem is not too many slugs, but too few ducks. Instead of focusing on how to kill off pests ourselves – the time-consuming option – we should think about how to encourage other creatures to rock up in our garden and do it for us. Ducks might not be an option for everyone, but birds, frogs, toads and hedgehogs also eat slugs.

The first step is to make sure you're growing wildlife-friendly plants that are attracting predators. Marigolds, for instance, attract ladybirds and lacewings, which will eat aphids, as do herbs such as dill and fennel. Meanwhile, poached-egg plants and stocks are adored by hoverflies – they should be encouraged because they feed on caterpillars as well as sap-sucking aphids.

Birds are your allies. They can easily be encouraged with a feeding tube or a bird table – blue tits, especially, hunt aphids. Not every garden will be suitable for hedgehogs but if yours is, their presence should also be encouraged as they eat slugs and caterpillars. Provide them with piles of wood so they have somewhere to hibernate.

You can always ship in some predators. Or more accurately, order them by post from green gardening websites, such as *www.greengardener.co.uk*. Different kinds of nematodes (microscopic worms) that you add to your watering can and water on to the garden kill vine-weevil and slugs. Lacewing larvae will arrive wedged between cardboard segments. You tap them out on to plants that are suffering from aphid attack and wait for them to get hungry – a lacewing larvae munches up to 300 aphids a day. One word of caution: release flying predators in the evening or you'll be helping your neighbour's garden as bugs love flying in warm air.

Harder to deliver in envelopes but very good at munching slugs are frogs and toads. A pond will keep them in your garden. As well as spawning frogs, this will encourage bathing birds and hatching insects. A large garden isn't absolutely necessary; a mini pond made from a sunken barrel or a bucket with a few plants and stones around it will contribute significantly to the diversity of your garden.

Obviously there are times when human intervention is required. One thing you won't be short of is advice on what can be done to discourage slugs and snails. They are the gardener's arch enemy. But what will work for you might not work for others. I've tried virtually everything suggested, from surrounding plants with eggshells and pistachio nuts to protecting young plants with cut-off plastic bottles. Sunken cups of beer have probably worked best, along with slug patrols at night to deplete their numbers. Whatever you do, don't give up. In the end, you will defeat them. Determination conquers all.

How to Deal with Weeds

I hate to be one of those relentlessly optimistic types who sees the silver lining however beastly the cloud, but you have to understand that organic gardening teaches you to look for benefits in what is traditionally seen as A Bad Thing. That weeds are proliferating in your garden at all is a good sign. It means your soil is fertile. Feel flattered that you have created an environment so many plants want to make their home.

Spare 'good' weeds. If they do not threaten other plants and don't look too bad, think about leaving weeds in peace. See your space as an exotic wilderness and thriving ecosystem rather than a failed attempt at a garden. Flowering weeds, such as purslane and milk thistle, look pretty and encourage a variety of wildlife, which in turn creates a balanced ecosystem in your garden. Weeds like this have shallow roots so they pinch fewer of your other plants' nutrients – very thoughtful of them.

Eat your weeds away. Purslane, dandelion leaves and stinging nettles are a few unwelcome garden guests that can be plucked from the soil and put in the pot. Some of them strike me as a duty to eat rather than a pleasure. I've made a delicious nettle soup before but came a cropper with dandelion leaves. Inspired by my success with the soup (see June, page 176) I returned to the undergrowth to snoop around for a second course. Braised dandelion leaves it was, treated as you might spinach. But they were bitter and unpleasant, even after a generous drizzle of honey. A forage too far, perhaps.

Show no mercy for sinister weeds. You don't need to be a weedologist to know when something you didn't plant is out to get what you did. If I had taken up a totally laissez-faire attitude to weeding, it would have seen off my broad beans long ago, strangled by bindweed. As soon as my back is turned, it winds its way around their stems. It does the same to my lettuces. I sometimes notice that a couple of them are looking peculiar and realize that they are bound up in the stuff, crying out silently to be freed.

Other pernicious weeds to look out for are couch grass, ground elder and creeping thistle. With deep roots, they blossom at the expense of others, stealing light and soil nutrients. As much as regular slug patrol is needed in an organic garden, there must also be weed patrol. A bit of weed education goes a long way, so you can separate the good from the bad.

Squeeze out weeds. Bare soil is a bad idea. Instead, cover your beds with a layer of mulch or heavy manure. Or you could plant green manure, which you sow in autumn and dig into the soil in spring. It's not much to look at, although some varieties flower, therefore attracting insects, but it's a good way of protecting your beds from winter weather and persistent weeds.

Wait to weed after rain. When the earth is soggy and loose, you'll find it easier to pull up the roots of weeds, rather than breaking off the bit above ground and allowing it to keep growing. Don't worry if you don't own a hoe; borrow a neighbour's, or do it with your hands. One of the benefits of hand-weeding is the opportunity it provides to come nose to nose with your plants. By doing this, you'll get to know them much better.

Seasonal Food

I used to be an **asparagus** purist, believing that the only way to honour this particular vegetable when its brief season arrived was to give it undivided attention on a plate; to serve it as a starter, smeared with butter and eaten in reverential silence. That was until I made a spring risotto that teamed asparagus heads with broad beans, peas and rocket. It was delicious, lighter than some risottos and dotted with lemon rind and tasty greens. By saving the tough bottom bit of the asparagus stalks to drop into the stock, I felt certain that I was doing the vegetable justice.

JUNE

GREEN LOVE

I T WAS ONE OF THOSE TAKE-THE-PLUNGE-AND-INTRODUCE-YOURSELF MOMENTS. EITHER that or stand there alone at the bar like a loser, pretending to look for something in your handbag or sending imaginary text messages. Much better to grasp the nettle. A deep breath first, and then: 'Hello, I'm Anna. I don't know anyone here. Do you?' That was how I met Alex, a chirpy Australian in his thirties who had recently moved from Melbourne to London to work for a campaigning organization called the Climate Group.

Turns out he and his friend – also called Alex, but female – had been to a Green Drinks event before. They were meeting a third Alex later on. I wondered briefly if this was not a gathering for people interested in the environment after all, but for people called Alex. Anyhow, what matters is that Alex and Alex rescued me from solitary cider-drinking.

I would have been more comfortable if I'd realized that Green Drinks is not, as I had first thought, a monthly dating event for those who want to bag an earth-friendly partner. Had I known that the worldwide network, which includes groups in 243 cities, exists primarily to bring people together who work in the environmental sector, I would have sunk casually on to a bar stool right away. Instead I had the impression that this was where greenies came to find someone to set up yurt with – and the idea of wading into this breeding ground for sustainable love made me feel uneasy.

Its founder, Paul Stott, puts me right. 'The aim when I started the group in 1989 was to provide like-minded people with an opportunity to share ideas, make friends and learn about job opportunities,' he says. 'I was working as an environmental consultant at the time and wanted to meet people doing similar things.' And find romance? 'I wouldn't rule out the possibility that relationships have grown out of the network,' he tells me diplomatically.

I should quickly add that curiosity had led me here, nothing more. Gervase and I had not experienced a particularly bad patch of eco-arguments. He hadn't left his mobile-phone charger plugged in one too many times. I had come to check out the kind of green socializing that takes place in my city – and obviously to sneak a peep at the talent.

The London branch of Green Drinks meets in the basement of a pub in Soho. Naturally the pub has been chosen for its fine selection of organic beer and Fairtrade tea and coffee. Most people have come with friends, not alone like me. When I arrive, everyone is busy drinking, eating crisps and discussing whether or not they could go out with someone who didn't recycle. The verdict, if you're wondering, is no – not unless they were willing to change their ways. A non-composter, however, is deemed acceptable, especially in the city.

'It's busy, isn't it?' I say to the woman next to me as we elbow our way to the bar.

'You should have seen it last month,' she replies. 'It was rammed. Tonight there's been a clash with CSR Chicks, so you can imagine what's happened.'

I nod, pretending to know who CSR Chicks are. Later I learn that it is a rival network set up by a group of women who work in corporate social responsibility and sustainable development. Founded in London, it now has groups in the Netherlands, Belgium, Canada and the USA. Operating as a Yahoo Groups network, it is first and foremost a recruiting ground for jobs in corporate social responsibility.

There is also a CSR Blokes equivalent, and another group called Carbon Drinks, which is mentioned later on in the evening. I'm assured that they are no competition. Green Drinks is the best established and apparently the most earthy. That's what Alex says. I wonder if he's joking about the earthy bit, but he's not. 'It's for normal people to get together; there's nothing pretentious about it,' he explains.

I must admit, I had deep and unforgivable misgivings about who I would meet here. I imagined a room full of the sort of people who don't have their own friends and have to join networking groups to make them. I was also sure the place would be packed with eco-droners: bores who bang on about how much they do for the planet and how superior their lifestyle is to everyone else's.

And yet what I find is a lively bunch, mostly in their twenties and thirties, brought together by a vague interest in greenery. From dreadlocked foreign students to academics and city accountants, the group represents all walks of green. It isn't nerdy. The people here look nice; they look as if they could be my friends. Whether I'd meet the green god of my dreams by attending regularly (if I didn't already have one at home, obviously), I'm not sure. Since most people I speak to are quick to mention their other halves, I doubt it.

Later on I meet Sarah. She is disappointed at the lack of singles at the gathering. It's one of the reasons she comes, she confides. Although she's spotted a lovely-looking fellow across the bar, but she's not sure how to approach him. Miranda, an American with a more direct approach to socializing, wishes there was some kind of compulsory circulation overseen by the organizers, speed-dating style. Otherwise you end up talking to the same people all night, she explains. Last time she came, she spent the entire evening at a table with students. By the way she raises her eyebrows, I realize that this is a very bad thing indeed.

Paul says he prefers to let the evenings run themselves. He sees his job as providing a venue and free-flowing alcohol. Sometimes he does the host thing and introduces people or rescues someone who looks a bit lost. At times, he helps things along by taking away the chairs. 'Networking is not sitting down,' he announces, with surprising gusto.

Luckily for me, Paul wasn't there when I arrived and the chairs remain. Alex and I slump down in a corner and discuss inevitable topics, such as how much impact celebrities who go green have on environmental awareness, council recycling schemes across London, and why the Government isn't bold enough to take decisive action against climate change, leaving it to overwhelmed individuals. It's good to get these things off our chests, away from our partners and the glazed expressions that sometimes descend on friends when we pipe up about them. If nothing else, Green Drinks is a place where the eco-interested can have a good rant, knowing that the people there will listen, not doze off.

Later, Alex and I tire of the planet. We have another drink and start talking about our relationships, our homes and, finally, what we make of living in London. I notice that around us other people have veered off green subjects too. They're tucking into pub food and talking about films. It's just like being in any pub. I feel strangely reassured by how normal everybody is. Alex is right – it's earthy. It's as though I had expected my fellow greenies in London to have two heads – and to talk about climate change from both.

Before I leave, I wander around the tables, stumbling a little after too much cider, eavesdropping on people's conversations. I detect some low-level flirting, which is encouraging. Someone tells me that the networking veneer only thinly covers the real purpose of the event. The founder might prefer to think of the lofty aims of Green Drinks, she says, but it is still where you come if you want a new job or a new partner.

Confirming this, a green dating site piggy-backed the event for a time, using it as a meeting point for members. Paul won't tell me which dating site it was, as he doesn't want to give them any publicity. He didn't like it at all. A dozen or so people would turn up, hoping to find a steady source of eco-interested singletons. But the website didn't discuss its agenda with Paul or credit Green Drinks. Paul suspected most of its clients of being poseurs anyway, not genuinely interested in the environment.

My own research into online green dating confirms Paul's view. Sites with names like *www.loveisgreen.org* and *www.greensingles.com* promise love to greenies of all ages and inclinations (although I wouldn't trust members to resemble their glamorous photos). The oldest UK agency is *www.natural-friends.com*, but I'm warned off it by someone with experience of these things, who tells me that it has a reputation for having members who are 'a little too homespun'.

Then there are many sites with vegetarian undertones – or overtones, as in the case of *www.veggielove.com*. Along with the usual discussions about the ups and downs of a green lifestyle, they feature debates on the morality of kissing a meat-eater and why vegan men are usually gay.

Some of this is intriguing, no doubt about it. I learn that certain sensitive vegetarians can detect unpleasant meaty aromas coming from a potential partner before they've even kissed, causing an immediate hitch in the budding relationship. I'm tempted to point out on the forum that a veggie diet heavy in pulses can lead to another smelly problem, but I hold back, not wanting to dampen the spirit of green dating. Other members complain about forums being swamped with fakers who claim at first to be motivated by 'peace to the planet' but are then spotted dropping cigarette butts and scoffing hamburgers on the second date.

Online green dating is clearly riddled with complexity, and I'm unconvinced by it. Would you want to go out with someone who was only willing to consider people with the right eco-credentials, anyway? I'd rather go about my life in a vaguely green way and hope that by doing so I'll inadvertently bump into other people like me. That way, I reckon I'm more likely to meet people who wear their green lightly – and more attractively. If you ask me, being green should be a secondary reason for bonding with someone, after the obvious ones. Do you get on well? Do you fancy them? Will they bring you tea in bed every morning?

That's not to say that bringing some leafy elements to your relationship isn't a good idea once it's established. By heading out to a nice place in the countryside, you can get to know each other all the better: lying on a rug, drinking wine and feeling at one with nature. On crisp autumn walks, you can pick blackberries and later share bowls of deep-red, bubbling crumble. You can dig the garden together and go off on weekend cycling adventures. And if this all sounds a bit homespun, you can balance it out with lavish meals and expensive gifts. The great outdoors is not only romantic, but also after all that fresh air you'll be too exhausted to argue in the evenings.

Green love blossoms through everyday activities, not via internet forums. Some say furtive glances between cyclists at red traffic lights can become the start of something, while others insist that the best course of action is to hang out at your local health-food shop – that hotbed of eco-activism – hoping you'll be roped into a worthy enterprise by the gorgeous guy stacking quinoa. Others enrol on permaculture evening courses in the hope of mulching with a Monty Don type, or join their nearest Green Gym (organized by the British Trust for Conservation Volunteers).

Not all singletons want a partner exactly like themselves. It is more admirable, after all, to preach to the unconverted. Why? Because if all the planet-nurturing people hook up with each other, there will be a glut of both super-smug couples and badly behaved ones, and there will be far fewer green conversions taking place within relationships. What we should aspire towards instead is cross-pollination: virtuous people teaming up with green sinners. One would balance the other and both would be more tolerable. Worry not about diluting your green values; think of it more as a way of helping darker greens to stay in touch with the real world. Much as I moan about Gervase's reluctance to embrace a pea-green lifestyle, he is very good at reminding me of how other people see things. Not everyone would want a water butt for Christmas, he'll say gently.

He also puts the brakes on unpleasant habits such as my tendency to overdo the lentil suppers and to reuse silver foil more times than is probably hygienic. Should we ever take the plunge and decide to get married, we would no doubt have a merry time quarrelling over whether to serve what he calls 'hippy food' at the reception and how to find ethically produced napkins. I can imagine it now: he would say that a wedding is a time to forget ideology and get on with the party. I would agree up to a point, but I would also want a few eco-twists. Not least because they would enhance the occasion.

These days, there's a lot to be said for wearing a vintage frock and flashing a conflict-free sparkler. It is, quite simply, the most stylish way to cruise down the aisle, and guarantees that your wedding won't be just like every other event of the summer. And crucially, given that the average wedding now costs over £18,000, you will be spared post-nuptial bankruptcy.

When my friend Charlie got married to Tom, they were keen to steer clear of what they called an 'off the shelf' wedding; not only for green reasons but also because it was not to their taste. They wanted something that reflected their approach to life as well as having an ethical dimension. Because Charlie works in fashion, running ethical T-shirt company Tonic T-shirts, she had no trouble finding inspiration for her dress. She called on the services of Junky Styling, a stylist duo who customize second-hand clothing. She told them how she wanted to look and they fashioned a dress using reclaimed fabric. On the day, most of the guests came by public transport and left with party bags containing a slice of carrot cake (the wedding cake), some bubble-blowing liquid and an acorn to plant to mark the occasion. For their honeymoon, sticking to their policy of taking only essential flights, they took the train to Montpellier. Charlie says this facilitated excessive champagne consumption, which, although feasible on a plane, gives you a much worse hangover.

The point is that a green wedding doesn't have to be a shoddy affair, light on fun and heavy on good intentions. Nor is it only for fully paid up, environmentally enlightened couples who have spent the duration of their relationship bonding over their green habits. Anyone can introduce a few green tweaks to the big day. All that matters is that you recognize some of the environmental consequences of your wedding, and take a few measures to combat them. The crucial areas are food miles, transport and the huge amounts of waste generated – never mind all the stress-related energy squandered.

The level of commitment is entirely up to you; it can be as light or dark green as you wish. While some couples may be happy recycling champagne bottles and printing invitations on recycled paper, others go hardcore, working out ingenious ways to reduce travel emissions by setting up tents within staggering distance of the party, or asking guests to make donations to charity instead of providing the usual toast racks and teapots.

It makes sense, of course, to ensure that whatever you do tallies with your interests and what you care about. If you're secretly longing to receive a heap of presents, it would be cruel to force yourself down the charity-donations path.

In my green wedding research, I came across Brighton-based Holly Aquilina who got married to Ben two years ago. She tells me that their guests would never have known that they were officially at a green wedding. 'The day was more creative and personal than a conventional wedding would have been,' she says. 'My grandfather painted old baked-bean cans to use as vases and we picked the flowers from my parents' garden.' Holly and her nine bridesmaids wore second-hand dresses, the total cost of which came to £470, and at the end of the party, at which an organic caterer served local sausages and mash, everyone camped nearby. The best thing of all, Holly says, was that it took the pressure off feeling that the day had to be perfect: 'I knew there would be a few hiccups and I didn't worry about it.'

Her only warning is to leave enough time for organization. 'Being green at a wedding often means doing it yourself,' she says. To prepare, she advises roping in as many friends and relatives as you can muster.

Gervase is probably right. What matters on the day is that you can put eco-worries to one side and have a darn good party.

WHAT'S IN IT FOR THE PLANET?

Green seduction . . . spreads the message

By drawing someone into your life, you can at least have a stab at bringing them round to your way of thinking. In an ideal world, it'll only be a matter of weeks before they are building you raised vegetable beds and insulating the loft. Another benefit of sharing your life with someone is the division of resources. Whether it's baths, bags of potatoes or houses, cohabitation is a more environmentally friendly way of living.

Green love . . . keeps you busy

By occupying yourself in the bedroom – or anywhere else your love life may lead you – you will be prevented from engaging in other carbon-hungry activities. In short, you'll be generating your own energy, so you can turn the heating off and dim the lights. A word of caution: practising for babies is all very well, but remember that making them has major implications. In turn, they will use up their own share of resources. Of course, this must be weighed against the fact that most people become more environmentally conscious after they have had a child.

Green weddings . . . cut down on waste

By using biodegradable and recyclable alternatives, you can cut down on the enormous number of different materials that a wedding involves many of which serve a one-off purpose and then end up in the bin, from ribbons in the bride's hair to name-cards at the dinner table.

By getting hold of seasonal, local produce, including food, flowers and drinks, you can also cut down on food miles and support the local economy.

By asking suppliers, venue owners and all the other people in the juggernaut that is the wedding industry for alternatives, you will be getting the message out that there's a demand for them, providing better options for future couples. The fact that guests will be bowled over by the success of the day and want to follow your lead is the icing on the (wedding) cake.

Throwing a party

There's no surer way to kill a party than to boast about its green credentials. I assure you this will go down like a lead balloon. The rule is that you set a honey trap – a promise of organic champagne, perhaps – and only later wheel in the recycling bins. That's not to say that you can't sneak a few eco-touches into the preparations. But don't get drunk on Fairtrade Chardonnay and bore everyone with tales of your hunt for biodegradable sparklers.

How to green your party secretly:

- Make it easy for people to recycle glass and beer cans by providing obvious green bins. Attach a balloon to them if they look a bit serious.

- Encourage people to car-share by mediating between friends to let them know who is coming from where and who might be able to give whom a lift.

- Celebrate our long tradition of ale and cider drinking by supplying British-brewed varieties. Some of the bottled ales are worth getting for their names alone, like Bishop's Finger, Fiddler's Elbow and my personal favourite, Blond Witch.

- Alternatively, have a British-wine-tasting party. Encourage everyone to bring only British wines and see how delicious – or foul – they taste.

- If you can't resist wine from abroad, think about whether the process by which it was made was ethical. Grape-pickers in countries such as South Africa and Chile are frequently underpaid; even in Europe, wine is likely to be harvested by badly paid itinerants from Europe's poorest regions. Try out different Fairtrade wines and, if you find one you like, stock up.

- Think not only about how far wine has travelled but also about its overall carbon footprint – that's the energy required for growing and bottling it, too. By this point, you'll be ready for a glass.

- Provide seasonal snacks. During summer, this is easy: chopped veggies, homemade dips and bowls of fruit go down well. Fairtrade nuts and other nibbles can be bought for parties in the autumn and winter for more of a squirrel theme.

- Have a 'free party' by asking people to forage for food on their way. It might not amount to much, but it is said that the best parties are those at which there is more booze than food.

- Buying balloons? Make sure they are biodegradable. Several online party suppliers have started catering for the eco-conscious customer by selling these, along with sustainably sourced disposable plates made from bamboo and cups and organic cotton bunting. Try *www.ecomyparty.co.uk*.

- Recycle decorations. Hunt out leftover sparklers, glittery tablecloths and party poppers from your last bash. Dedicate a drawer to all this stuff, so you can always find something quickly for a pre-party spruce-up of your house.

- Invite your neighbours, to enhance community spirit – and to avoid being told to turn down the music.

Going green . . . in the bedroom

I'm all for bringing new twists to bedroom antics, but I'm not easily convinced by turning them green. First, it's not very naughty, is it, worrying about the carbon footprint of your sex life? Secondly, the bedroom is the last bastion of privacy, the one remaining place where no one is going to suggest that you reduce, reuse or recycle. For many, this is one territory that should be spared a green makeover – we should be able to drop our ideals, as well as our organic hemp knickers, at the bedroom door. Finally, making babies is not particularly green anyway – unless you're only practising – so you're on a losing team already. Wouldn't it be more worthwhile to commit to good sex, rather than green sex?

That said, I was rather taken by the concept of an eco-boudoir – soya-wax candles burning virtuously, organic massage oils and a bamboo bed with plumped-up cushions made from recycled materials; perhaps an organic rug strewn with a couple of solar-powered sex toys. Actually, that last bit broke the spell. I don't think I'd want to be reminded of the latest developments in renewable energy in vibrator form. But in case you are more willing than I am to find room between your organic sheets for environmental matters, here are some tips on how to be a green lover:

• Take baths together. Even better in the water-saving stakes is to take brief, flirty showers.

• Undies should be organic. Non-organic cotton is one of the most heavily sprayed crops around; roughly a quarter of the world's insecticides are poured on to cotton fields each year, with about 150g being used in the making of one T-shirt.

• Too embarrassed to charge a solar-powered sex toy on your sunlit balcony in full view of the neighbours? I would be, too. Stick to one that takes rechargeable batteries. And keep it in the bedroom.

• The most biodegradable contraceptive on the market is a condom made from the intestinal membrane of lambs. Suitable only for lovers with a strong stomach. Definitely not for vegans, who have their own special brand, called condomi, which uses cocoa powder instead of the milk protein required to process latex.

- Don't throw normal condoms down the toilet. The Environment Agency estimates that two billion items of sanitary protection, of which condoms form a big part, end up in the UK's sewers every year.

- Petroleum jelly as lubricant? Forget it. What you need is organic lubricant with added aloe-vera extract (see *www.organiclubricant.com*).

- Choose your moment carefully. Just before bedtime means that you'll warm up the bed and yourselves, and you can turn the heating off.

- Do it for the planet. Having sex is carbon neutral and a darn sight less damaging than most other leisure activities. Providing it doesn't always end in babies.

Going green . . . on a date

Some couples bond instantly over a shared love of mung beans and are happy to discuss the planet-warming consequences of cow dung until the herd comes home. But would you want a partner like this? I thought not. The rest of us have to ease green issues gently into our love affairs. While love may conquer all, it won't survive an in-depth interrogation about a man's recycling habits on the first date. That I've been out of the game for nearly eight years hardly equips me to dole out green dating advice. I'm at a point in my relationship where I can happily hurl abuse at Gervase if he so much as leaves the tap on for a moment longer than is necessary to rinse a plate or dampen his toothbrush. I don't even worry about him thinking I'm an eco-facist. He knows I am. Nevertheless, here are my top tips for a successful green date:

- Don't mention the C word. Climate change should not be introduced too early on in a romance. Instead, indicate your interest in green matters by suggesting eco-friendly restaurants. For a list, see information section on page 380.

- While at the restaurant, drink tap water (along with the hard stuff, obviously). Should your partner ask for mineral water, frown slightly, while being careful to maintain a mischievous smile.

- Eat by candlelight. It will save energy and guarantee a flattering glow. This is easy at home, harder at a restaurant, but you could try asking the waiter for dimmer lights and more candles. Whatever you do, don't make this request in front of your dining companion; it will make you sound romance-deprived.

- Don't count carbon calories. There is nothing more unattractive than a lady who won't enjoy her food because she is too busy totting up its environmental impact. On a first date, forget food miles completely, or at least don't talk about them.

- By all means, enquire if there is a sustainable-fish policy at a restaurant. Stop short of asking for the CV of your sea bass and the lowdown on who its grandparents were.

- Let the man pay. Isn't being green all about conserving the best bits of tradition and altering the worst? Exactly.

- Insist on a moonlit walk home to save your carbon footprint and to provide plenty of kissing opportunities.

Try it in in June . . .

Light Greenies
Learn to make nettle soup

For the rural novice, cooking with stinging nettles may sound terrifying: a green leap into the unknown, otherwise known as the hedgerow. It is the sort of culinary challenge that one imagines is best reserved for country types who can identify a bilberry bush at twenty paces and spend their free time pickling things. But why should they have all the fun?

In a spirit of defiance, I set about brewing up a bag of nettles last summer. I did it while spending a weekend alone at my mum's house, in case it was a disaster. I didn't want anyone laughing – through stinging lips – at my feeble attempt to subdue the Cambridgeshire countryside. But making nettle soup was a piece of cake and totally painless. I made a tasty and nutritious dinner that I then wished I could share with someone. I rang as many people as I could think of, announcing, 'Guess what I'm eating? Nettle soup. It's delicious and it cost me nothing.' I didn't mention that I'd been stung a couple of times while picking my nettles because I'd forgotten to take rubber gloves and had tried to do it with a tea towel, or that I'd been scared to take my first sip of soup and had involuntarily shielded my lips from the mixture so that it dribbled down my chin. The fact remained, I'd done it; I'd conquered the nettle.

If you've suffered years of summer walks that end with rows of itchy red bumps on your legs, cooking nettles is deeply satisfying. First, you get to snip the tops off as many as you feel like punishing, using scissors to lever them into a plastic bag. Then, when you've brutalized enough, you take them home to wash them (worth doing well if you've picked them in a city or anywhere with dogs around) and treat them like spinach. It's the gentle simmering that removes the sting. I like Hugh Fearnley-Whittingstall's simple recipe which involves a final beating in a blender (you'll find it on *www.rivercottage.net*). He recommends using young nettles in May or June before they've flowered, although I made my soup in July and I'm still here to tell the tale.

The results were a pleasant surprise. I'm still not quite sure of a nettle's exact flavour as my soup tasted mostly of the other ingredients – garlic, onions, celery and stock, which was no bad thing – but the nettles gave it a lively green colour. Amazing, isn't it, how easily you can conquer a vicious weed with some scissors, a hob and a blender? After a second bowlful and an extra grinding of pepper, revenge tasted even sweeter.

Dark Greenies
Make your own cosmetics

For many of us, the first wedding or party of the summer is accompanied by a rising sense of panic. We realize that a super-duper outfit must be pulled together, followed by the sort of instant radiance that is unlikely to have been on show since last year's holiday. For the dress, a few trusted outfits that have already had multiple outings can generally be relied on. For skin revival, you might want to try the DIY approach to beauty.

For an invigorating face mask, I use an avocado mashed up with a dollop of honey. Rich and hydrating, avocados contain a number of fatty acids that nourish the skin. Dab the green goo on your face and recline on the sofa (to stop it sliding off). As you lie back and experience a strange tightening sensation – could this be a natural version of Botox? – tot up the eco-advantages of DIY cosmetics. No unnecessary packaging, or chemicals and preservatives, and you know exactly what you're putting on your skin – something no amount of organic labelling can guarantee. You can banish concerns about the scary-sounding ingredients listed on the back of those bottles of slap – foaming agents, emulsifiers and phythalates, to name but a few. It's a recipe for success for the modern woman, sick of forking out high prices for pointless tubs of gloop. It's not an approach I use all the time, only when I'm broke or appalled at the number of ingredients in my latest exfoliator. Remember: keep it simple. There's no need to get all Gordon Ramsay about the recipes, and when you've mastered the basics, you can move on to making more complicated skincare products, such as moisturizers and toners.

Don't, however, expect your mixture to last. Before the day is over, it will have turned brown and will have to be scraped into the compost bin. It's a daily commitment, DIY beauty. And it doesn't always work – I remember making a rather unpleasant potato cleanser once. Consistency issues, you see. Blobs of semi-mashed potato mixed with egg yolk and milk dropped off my face and on to my clothes. But don't let that put you off. I've had successes too, like the yoghurty hair cleanser (recipe below) that smells so much like an old-fashioned lemon fool that I'm always tempted to serve the leftovers for pudding. Why not? Once you start smearing food on your face, boundaries become a little blurred.

Recipes
for Your Own Cosmetics

Avocado and Honey Face-mask

Mash one teaspoon of honey into the flesh of a ripe avocado until creamy. Massage into the skin, leave for 10 minutes, then rinse and moisturize. It gives your face an instant glow – and no, that's not just a mushy sheen of avocado that's been left behind.

A word of caution: because avocado is so oily, this might be best avoided if you have greasy skin.

Yoghurt hair cleanser

Mix an egg yolk and the juice of half a lemon with 50ml of yoghurt. If you have greasy hair, throw in a capful of cider vinegar. Work through hair, leave on for 10 minutes, then wash off. This is supposed to be a shine-enhancing shampoo. When I did it, I was impressed at how clean it made my hair feel, yet not in that sheeny way that conventional shampoos do, which make your hair feel as though it has been coated in something. That said, I would definitely want to complement the treatment with some conditioner, if only so I could get a comb through my knotty locks.

Oatmeal hand scrub

I can't say I've ever spent much time worrying about the welfare or appearance of my hands. They've always got along fine without any special treatment. But since my mother has started drumming it into me that they give away your age, I've begun to wonder how mine fare. They'd be better, I'm sure, if I could remember to submerge them regularly in this exfoliating hand scrub. It smells delightful, like a bowl of summer porridge, and all the ingredients are common-store cupboard items, so you shouldn't have to spend any extra money on them.

Mix a quarter cup of rolled oats with a quarter cup of hot water, a splash of orange juice (ideally from an orange, but if you use stuff from a carton that's OK) and a tablespoonful of olive oil. Slather it over your hands and go and sit quietly somewhere without dripping on the furniture. It can help to put each hand in an old plastic bag and get a family member to tie them up around your wrists. Thus incapacitated, you can avoid all domestic duties for the sake of soft hands.

Homemade toner

I've never seen the point of expensive toners when you can buy a simple solution of rosewater and glycerin cheaply in most chemist's. It has a lovely scent and comes in an old-fashioned bottle that you can reuse afterwards. You could even fill it with your own homemade rosewater, made by gently simmering a couple of handfuls of rose petals (straight from the bush – don't use fallen ones) with a litre of water. The reason I don't do this is mainly because rosewater is cheap to buy and, unless you faff around adding alcohol, the mixture won't last for more than a couple of days. But also because, if truth be told, I'm not entirely convinced of the importance of toner. The longer I live with Gervase, the more I suspect that his approach – hot water splashed on the face and a splodge of any soap or cleanser that is kicking around in the bathroom cupboard – is worth considering.

Eco-Cheats

• For an earthy swing to your home, there needs to be a few muddy root vegetables and leafy greens hanging around the kitchen, and perhaps a string of garlic. A good way to make sure that you have a constant supply of such things is by signing up to an organic box scheme. A six-month subscription also makes a good wedding present. Find your nearest one on *www.ecologist.org*.

• Looking for an excuse to give the gym a miss? Easy. Think about the energy consumption involved in plugging yourself into cardio machines, and all those steaming-hot showers, tumble-dried towels and air-conditioned lobbies. Chances are you probably drive there, too. At this time of year, it makes much more sense to exercise in the great outdoors. See hills as exercise machines and outdoor lakes and rivers as swimming pools (see *www.outdoorswimmingsociety.com*). Or you can opt to sweat it out clearing woodland with the Green Gym (*www.btcv.org.uk/green gym*). Best of all, it's free.

• Neglected saucepan lids, rusting from disuse, are a common sight at the bottom of many a kitchen drawer. Lid use has been in decline for years. We tend to favour a devil-may-care attitude to boiling; we whack up the gas and let things bubble away, open-topped. But using a lid – when you're boiling potatoes, say – gets the job done in half the time and saves on gas or electricity. First you'll have to find one that fits.

A Green Guide to Getting Hitched
From Hen Parties to Honeymoons

Travel

Make it easy for guests to shed carbon calories. Since travel to the venue is likely to be one of the biggest environmental costs of your wedding, provide information about public transport, keep venues close together, and encourage lift-sharing. Website builders (such as *www.theweddingracker.co.uk*) can create a wedding website for you on which guests can find out who is driving from where. This will also save you from sending out bulky invitations packed with all this information.

Have your hen- or stag-do locally. It reduces carbon emissions and beats spending most of the weekend in an airport lounge.

Do it on the train – your honeymoon that is. You don't have to forego foreign travel. A luxury couchette in a sleeper-train whizzing through Europe is a fine way to start a marriage. Or consider booking your trip through *www.responsibletravel.com* and offsetting your carbon emissions.

The Dress

Why wear it once? When tackling the question of the Big Dress, think about post-wedding opportunities. Could it be dyed and worn again? Could you alter it to make a less dressy outfit? Could it be cut up and turned into polar-bear outfits for your children in their school play (my mother's own resourceful approach to wedding-dress recycling)?

Second-hand secrets. eBay is a fantastic resource for wedding dresses and morning suits – no one need know your dress has been down the aisle before. Oxfam also has a vintage-wedding-dress section.

Custom-made styles. For something fresh, try one of the new breed of eco-designers who have turned their sewing machines to the task of creating wedding outfits. For a reasonable fee, they will craft you a dress made from recycled materials, organic fabric, or perhaps even compostable fibres if you're really lucky. Try *www.enamore.co.uk* or find ethical fabric from the wedding services offered by *www.thenaturalstore.co.uk*.

The Party

Check that your venue recycles. If not, harangue staff until it does. If it doesn't collect food waste for compost, you could see if the mountains of meringues or other leftover food could be donated to a local homeless shelter.

Find a wild green space. It will reflect an earthy commitment to your day. Camping should be encouraged nearby, as should imaginative forms of folk dancing.

Treat guests to an organic, local and seasonal feast. No need to serve lentils to make your point. Instead find a decent caterer who can provide quality food with ethical credentials.

Sample local ales and ciders. Preferably not the night before the wedding. If you're impressed, what about complementing your chosen wine with something brewed in the region?

Organic champagne is the ultimate in green flashiness. Although be careful you don't end up serving it with nettle soup after blowing your budget.

Don't mention your green commitments in the speeches. While having several eco-twists to your big day is a good thing, bragging about them is not.

Flowers

Plan ahead if you want eco-flowers. Speak to a local florist and ask them to source local flowers – or they might even be able to grow some especially for you.

Growing plants can be given to guests at the end of the day as souvenirs, or taken home by the bride and groom to be nurtured along with their newly made vows.

Homemade confetti is the best kind. Ask a florist on a Friday night if they have any flowers that will be chucked away. You can make petal confetti from blooms that are past their best. Otherwise look for biodegradable confetti that doesn't contain chemicals or swell in the stomachs of birds, like rice does (*www.confettidirect.co.uk*).

Presents

Charity donation. A popular alternative to a wedding list is to set up an online account where guests can contribute to a chosen charity. Don't expect everyone to play ball; there will be a few surprise toasters.

You don't have to relinquish your right to presents. What about giving out a list of gifts with a green slant? I like the idea of staying within the confines of traditional wedding gifts, but asking for a six-month subscription to an organic vegetable-box scheme, say, or champagne flutes made from recycled glass. Or you could be encouraged to create compost together with the gift of a wormery or a beehive-shaped composter, made from sustainable timber.

Closing the loop. You could specify that you want gifts made from waste, so helping to create a market for recycled materials. By giving the website for a database of recycled products (*www.recycledproducts.org.uk*) on your invitation, guests will be able to choose between picnic blankets made from scrap textiles, lampshades made from recycled cardboard and the best chicken doorstops I've ever seen.

The halfway-house option. You could offer the opportunity to donate to a charity or to buy from a list of green gifts.

All That Glitters . . .
How to find ethical jewellery

A girl's best friend? These days 99 per cent of diamonds sold in the UK are 'conflict-free', but you'll still want to make sure that yours doesn't fall into the remaining 1 per cent. So ask questions. Is your jeweller's a member of the Council for Responsible Jewellery Practices? Does it have a written ethical policy? Has the diamond that's caught your eye been certified by the Kimberley Process, an ethical certification programme introduced in 2003?

Gold-diggers should look for rings that have been made in association with Green Gold. According to Cafod, an international aid agency, gold-mining creates toxic waste, and open-pit mines have left such a dent on the landscape that some of them are visible from space. Green Gold works to reverse the ecological damage done by mining; Cred (*www.credjewellery.com*) and Green Karat (*www.greenkarat.com*) are two reliable ethical jewellery companies.

Make your own wedding rings. There are short courses available in jewellery to enable couples to make their own rings (*www.weddingringworkshop.co.uk*). If you trust yourself to create something that symbolizes your union, this could be the way to go.

Plunder your family's hands. Is there a ring in your mother's jewellery box that she would donate? A jeweller could spruce it up and make any required adjustments. It might not shine as brightly as a brand-new bit of bling, but everyone coos loudest over a ring that has been 'in the family'.

Ingredients for a Successful Summer Picnic

Any form of picnicking is to be encouraged. And far better to reach into your bag and pull out a cheese-and-pickle sarnie made in the kitchen earlier that day – or even yesterday – than succumb to an overpackaged shop offering. Taking food with you when you venture outside is always worthwhile. As well as saving money, there's the feeling that you won't be caught short. An emergency stash is on your person should hunger strike.

But there is a dark side to ferrying food around. Namely, packaging. If you've had the misfortune to be left with a hummus-smeared rug to clear up after a picnic, while everyone else skips off to buy ice-creams and play frisbee, you will know about the ungreen quantities of waste that picnics can generate.

It wasn't always this way. Before the age of sliced chorizo that arrives in plastic body armour, sandwiches boxed rigid and pasta salads in pots with their own fork tucked under the lid, ingredients would be chosen because of their suitability for travel. Boiled eggs, bananas, pork pies, a lump of pâté, a couple of cold sausages and a sturdy fruit loaf were the picnic materials of my childhood, eaten with my grandparents in Herefordshire during the summer holidays.

Squash-resistant foods such as these would be combined with items that squashed horribly, but which we ate anyway. Sandwiches and strawberries fell into the latter category. All would be packed up with the minimum of fuss and barely a plastic bag in sight.

Unpack these ingredients today and they'd look a little dated compared with sun-dried tomatoes and slices of expensive Parma ham, but we can still pick up some tips from the picnics enjoyed by our forebears.

Plan ahead. A last-minute raid on a supermarket is convenient, but it will not help you to minimize waste.

Look for natural packaging. Wherever possible, choose food that doesn't require extra packaging. Bananas and hard-boiled eggs are good examples.

Bring as much as possible from home. Both food and crockery. Nothing beats a simple homemade cake on a picnic, eaten from a proper plate.

Make the most of recyclable containers. Jam jars can be used to store salad dressing; old ice-cream tubs make a perfect salad container, as do empty take-away cartons.

Stick to the 'anything but clingfilm' rule. As a one-use-only plastic product that cannot be recycled or easily reused, clingfilm gets the thumbs down. On top of this, it is rumoured to leak 'plasticizers' (chemicals that soften) into food. There is no concrete evidence that this adversely affects your health, but it rather puts you off.

Find recycled aluminium foil. It is out there, available at *www.naturalcollection.com*, among other places. Once used, you can easily fold it up and reuse it again.

Dig out your thermos. Ideal for transporting homemade soup, tea or hot chocolate laced with a glug of whisky.

Don't worry about picnic hiccups. Should the Fairtrade chocolate melt en route, it can become a dip for the strawberries. Not enough plastic cups to go around? No problem, you're saving on plastic waste.

A final word on barbecues: don't fret, I wouldn't dream of trying to put the brakes on this important summer tradition. Goodness, no, I like a bit of charred chicken myself. And what starts with a few sausages sizzling outside your back door leads to camping on hills and other back-to-nature pleasures. Alfresco eating is a step towards greener living, I'm sure of it. But I would say keep it simple. The monsters that are cropping up on some patios, with several burners and more knobs than a spaceship, are real gas-guzzlers. Disposable BBQs create large amounts of waste too and, let's be honest, it doesn't feel like a proper occasion when you've only got a tiny foil tray of coals. At least with a charcoal-based permanent affair your fuel source is carbon neutral, unlike with a gas BBQ (and the food will benefit from a proper barbecued taste). By burning charcoal, you are simply putting back into the environment the carbon dioxide that was removed in growing the wood. And make sure your charcoal is sustainable. British charcoal comes from renewable coppiced woodland; look for the Forest Stewardship Council tick on the packet.

Seasonal Food

Last June I became mildly obsessed with **bulghur wheat and feta salad**, originally inspired by a Gordon Ramsay recipe.

It involves mashing the feta in a bowl with olive oil and lemon juice to start with, then adding chopped cucumber, lots of herbs and finally the cooked but cooled bulghur wheat. By the end of the summer, I had started piling black olives, sliced celery and rocket into the bowl too, along with anything else I could lay my hands on. I'm not sure if I improved the recipe, but the salad was always popular with friends. The crucial thing is to make a decent dressing for it – as well as the oil and lemon juice you've mashed the feta into, add lots more lemon juice and black pepper.

June is also the moment for **gooseberries**, always called goosegogs by my grandpa. Part of the fun of doing anything with them is the opportunity to sit out in the garden topping and tailing them. There's nothing quite like it on a sunny evening, astride a bench or a garden wall with a couple of bowls around you. Sadly, the sour little fruits can be hard to get hold of. I'm planning to plant a couple of bushes this autumn. Soon I will have fool on tap, so to speak. And when I'm bored of creamy puddings, I'll be happy to stew the fruit with plenty of sugar and freeze it, pulling it out throughout the winter for crumbles or for last-minute dollops of gloop to accompany mackerel fillets.

JULY

DO I REALLY HAVE TO
STOP FLYING?

IT'S HARD NOT TO PERK UP IN JULY. IT'S FAIR TO SAY THIS MAY BE A HANGOVER FROM schooldays, when the month would stretch out as one long, blissful expanse of holiday, but it hardly matters. It still manages to coax out of us a cheery side we do an impeccable job of covering up the rest of the year. Post-Wimbledon, pre-August summer fatigue, nothing seems that bad.

City-folk start drinking in outside bars and pretending it's the Mediterranean; parks spring to life, dotted with picnics and impromptu games of cricket. Meanwhile, in the countryside, there are fetes to attend and rivers to swim in, when temperatures rise.

You would think all this might stop us packing our suitcases. But no, as Britain basks in its finest hour, what do most people do? Plan their escape. It's the holiday season. Time to leave it all behind to roast your lily-white skin on foreign beaches and spend longer than is probably advisable with your loved ones.

That's fine by me. Anyone craving two weeks of crowded beaches with airport delays as bookends is welcome to them. I prefer to stay put during the summer. When well-meaning people ask me, innocently, where I'm going on holiday, I'm likely to respond with a frown. 'Go? Why should I go? It's very nice here, thank you.'

Lucky enough not to be bound by school holidays, I see no reason to flee the country as soon as the sun comes out. That my distrust of joining airport queues prevents a sudden inflation of my carbon footprint is an added bonus. As someone who cycles, composts and belongs to a car-share scheme, it hasn't passed me by that I shouldn't really be taking to the skies in an enormous CO_2-belching vehicle with wings.

Instead, I should be doing something green and UK-based. Yes, that's right, I should be going camping. It is ideal, as a method of holidaying, for short jaunts around Britain to explore unlikely corners you never knew existed. Take the wilderness that is the West Hampshire/Berkshire border. It might not sound exotic but unless you've seen the famous grazing cows of Hungerford common and tasted the local ale on a Sunday afternoon sitting by the river, you don't know what you're missing.

My friend Jo lives there and last summer she befriended a farmer who let us camp on his land for a weekend. He even lent us his Land Rover so we could explore – demonstrating the munificent rural spirit that us city-dwellers like to imagine runs riot in the countryside (that's usually before we get shouted at for scaring the livestock with our floral wellies and want to go home).

It may be hard to convince everyone that jacking in the comforts of a boutique hotel for a lump of bumpy ground without a bathroom is a sensible thing to do, but I have come to realize that camping is exactly how I like my nature. In small, controlled chunks. A few nights in a tent sets me up for months of London living. Should I get fed up with the hustle and bustle of the city, I simply think back to the time that I popped out of the tent for a pee in the night and stung my behind on nettles. To help me appreciate bland urban surroundings, it works wonders.

Honestly though, what I like about camping is the way it strips away your comforts. That may sound like a bad thing but it's just what you need every once in a while. When you reintroduce them, each one is a blessing. Camping cleans the slate and lets you start again. After a few nights with no electric lights, no kettle or running water and nothing to sit on except – if you remember it – a rug, returning home, your place will seem like a palace. Your bed alone is surely the most comfortable in the world. In normal life, my expectations creep up. I start wanting a bigger, softer sofa, a better kitchen, a cleaner house. Then I go camping and what I've got already seems more than enough.

Recently Gervase and I camped on the land of a family we knew vaguely through friends. After a few nights of torrential rain and general gritted-teeth endurance, we were persuaded by the mother of the house to come in for breakfast. We sat in her kitchen eating hot buttered toast and drinking instant coffee and nothing could have seemed more luxurious. You might scoff, saying you'd prefer to stay indoors and eat hot buttered toast whenever you want, but I promise it won't taste as good as it does to a recently returned camper.

Of course, staying in the UK over the summer is the easy bit. The real test comes later on, during the dark months of January and February, when camping is not an option. Or not for me it's not. That's when I crave a long-haul flight. And that's when I have to address the queen-bee of eco-quandaries. To fly or not to fly.

Compared to other aspects of going green, how to address air travel has caused me considerable internal strife. The only explanation is that I haven't yet been able to persuade myself that I'm as happy on wet walking weekends in the Peak District all year round as exploring the souks in Damascus or eating tapas in Madrid. I'm not bold – or green enough – to give up flying completely.

My ethos has always been that eco-alternatives are fun and creative; opening up a more satisfying way to live your life, as well as one that is better for the planet. Not buying new clothes, growing vegetables and cutting back on food miles has been easy because I have found – or managed to convince myself, I'm not sure which – that I don't like cheap clothes anyway, and I prefer to grow my own lettuce, thank you very much.

But, if I'm honest, I don't relish giving up the shift in perspective that a few weeks in a foreign country grants, if only as a reward for many months of good green behaviour at home. I love the opportunity to explore little-known corners of the world that challenge the way I see things. And I'm reluctant to deprive myself of this completely.

And yet, I am uneasy about flying. It began when I got back from a trip to India, in 2006. Due to the distance I travelled, I became acutely conscious of my carbon trail. Whatever way I looked at it, it hit me that flying was likely to be the most significant of my personal emissions and that it was the fastest-growing source of greenhouse gases. By continuing to do it, I was making a mockery of all the other meagre ways I obsess over slimming down on my carbon consumption at home.

Confusing the matter further, it was also my trip to India to write an article about a company that had won a Responsible Travel award that brought home how precarious the climate is in parts of the developing world. Known as climate canaries, these areas close to the equator which experience intense weather cycles will be the first to be affected by climate change. Had I not visited, I would not have witnessed in Rajasthan the devastation wreaked by droughts that are becoming more severe every year, or heard from my guide about the thousands of farmers in the region who abandon their parched land and flock to overpopulated cities.

It is an unfortunate paradox that the trips that pollute the planet also open our mind and persuade us that the world needs our attention. They trigger our consciences and bestow a sense of the global as well as the local. My friend Coco believes that when people see other parts of the world, they return to their own countries more open-minded; travel therefore making for a more tolerant, liberal society. But is this broadened outlook worth the price of polluting the skies?

Not all greenies appear to get in such a pickle about this. Rational types make confident decisions and stick to them. Either they grace the finest parts of the UK during August, occasionally taking trains and ferries further afield, or they conveniently side with those who argue that a few well-meaning individuals staying on the ground voluntarily isn't going to make a difference. If we want to reduce significantly the number of flights that are taken, this needs to be imposed from above. This last lot, I see as the flaky greens, and when I'm hankering after sunshine, I'm tempted to join them.

But, generally, I'm more the dithering variety. Sometimes I pass up on an opportunity to fly, looking upon the person proposing the trip with exaggerated outrage, as if they had suggested Al Gore be given a patio heater for his birthday. Other times, I accept eagerly and try to banish thoughts about my obvious hypocrisy.

I read up on the various arguments, try to take comfort from the fact that electricity generation and emissions from industry are bigger problems in terms of their share in causing the UK's total greenhouse emissions.

Then I dither some more, learning that by burning kerosene at high altitudes, the damage done by planes is increased, more than doubling its impact. What's more, flights are increasing at such a pace that it is estimated that they will account for 25 per cent of the UK's carbon emissions by 2050.

Only a month after getting back from India, I got a call from *The Times* travel desk which provoked an epic episode of dithering. They asked me if I would go to Gabon, West Africa, to report on its fledgling tourist industry. As with my trip to Rajasthan, this one could be justified by claiming it was work. I wasn't choosing to fly in my spare time. But work or not, the carbon emissions remain the same. It was a poor excuse, I knew.

I'd be visiting conservation projects and community lodges – not that I'm pretending this would redress the impact of my flight, but it would be an opportunity to explore the positive impact of tourism. On the other hand, what is the point in demonstrating how valuable it is to support tourism in Gabon when it is a sixteen-hour flight away, which packs a punch of 1.59 tonnes of CO_2 per person (for a return trip, according to *www.climatecare.org*). However sustainable the tourism might be once you get there, the journey is anything but.

I was faced with an opportunity to either put my money where my mouth is, or acknowledge that I'm not ready to stop doing work that involves visiting other countries.

Before deciding whether to accept, I asked my readers both on the blog and in my weekly column whether they thought I should go. The responses ranged from furious indictments of journalists who write about the environment and then flit around the world, to explanations of the importance of tourism in relation to conservation. Chris Breen, who immediately declared his interests as the founder of a travel company called Wildlife Worldwide, got in touch to point out that if we stop visiting many countries in Africa, the incentive to preserve their wildlife disappears. 'Without visitors to Gabon, the wildlife could well be poached out of existence, which would be a global tragedy,' he writes. 'It's one of the few places in the world where there are Western Lowland gorillas.'

Not only are rare animals reliant on tourists for their survival. The economies of developing countries would suffer if visitors stopped coming. That tourism is not always the dream ticket to prosperity has been made clear by research into its impact in places like Benidorm, southern Spain, where it has drained already overused reservoirs and trashed beaches, but there's no getting round the damage that would be caused to fledgling economies around the world if we all holidayed in Wales. It would hit the beneficial, often known as 'responsible' strand of tourism – that provides training and employment for local people and encourages communities to preserve their heritage – as well as the destructive variety.

Many people argue that this kind of defence of flying is simply a way of justifying ongoing holidays to exotic locations. Are we clutching at straws because we don't want to make the real changes that will benefit the environment? This was the view of the majority of readers who wrote to me. Theirs were stern words. 'Accept that you will have to abstain from trips that you may like to take,' advised one. 'It's the sort of sacrifice that we will all be obliged to make if we wish to save our planet.'

So it was with tail between legs that I 'fessed up in a follow-up blog post that I would be going to Gabon. I explained that I had made a decision to fly less rather than to stop taking flights completely. I would take a stand against my reliance on the skies by setting myself an annual flight quota. This voluntary commitment would allow me only one long-haul and one short-haul flight a year, including work flights, whittling away all but the most valuable trips. My trip to Gabon would splurge the bigger half of my quota for 2007.

In the meantime, I have settled down to substantial amounts of train travel. Given the option, I might have chosen this anyway. I like rattling across the countryside, papers on my lap, Fairtrade cappuccino to hand. That global warming has made it the admirable choice suits me very well. I'm certainly not a car person – too much concentrating and no chance to get my nose into a book. The only hitch with trains, other than the small fact that you have to remortgage your house if you forget to book a cheap ticket in advance, is how far they can take you.

Until a few years ago, I would have said the limits were obvious. I would have told you that to get to the really exciting places you have to leave the ground. Early eco-adopters have always argued the opposite, but I never believed them. Not on this one anyway. I was suspicious. Maybe what is a thrilling weekend for them wouldn't float my boat. It didn't help that they always cited Paris and Brussels as examples of where you could go by train. Charming as these cities are, they are not exactly Buenos Aires.

But then I went to Marrakech. By train. And it was one of the best trips of my life. Inspired by a train travel website (*www.seat61.com*), run as a hobby by a train aficionado called Mark Smith to show how far trains can take you and how much fun they can be, Gervase and I plotted our route through Europe. It involved two night trains, two long day journeys and a ferry. Our mission was to remain on the ground (or sea). With only ten days' holiday, we wanted to spend at least three of those days in Marrakech. The planning stage was a blast, but we weren't so sure about the reality of cramped compartments and mad rushes across cities to catch our trains.

In the end, it was better than we could have imagined. To give you a snippet, here we are in Paris at lunch-time. We had left our London home a few hours previously and headed for the Eurostar. Stumbling upon a little bistro in the Bastille district, we slurp glasses of Bordeaux in suitably Gallic fashion, while hacking off chunks of cheese from a board the size of a small ping-pong table.

Tummies groaning, the afternoon passes hazily in the unashamedly romantic Place des Vosges, before we take our places on the sleeper to Madrid.

We went all out on a grand class ticket and were not disappointed. As the *Trenhotel* rattled through France, we watched the sun plunge into the deep greens of the countryside and toasted our trip with champagne in the dining car. More than any other leg of our journey, it was this part that reclaimed the art of old-fashioned travel. It was as I imagined it to be, before the stress of airports and the disorientation of jetting across thousands of miles in a matter of hours ruined everything. Here, at last, was the proper way to go on holiday: a touch Agatha Christie with some James Bond-ish moments.

By taking the train, there is time to consider the journey you are making and the distance you are travelling. In fact, there is a lot of time. Luxurious hours unravel before you with only the shifting landscapes to watch out of the window – and of course the sparkling conversation of your loved one. Surely there could be no better way to seduce someone (especially an earth-aware traveller) than over a three-course dinner served by waiters in starched shirts on the train to Spain?

That the average age of our fellow passengers was greater than our combined ages (plus those of our pets) didn't matter a jot. It added to the Miss Marple-esque atmosphere in the dining car. Among ancient Americans and dozing German grandpas, we scoffed our supper and polished off the whisky provided. Staff, meanwhile, transformed our couchette from living room to bedroom. It began its evening as a salon with two comfortable chairs and a tiny bathroom opposite. When we returned, the chairs had been folded up, the beds brought down and a chocolate left on our pillows as a final flourish.

After another day and night in Madrid, we felt as though we'd already had several holidays. This is one of the greatest things about an extended overland journey. Before you even arrive at your destination, you've had a range of minibreaks.

Before catching our next train, we followed the crowds on their Sunday pilgrimage to El Rastro, a sprawling flea market in La Latina district, to buy stripy leggings (for me, not Gervase) and gobble tapas while perched at bars around the city. Inching further south to Algeciras, we noticed the changing faces of Mediterranean people and the sun's rays strengthening.

A ferry across the Straits of Gibraltar, followed by another sleeper from Tangiers to Marrakech, completed the final stretch of our journey. On the last morning a wizened Moroccan man woke us to announce that we had arrived in Marrakech, thrusting cups of hot chocolate into our hands. It was almost a disappointment to arrive.

The awful truth – that I've been wondering if I could avoid mentioning – is that in the end we were defeated by time and flew back home. A terrible way to end our adventure, I know, and I'm sorry to disappoint you. It's not a decision I'm proud of – we offset our flights, of course, but I don't kid myself that this makes everything better (see page 211) – and I like to think I'd do it differently now. But there is no getting around the time and money required for long-distance train travel.

Our return flight to Gatwick from Marrakech, as well as being guilt-ridden, was supremely dull. But it took a swift three and a half hours and cost less than a third of the train.

The reality is that the pace of life makes overland travel to destinations such as Morocco a challenge. It's a luxury that few can afford – and only those with understanding bosses who grant you plenty of time to holiday the slow way.

Sticking within the boundary of Europe might have been more sensible. This is what Dan Kieran and his young family do for their holidays. The writer and deputy editor of *The Idler* began holidaying by train because of his fear of flying rather than environmental concerns. 'I'm a scaredy-cat,' he admits. 'But something good has come out of it. I've discovered that by avoiding planes you have a richer, more exciting, life-affirming experience. Slow travel allows you to genuinely go on a journey.'

Dan compares flying to a ready meal: 'It might be cheap and easy but that doesn't mean it will taste very nice or be good for you.' Instead, with his wife Rachel and young son Wilf, who has become an avid train fan, he gallivants around Europe, mostly sticking to a two-week framework. When we speak, he's about to take the overnight train to Sorrento, in southern Italy, which involves the Eurostar to Paris, then the overnight train to Rome and on down to Sorrento. In the past, they have taken trains to the South of France and to Spain. Interestingly, it is the experience of train travel that has sold it to them, not its green credentials.

Similarly, my journey to Morocco proved that cutting back on flights doesn't have to kill off your adventures. My concern that the spirit of exploration would be crushed without cheap flights to jet you around is unfounded. Quite the opposite, restrictions make you more creative when you're planning a holiday, so you're likely to have more adventures.

Instead of scanning *lastminute.com*'s offerings and heading off to any-where that's cheap and sunny, restricting your flights encourages you to think long and hard about exactly where you would like to go, why, and how you might get there. In his book *The Art of Travel*, philosopher Alain de Botton recommends that we travel less, stay for longer and invest more in the places we go to. A longer trip makes the environmental cost of the journey more worthwhile, and it also gives the traveller time to explore the different culture and invest in the local infrastructure. The experience becomes not only more ethical but also more enjoyable.

With this in mind, Gervase and I are planning a trip to Senegal. We're hoping to scrounge three weeks off work and combine some travelling around the country with a week's relaxing in one place. It's easier to stick with two flights a year if you know that you can store up some carbon credits and take one whopping great holiday once in a while. And, yes, we will carbon-offset our flights – as good practice, not because we think it makes flying sustainable.

The anticipation and planning stage has already provided considerable excitement. I've been hunting down beaches on the *Lonely Planet* website and wondering how to speak French with a West African accent. Of course, I still dither. Mostly about whether two flights a year is a firm enough stand against the growth of air travel. I worry I'm being too soft on myself. But I usually conclude that, for now, it's acceptable. At least it helps me to overcome my crabbiness when summer holidays are being discussed. When asked if I'm taking a week off, I smile sweetly and say, 'Actually, I'm going to take a month off in the winter.'

WHAT'S IN IT FOR THE PLANET?

Fly less and you will . . . significantly reduce your overall contribution to climate change, since air travel – along with car travel – is likely to be the biggest factor. A flight to Florida produces as much polluting greenhouse gas per passenger as the average car does in the UK in a year. Compared with this, trains are responsible for six times less CO_2-emissions-per-passenger-mile than aircraft, and ferries roughly half.

Remember . . . figures that show air travel's share in global greenhouse emissions are going to be unreliable given that greenhouse gases released at a high altitude enter a vulnerable part of the atmosphere, making them over twice as damaging as those released on the ground. This is compounded by the fact that researchers don't always include return flights in their calculations, as *The Times* reported recently.

Take fewer but longer trips abroad . . . and you will have time to find out about your destination and any specific environmental problems to watch out for. For example, if soil erosion is a problem, you'll know to stick to foot-paths. If endangered animals are poached to make souvenirs, you can make sure to avoid buying them. More time also enables you to escape the big hotels and tourist traps and explore other areas, allowing you to spend your money in the local community rather than giving it to foreign-owned corporations.

How to be a 'good' tourist

• Stay in small, locally owned accommodation rather than chain hotels. In some parts of the world, including the Caribbean, it is estimated that only 20 per cent of the money spent by tourists goes into the country; the rest bypasses local people and lines the pockets of big corporations in the developed world. As well as accommodation, think about who else will profit from your holiday. Who owns the airline and restaurants you visit? Don't opt for full board as this limits your chance to support local restaurants.

• Drink local beer and eat local produce, not imported stuff. Don't believe a hotel that insists it is only safe to eat within the four walls of the hotel. Even street food, if it smells fresh and is cooked in front of you, is usually fine. I trust it more than some restaurants because you can see whether work surfaces are clean and assess the state of your food before it is cooked.

• Drink local brands of mineral water. Bottles made by multinationals such as Nestlé might seem a safer option, but it would be better to buy a local brand. It'll have a lighter carbon footprint and you'll be supporting local industry. So long as the top is sealed, there's no need to fear for your stomach.

• Use water sparingly. Often tourists are responsible for draining precious resources with their twice-daily showers and hotel whirlpools. Do you really need your towels to be laundered every day? If not, say so. This will also minimize pollution from detergent use.

- A word on toilet paper: while it is usually only gap-year students who decide to take their cue from locals and forgo it altogether, it is worth remembering that since the influx of tourists, countries in the developing world have not only had to provide toilet paper but also to adapt their waste-disposal systems to cope with it. In many areas, the plumbing is only halfway there. If you see a sign asking for used paper to be put in a separate bin, don't ignore it. You don't want to leave a trail of blocked toilets in your wake.

- Use electricity sparingly. Leave your air-conditioning on in your hotel room all day and somewhere someone will probably have to cope with a power cut that evening. Many parts of the world have started to prioritize the needs of tourists over local people, so if we use up the lion's share of the resources, local people suffer.

- Don't give to street children. Most organizations promoting responsible travel agree that giving to children encourages begging. Instead of handing out sweets or pens, why not donate to a school or charity working in the area? Remember that the chance of acquiring a pen, which will quickly become a commodity, is reason enough for a child to stay out of school.

- Don't buy anything made from endangered animals. The idea is to encourage the notion that wildlife will bring in money alive rather than dead.

- Don't over-haggle. Unlike Brian in Monty Python's *Life of Brian*, many of us take to haggling enthusiastically. But remember that the idea is to find an amount that pleases both parties, not to force the price down as low as you possibly can. An extra 50p won't make much difference to you but it might to the seller.

How to find a truly 'eco' destination

Questions to ask:

- Don't accept the word 'eco' without questioning it. Ask to see a written eco-policy. If there is no such thing, be sceptical.

- Ask for examples of ethical practice. What is your hotel or travel operator doing to improve the lives of local people? Are they contributing to conservation in the area?

- Are there examples of eco-practice? Find out if your accommodation uses renewable energy, recycles waste water or does anything else to limit the resources it uses and back up its 'eco' status.

- How many local people are employed? What proportion is this of total staff? And are any in management positions?

- What kind of food is provided at the hotel? Is it being imported or provided locally? Cooked by foreign chefs or local ones?

- Is there a spa? If so, does it use cosmetics from multinational companies or support local products? Who will be doing your massage and will the treatments be inspired by local therapies? In any case, spas in areas where water is scarce are questionable. How is this conflict addressed?

- Does the travel company use local guides? Insist that it finds you one. Language barriers can be a challenge but they are half the fun and it is often the highlight of a trip to be able to chat to someone about their family and plans for the future.

For more tips, visit *www.responsibletravel.org* and *www.tourismconcern.org.uk*.

Try it in July . . .

Light Greenies
Swap one holiday abroad every year for an eco-break in Blighty

Tell your friends that you've decided to swap two weeks in Thailand for a holiday on the English Riviera (that's Devon, if you didn't know) and they'll probably think you've got the short straw. But the fact is choosing not to leave the country too often can come as an enormous relief. It'll make you wonder why you've wasted years of your life waiting in queues to have your passport checked and panicking about whether you remembered to take out travel insurance. And the extra money that you would have spent on flights can go towards superior accommodation.

Over the last few years there's been a boom in travel operators supplying UK holidays. From organic farms where you can get your hands dirty (*www.responsibletravel.org*) to those where you are allowed to refuse bovine interaction (*www.luxuryinafarm.co.uk*), then there are solar-powered cottages (*www.naturaldiscovery.co.uk*) and sleek city boutique hotels (*www.bestloved.com*). That's before you've started squinting at the families of teepees, eco-cabins, yurts and gypsy caravans that have mushroomed all over Britain, the ideal places to play out your *Little House on the Prairie* fantasies. If you're after somewhere deemed officially 'green', go to the website of the Green Tourism Business Scheme (*www.green-business.co.uk*) where you can search for accommodation that has been given its seal of approval. Keen for a *Carry on Camping* meets *Hi-de-Hi* adventure? There are 600 places to stay, mostly 1970s chalets and trailer-style caravans, offered by UK Parks (*www.ukparks.com*), which are approved by conservationist David Bellamy. Those chosen to hold his endorsement have carried out conservation work in the surrounding area. Won't holiday without a decent beach? Look no further than the Marine Conservation Society's Good Beach Guide that points you to the best bathing spots around the country (*www.goodbeachguide.co.uk*). I'm not saying that with all these glowing green holiday options you'll never want to head to the Med again, but it will make you realize that leaving our shores is not the only option if you want a break and, just maybe, a suntan.

Dark Greenies
Become an anti-expansionist

Join the grassroots movement that is fighting against Government plans to expand airports. In George Monbiot's book on global warming, *Heat*, he argues that limiting the capacity of airports is the most certain way of holding back flights. Unless the Government intervenes, he writes, demand will surely rise to fill the growing provision of space.

Taking a personal stand against flying is important but it's easy to feel

LEEDS COLLEGE OF BUILDING
LIBRARY

defeated when plans submitted by the Government involve a third runway at Heathrow and to treble the number of flights by 2030 (outlined in Aviation White Paper 2003). Especially since they are totally at odds with promises from politicians that climate change will be tackled and carbon emissions cut.

The good news is that groups across the UK, fuelled by a potent blend of global and local concerns, have come together to form a powerful lobby. It's not just environmentalists camping outside airports swelling the ranks but also pensioners concerned about noise and air pollution and young families worried about increased traffic. Banner-waving with your neighbours isn't everyone's cup of tea but it seems to work. Plans to expand Manchester airport on to Cheshire green-belt land were thrown out, along with those for a new terminal at Coventry that would have been capable of handling a further two million people. Birmingham's second runway project was recently shelved and the company that owns Luton airport inexplicably cancelled its plans to develop a new terminal. So it's good to know you'll be backing a winning horse. For a list of over a dozen local groups, go to campaigning group Plane Stupid's website (*www.planestupid.com*).

• Sunny outside and stuck in the office? Have lunch al-fresco, not al-desko. This might be easier said than done if you work in a city but there are often plenty of parks to explore as well as smaller patches of green hidden behind churches and along canals. Grab your lunch – homemade is best, obviously; see below – and head to your nearest bit of green to sprawl out and munch your lunch in the company of birds and squirrels.

• Make your own flavoured water. Instead of those sweetener-filled shop bottles, fill a jug with tap water and squeeze some fresh lemons or limes in. Drop the slices in with a couple of leaves of mint. For a sweeter drink, start off with a tablespoon of sugar and a splash of hot water (to help the sugar dissolve) and then add cold water and the other ingredients. Always keep a jug in the fridge so that you don't have to run the tap for minutes to get the water cold.

• Create some tasty salad lunches to take to the office. Forget limp lettuce and traditional salad materials, be creative and think about what won't end up soggy after it's been dressed – or take the dressing separately in a jam jar. One of my favourites requires only pasta, new potatoes, green beans and a dollop of homemade pesto (see page 152). It takes seconds to make. Bring one large pan of water to the boil, crumble in some salt, then add the halved new potatoes (the smaller the better) as they'll take the longest to cook (depending on how long the pasta takes). Pasta goes in next, followed by the beans for the last five minutes. Mix it all up with a tablespoon of pesto and some black olives, if you have any lurking in the fridge.

The Great Carbon-Offset Debate

Should I stump up for saplings?

Of all the ways that we have tried to address environmental problems over the last decade, carbon offsetting has been the most controversial. In case you've been living in a cave and have no idea what I'm talking about, it works like this. You fly; then you pay a fee to a carbon-offset company, and this goes towards planting a tree or building a wind turbine somewhere in the world where it will cancel out the carbon that your flight created. There, problem sorted.

Only it's not that simple. It is far better to reduce the amount you fly than to offset. 'Offsets do not reduce emissions overall and should only be seen as a last resort after other measures to reduce or avoid emissions have been explored and acted upon,' says a statement from Friends of the Earth, Greenpeace and WWF.

Why do it?

It's a good start, helping people to engage in the environmental debate and realize that travelling around the planet has an impact on the environment.

It's better than doing nothing. If you're going to visit your sister in Australia whatever the environmental implications, it is obviously better to give £20 to a company that is providing biogas digesters in India and solar panels in Africa. As long as you do this as well as, not instead of, making other green changes in your life.

Given the problems with using trees to offset, companies are moving over to green technology. By funding diverse renewable-energy projects, there are fewer uncertainties about how they will reduce CO_2 in the atmosphere and fewer problems with local communities being displaced by reforesting plans (see below).

Why think twice?

It encourages the wrong mindset, that you can pay your way out of environmental guilt, and that we can carry on doing what we know is bad for the environment instead of mending our flighty ways. We cannot undo the damage that has already been done by flying, but we can make sure that we curb our damaging ways in the future.

It distracts from the real question of how we are going to reduce carbon-dioxide emissions from air travel.

Tree-planting offset schemes have limitations. Trees only trap CO_2 when they are alive; it will be released back into the atmosphere through fire, decay or harvesting, so the positive impact of a tree only lasts for its lifetime. And carbon-offset companies cannot easily guarantee the survival of trees they are planting. If they are cut down too soon, they will not have fulfilled their job to remove the emissions from the flight they were supposed to be offsetting.

There has been controversy surrounding land use in developing countries. There is a risk that locals will be moved from their land so that we can assuage our guilt by planting trees on it.

Again, with tree-planting offset projects, convincing indigenous people that they shouldn't chop down trees or use forests for their own purposes is not easy and its ethics are questionable.

How to choose an offset company

Find out about the different projects your money will go towards. Are you convinced by them? Are local people involved?

Find out how much of your donation goes directly to projects, and how much goes to VAT, running costs and salaries of staff. If it's less than 50 per cent, don't even consider it.

Make sure the company doesn't only offset by planting trees (for the reasons above).

Is the company profit-making or a charity? How much profit does it make? Although the CarbonNeutral Company is profit-making, it made a loss in 2005, citing the costs involved in seeking out and auditing appropriate projects as the reason why. This is comforting in some ways, but it might be safer to support a non-profit-making carbon-neutral company.

Look for projects certified by the independent, internationally recognized Gold Standard (*www.cdmgoldstandard.org*).

The Triumph of Chutney

Right now, the garden is full of bounty. It's so impressive, I wouldn't be surprised if you ended up taking pictures with your digital camera, if only to capture the first courgette-plant flower and the height reached by the runner beans. But where is everybody? Who is going to appreciate the sweetness of your raspberries and the first home-grown tomato salad of the year? Typically, they've all gone on holiday to stuff themselves with boring old pasta in unimaginative Tuscan villas when they should be staying loyal to the motherland and being rewarded with a glut of summer produce.

To ensure that you don't miss out on the praise that is, after all, your right since you so cleverly created something from nothing, I recommend preserving some of your produce. Then, when the hordes return, thinking they've escaped the annual ritual of showing deep gratitude for your gift of one mini courgette (the one that didn't go rotten in the wet spell, that is), you can offer them chutney and pickled peppers, before setting up a slideshow featuring photos of your vegetables at various stages of growth. The best thing about jars of preserved produce is that they enable you to carry on harvesting praise for your efforts, not only in the summer months, but on and on into the winter. Until your friends stop coming round.

This recipe is a blend of many different tomato chutney recipes. I have no idea which bit came from where but it usually works out for me and it's a satisfying way of using up old jam jars.

A word on seasonality: July is a bit early in the year for tomatoes to have reached their full, rosy sweetness. You'll be more likely to be making tomato chutney next month or in September, but a practice round, replacing the tomatoes with courgettes, won't hurt.

Slice the tomatoes, apples and onions. How small you make the pieces will dictate the final consistency of your mixture. I try to chop everything as small as I can manage because I like a well-blended chutney, but sometimes I get bored and some large lumps of tomato and apple end up in the pan – you can always batter them into submission with a wooden spoon while everything is cooking.

Throw all the remaining ingredients into a pan and bring to a boil. (A professional chutney maker would put the ginger, chillies, cloves and cardamom in a muslin sack first. I tend not to, which means I have to fish around to remove them before filling the jam jars. Sometimes they stay in, which is hardly a disaster.) Then simmer for roughly an hour and a half or until the mixture has thickened slightly.

Pour into sterilized jam jars. I sterilize mine by soaking them in boiling water, which also helps to loosen the old labels. Put on lids tightly, label and store for at least three months before tucking in.

NOTE: A tasty variation of this is to bake an entire bulb of garlic for half an hour in the oven. Squeeze each clove, so roasted garlic paste shoots into your simmering chutney mixture.

700g (1 ½ pounds) tomatoes
350g (¾ pound) apples
450g (1 pound) onions
200g raisins
Generous pinch of salt
400ml vinegar (I use a mixture
    of malt and cider vinegar)
175g brown sugar (if you're
    using green tomatoes,
    add an extra 100g)

Two or three cloves of garlic,
    sliced
A lump of ginger
Couple of chillies
Couple of cloves
Couple of cardamon pods,
    bashed with a rolling pin
Any chopped herbs you can lay
    your hands on; I use sage
    and parsley

How to Camp in Style

Pillows. Don't even think about leaving the house without them. No, before you ask, rolling up a spare jumper won't work. It'll be lumpy and you'll get dents on your face from the pattern.

Rugs, rugs and more rugs. They're good for curling up under around the fire and the more you layer on the floor of your tent, on top of the more conventionally used camping mats, the less your hips will complain in the morning. Serious comfort lovers like to use blow-up mattresses. I find they pop.

A hurricane lamp. It casts a romantic glow and, unlike candles in jam jars, and as its name suggests, it won't blow out. It'll also come in handy when you stagger off to the loo in the night. If you are sensible, you'll use it to check for stinging nettles.

A gas stove. Back-up in case your cavewoman instinct fails, along with that of your co-campers.

A water carrier. So you don't end up buying mineral water and then having to use it to wash up and clean your teeth, which might sound very decadent but, really, is a bit of a waste. I like the lightweight Platypus water bottles, available in most camping shops, which fold down when they are empty.

Proper food. All is lost if you sup on instant noodles. Think long and hard about meals. I always do. Banish anything immediately associated with camping, with the exception perhaps of cans of rice pudding and porridge. Plan something simple but nourishing. Jacket potatoes can be wrapped in silver foil and placed in the glowing embers of your fire. In the same way, a box of brie can be converted into a cheese fondue to be dipped into with crusty bread.

Cutlery. Otherwise you'll have to eat everything fondue-style and you'll run out of bread.

Saucepan lids. Another oft-forgotten utensil that will transform camping cooking. As an eco-measure it serves the important function of enabling you to cook with less gas, but what matters most is the fact that it halves the time it takes to boil water, so converting the desire for tea into a cuppa is much less agonizing.

How to make the perfect camping chai

This is dead easy, sweet and flavoursome and should disguise the strange odour coming from badly washed camping mugs.

• If you have lots of milk, put enough in a pan to fill your cups and place it on the fire or gas cooker to boil. If you've got to go easy on the white stuff – must have enough for breakfast – don't worry, you can use up to half water and it'll still taste creamy.

• When the milk starts getting hot, but long before it boils, add a couple of teabags, a generous pinch of cinnamon, a couple of cloves and a few squashed cardamom pods, along with lots of sugar.

• Watch as your delicious concoction starts to take form. You might have to stir it a bit to get the powdered cinnamon to blend in. If you've brought proper cinnamon sticks with you, well done you.

• Just as it starts to boil, remove the teabags, cloves and cardamom pods, if you can find them, and pour into mugs. Spike with whisky if you have it, or even better Amaretto.

NOTE: It may sound fiddly to have cloves and cardamom on hand when you're camping, but actually it's not. I always bring them wrapped in silver foil. Stored in a mug with your camping gear, you need such small quantities that a wrap could last a few years. I made mine ages ago.

I've tried to make **pea soup with bacon** as well as my friend Alex did, but to no avail. When I asked him for his secret recipe, he told me: 'You need to blend self-doubt and self-love sufficiently that you see your own face reflected in the surface of the soup,' which I assumed was a polite way of saying no. After a second request, he was less cryptic, admitting that he had adapted one of Elizabeth David's recipes. Start by dissolving lettuce in a large amount of butter and frying some bacon in it, then add fresh peas – of which there are lots around at this time of year – and instead of blending the soup, mash it lightly, leaving some peas whole. Add plenty of mint and stock, for a final touch, break a couple of eggs into the mixture just before serving, which cook slightly with the heat of the soup, so you don't have to worry about eating raw egg. It being the first time he had made the soup, he was chicken about the egg and only used one. Next time he promises to be bolder.

If you have any **broad beans** left and they're getting a bit tough, whiz them up in a blender with garlic and lots of olive oil to make broad bean dip; alternatively, boil them for 5 minutes, then mash them into a frying pan in which finely chopped rosemary is slowly warming with slices of garlic and a good slug of olive oil.

AUGUST

HOW TO SAVE WATER
(WITHOUT SHARING BATHS)

BEFORE WE START, A BRIEF WORD ON THE TITLE ABOVE. PLEASE FEEL FREE TO SHARE baths if you like, I would hate to deter you. As a method of both water saving and as a demonstration to loved ones that your feelings go beyond anything that you might find in their water, it should be encouraged. The only reason I mention that it's not obligatory is because I know how attached some people are to their private supply of H_2O. In fact, I know people for whom it is bad enough to share the same tub. My ex-flatmate Tom would vigorously disinfect it between my evening bath and his own. I'd see him on his knees scrubbing the life out of the enamel sides with what I considered to be inappropriate ferocity. Doing my best not to feel offended, I'd wonder if it was only after me he did this.

The funny thing is, Tom is actually the bath-sharing type. A gentleman of courteous manners, he regularly offers up his dirty water and a portion of bum space to his girlfriend Louise. That he was wary of my washing habits, I fear, may be a reflection of the fact that I am not what you would call a fanatical self-cleaner.

Before I go any further, let me assure you, I bathe and shower quite enough to keep myself respectable and relatively fragrant. I would hate to risk the reputation of the green movement, conjuring up old terms of abuse such as soap dodger, by doing otherwise. But I am not one of those types who insist on several showers a day.

Not like some of my friends, who claim to feel unclean unless they have showered at the beginning and end of the day and freshened up several times in between – whatever that may mean. That to me is excessive: a waste of water and time. It suggests an unnecessary fear of body odour, and I don't imagine that it is particularly good for your skin. Washing and applying products, I've always been led to believe, deprives it of natural oils – and disguises pheromones, which make up your unique scent of attraction. Hence, the letter Napoleon allegedly wrote to his lover Josephine to announce that war was over: 'I'm coming home – please don't wash.'

As a child, I was encouraged not to overdo it with the soap and water. Not for environmental reasons but because I had eczema and washing dries out your skin. By the time I reached double figures, I had shaken off the eczema, but habits had formed. The Sunday-night bath was a grand affair, including hair-washing, back-scrubbing, toe-clipping and rounded off with tea in bed and an episode of *The Two Ronnies*.

Worryingly, I can't remember much soaking and scrubbing going on during the week, but a little must have taken place because my mother has always advocated washing every other day. A commendable water-saving message, but to modern tastes, it may seem on the grimy side. In terms of how clean we need to be to stay healthy – by keeping bacteria at bay – it is enough. But, these days, taking a bath or shower has moved beyond its original purpose.

Washing is a pastime rather than a necessity, a pleasure rather than a chore. We do it to relax, to make ourselves feel and look good, as much as to keep ourselves odour-free. I bring this up in the pub with my friend Rosie. She says she doesn't run a bath because she needs to wash but because it's a nice thing to do. She might have already showered that day and she probably won't bother using soap second time round, but it won't stop her wallowing in the tub.

I'm not saying this is a bad way to go; you've got to weigh it up against the impact of the activities you might otherwise be doing. Watching TV, driving somewhere or going out for dinner, most things we do have environmental consequences. As it is, Rosie doesn't have a telly; she takes long baths instead.

But when it comes to water saving, I'm afraid baths are the baddies. Short, perfunctory showers are the thing. A five-minute shower uses roughly a third of the water needed for a bath. In you go, no dilly-dallying, do what you need to and then out.

Gervase is more committed to the shower than me. He takes one every morning without fail and most evenings. I rely on him to give me a nudge bathroom-wards if need be. While this provides an excuse for him to humiliate me every so often by pointing out grubby marks on my neck, it gives me the edge in the green stakes.

Given that rainfall is becoming more unpredictable and climate change is on the horizon, we are strongly encouraged to save water in the home. My slovenly habits, in other words, have received a green sheen. That they stem primarily from laziness, I keep quiet about. Should I forget to flush the loo, I'm not seen as careless and sloppy; I'm eco-friendly. I'm saving water. Another resource to consume frugally (although my advice on this is that it's fine in your own home, but in other people's it's best to be on the safe side and flush).

In August when our green and pleasant land is thirsty, saving water is instinctive. It's hot and dry and our reservoir supplies are not as full as they were during the winter months. It makes sense to go easy on the hose and cut back on baths. For sustained good behaviour, however, involving year-round commitment, it helps to appreciate how the water system operates and why, even in a rainy country like the UK, we should not take water for granted.

It may come as a surprise to you to learn that I, so proud of my spartan home habits, until recently knew very little about how water reaches our homes and where it goes when it leaves. Of course, I understood the basics. Dirty water disappears down waste-water pipes and clean water arrives in its place, through a different pipe. But what exactly happens to the dirty water, and, more worryingly, does it get turned into the clean stuff?

I'm sure I learnt this at school, but somehow the water system has become more of a mystery as I've grown older. In an attempt to get to grips with it, I make a brave decision. I choose to visit a dark and smelly underworld: a sewage works in South London.

Of all the experiences that have arisen from my attempts to go green, you might imagine that this one would fall to the bottom of the heap. What happens to human waste and what we flush down the sink, frankly, is not a popular subject. It's pongy and unpleasant.

But it is also peculiarly fascinating; it affects us all. Just as we should think beyond the moment that we drop rubbish bags outside our home for collection, so too should we spare a thought for what we wave away down our waste-water pipes. In both these cases, there is no such thing as 'away'. There is only 'somewhere else'.

And that place is not as bad as you might imagine. Late on an August afternoon, when most sensible people are sipping their first pints in beer gardens or heading home for barbecues, I find myself peering into the murky depths of a London sewer. Clad in hefty boots, a luminous jacket and a hard hat, I am standing at the point at which a network of tunnels – some of London's 40,000 miles of them – delivers South-east London's waste water to the sewage treatment works.

Here, it will be cleaned, the debris filtered out, the solid matter (OK, poo) burnt in an incinerator to provide energy for the plant, and the remaining water will end up clean enough to be flushed into the river (the Environment Agency has varying required levels of cleanliness for this final product, depending on the size of the river in which the water will be deposited. In the Thames, a higher degree of sediment is acceptable than in smaller rivers).

So, in answer to my first question, no, waste water does not come directly back to incoming water pipes. I can relax; we do not drink water that comes out of a sewage works. What gushes from our taps is from rivers and ground-water supplies, but first it will have come through a Water Treatment Centre, where it is chlorinated and rigorously checked for purity levels.

As for the light brown water flowing in front of me, this is its story so far.

It has disappeared down the toilet or sink, been flushed into a pipe which has joined up with a bigger pipe, which has eventually found its way into a sewer (like blood vessels slotting into each other, says Don Sharples, the Thames Water press officer accompanying me).

Relying on a combination of gravity and pumping, it has wound its way to Crossness Sewage Treatment Works. And here it is, waste water from 1.87 million people, arriving at a rate of 600,000 cubic metres every day. My own not included, as it is piped to another of the three treatment centres that serve London.

What's odd about the sewage plant is that while it is whiffy, the appearance of the water coming in and its odour really aren't that bad. I expected to be breathing into my sleeve, feeling faint and calling for the smelling salts, but actually it's a manageable pong. No worse than a cow shed on a hot day. Brian Phelps, the production manager, explains that sewage is not as foul as most people think: 99 per cent of it is water, much of it run-off rainwater. Human waste makes up less than 1 per cent. But he admits that his wife still complains he stinks when he gets home.

Far more rank than the dirty water itself or the smell in the air is the debris floating in it. Detritus of our urban society, it is stuff that people think they magic away when they flush the loo or jam it down the sink. But here it all is, looking at first like bits of rag. I peer cautiously down the three-metre-wide tunnel. As the bits drift closer, I start to make out what they are. Baby wipes, bits of plastic bags, dishcloths and more than a few condoms.

Brian chooses this moment to tell me about a dead horse that turned up at the works not long ago, along with a dark tale about a young boy who slipped down a sewer in the 1970s and travelled over half a mile in its flow until he was pulled out by the sewage workers. They heard his screams as he was swept down the tunnel. I try not to dwell on what it would be like to be submerged in this water.

This stage is called screening. It involves a dozen rotating metal claws that descend into the gloom of the sewer and scoop upwards. Of course, none of the floating stuff should be here. It should have been binned since it risks blocking the sewers and it costs the water authorities a fortune to remove. Here, every last ear-bud must be taken out before the water continues its journey. Because health and safety regulations prevent sewage-soaked material being dumped in landfill, all the materials extracted from the water must be washed and dried first. They wind up in landfill eventually, after a slow, water-wasteful journey.

Brian says that if he could change one thing about our attitude to water, it would be to make us stick to the 'Bag It and Bin It' rule promoted by the water authorities. 'Toilets must not be used as guilt-free rubbish bins,' it says on the campaign's website (*www.bagandbin.org*). 'Nothing except waste from people's bodies and loo paper should disappear down the loo.' There is focus on tampons and tampon applicators, perhaps because many brands advertise them as toilet flushable and it is widely believed that this is the best way of disposing of them.

I'm embarrassed to get into the details of this with Brian, so I wait until later to get Thames Water's official response. Aren't tampons flushable? Yes and no. Yes, they will go down the toilet – an estimated two billion sanitary protection items, such as condoms, tampons, razors and cotton buds – are flushed down toilets each year. No, it is not the ideal place for them. They will block the screens that filter sewage at the treatment centre. Even worse, they might escape the system and end up on beaches and river-sides. If there is a bin provided, water companies ask that we use it.

What's known in the industry as sanitary-related debris (SRD) is not the only problem that clueless water consumers create. If you are one of the brave men whose job it is to maintain the sewers, fat is enemy number one. As hot liquid, it disappears effortlessly down the drain. But here it quickly cools, hardens and joins up with other lumps, which attach themselves to tunnel roofs. It's a nasty substance, not unlike cholesterol clogging our arteries. Or, as Rob Smith puts it – and he should know – 'like feta cheese'.

Rob has hacked into enough of these foul chunks to feel strongly that we have lost our regard for sewers. 'They are not being used as they were intended,' he says. 'For the transportation of bodily functions.' His official title is catchment engineer, which thankfully involves work above ground as well as below. But he's done his time. At 58 years old, he's spent the last sixteen years as a 'flusher' clearing blockages.

'Getting rid of fat is not a nice job,' he says, with epic understatement. 'Imagine a block of rancid fat. Caught up in it is all the other usual stuff you find in a sewer.' Not nice. Using a variety of tools, from jets of water to shovels, Rob and his teams of flushers break up and remove the fat. Like everything that shouldn't be down there in the first place, once fished out it is taken to landfill.

Which is where we should have sent it in the first place. According to Thames Water, this is what we should do with hot fat: 'Pour it into an old tin or sturdy container; and then put it in the bin once it has cooled and solidified.' That's all very well, but it strikes me as a waste of an aluminium tin or jam jar to use it as a receptacle for fat that you are going to send to land-fill. I prefer to pour it into leak-proof plastic packaging, such as meat trays, that are non-recyclable anyway.

When you eat out, it's more of a problem. You can't very well enquire after the vegetable oil your chips were cooked in. Or you could, but it would probably kill the atmosphere of your dinner. Restaurants are a major cause of fat clogging up the sewers, increasing Rob's workload more than anything else. 'Since it costs money to get rid of the stuff, the cheapest thing to do is pour it down the drains,' he says.

The responsible alternative is to buy a 'fat trap', sometimes known as a 'grease interceptor', which sits under a restaurant's sink and collects oil and fat. It is emptied regularly by the manufacturing company. Calls to make them obligatory in the catering industry, as they soon will be in Dublin, have so far been ignored; an indication of how slow we have been to appreciate the impact that our restaurant boom has had underground.

Back at the sewage treatment works, I've got to the really yucky bit. So that you don't think I'm being coy, let me tell you about what happens to the organic sludge, a posh word for poo. After the screening process, the flow of the water is slowed down, which encourages the solids to fall to the bottom. 'Good healthy sludge, this is,' shouts Brian as he lifts the lid of a bubbling cauldron of gunk that has been separated from the rest of the water. Not being an expert and not wanting to get too close, I nod my agreement, narrowly avoiding being splashed by a sludgy pool of God knows what.

From here it is scraped into a different tank. Half of it will be thickened to make mud cakes, which are burnt by the incinerator. The other half will be treated – to kill the pathogens – so that it can be given to farmers as agricultural fertilizer.

The sludge power generator, which houses the incinerator, looms in the distance. It's a futuristic monster of a building. The fact that it manages to make energy from human waste adds to its imposing, faintly evil, appearance. Brian explains that it works like any other power station, but instead of burning coal or gas, it is fuelled by human turds.

It provides only just over a third of the sewage plant's energy requirements. The rest of the energy comes from non-renewable sources, which is a reminder that using water, and treating it, produces a carbon footprint. The two processes that use up the most energy, I'm told, are the pumping stations that get the water to the treatment centre, and the business of aerating it (after the solids have been removed), which encourages bacteria to breed in it and thereby clean it.

Rarely do we think about the energy required to treat our water and pump it to and from our houses. Only during the Second World War, when posters recommended saving fuel by not running a bath over five inches deep, did the relationship between water and power garner attention. Nowadays, it's a tough job encouraging people to consider the implications of their bathwater.

Like turning off stand-by buttons, the problem is that you don't feel any direct benefit from saving water – beyond financial savings if you swap to a water meter (see Light Green section in this chapter).

There is not a wholesome feeling in your tummy like the one after a plate of organic food, or the rewarding ache in your calves after you've cycled to work. You have to be content with the knowledge that you are doing the right thing. And sometimes, just sometimes, you can find yourself thinking, but why do we need to save water anyway? We live in a rainy country, there's lots of it about.

But rainfall does not always translate into replenished water supplies, as the charity Water UK is at pains to point out. The journey between sky and kitchen sink is not straightforward. Much of what falls runs into rivers and into the sea with only a certain amount being captured for future use. Over the past few years, downpours in the UK have increased in intensity, becoming shorter-lived but heavier, and we have more of them.

You might think that a summer storm justifies your extra-deep bath, but many people's water comes from underground aquifers, and these are restocked during the winter. It is winter rainfall that counts for more. Between spring and autumn is the growing season, so little of what falls during summer makes it to the underground aquifers. Either it evaporates or it is used by gardeners and farmers. Then, in late autumn, the 'recharge period' begins, which continues until spring. There is usually more rain, and less of it is siphoned off for agricultural use.

Of course, this has always been the case and at least our ability to store rainwater has improved over the years. I ask my mother if she remembers being encouraged to save water as a child. She doesn't, but she makes the point that there was not the same number of water-using appliances in people's homes in those days. No dishwashers, power-showers or wet rooms with Jacuzzi functions. And thriftiness with any natural resource was inbuilt. Back then, you wouldn't waste water, in the same way that you wouldn't waste food, she tells me.

These days, we use more water than ever before. Bathrooms have become elaborate temples to the watery worship of our bodies. The trend for 'monsoon' showers and baths the size of small swimming pools is exploding water consumption. As is our swelling population, which leads to many areas of southern England being labelled as 'water-stressed' by the Environment Agency. Don, the press officer, tells me that (according to Thames Water's figures) each person in the UK uses an average of 150 litres of water every day.

As an Australian, brought up in a place where water was 'a big deal', he is quietly appalled. 'Back home, nobody takes two showers a day or waters their garden more than twice a week.' What's more, he tells me that people dob their neighbours in, reporting them to the authorities if they use too much.

He understands that with our soggy climate, saving water has not been seen as a priority. But numerous factors, including climate change, freakish weather, depleted groundwater levels and a growing population of heavy users, are pushing water higher on the eco-agenda. Frittering it away is becoming more of a problem, putting pressure on both ends of the water cycle: our supplies and our sewers.

Back at Crossness, Brian thinks there is a problem of attitude. 'People don't want to think about what happens after they flush the loo,' he says. 'There is an "out of sight, out of mind" culture when dealing with all aspects of waste.' Half joking, I suggest he organizes educational trips to the sewage works for businesses and schools. Isn't it an ideal 'team-building exercise'?

'We tried that,' he replies. 'We organized community visits, but there wasn't much interest. No one wanted to come.'

It's a shame because I enjoyed my trip to Crossness. I've dined off it at dinner parties for months – once we've finished eating, obviously. When I mention London's sewers, there is always interest – in their structure and the mastermind behind their construction, Joseph Bazalgette, if not their contents. Some people want to know what the sewage actually looks like, how bad it smells and what happens to it. Murky matters, but much better to think about them than brush them under the carpet, or in this case, down the loo.

There is a grim but underlying curiosity about sewers and human waste. It's part of life, after all. We all go to the loo; we all require water to survive. It makes sense to understand enough about the relationship between the two to stop us abusing the cycle.

Since my visit, I have treated my own loo, and others that I have visited, with the utmost respect. Not once have I been tempted to post down an ear-bud – definitely not a dead horse. The only disturbing thing that has occurred is I have caught myself more than once gazing down the disappearing curve of the toilet basin, wondering about interlinking pipes and their journey to the sewage works.

I envisage the screens scooping up misplaced debris, the organic sludge swirling in its tank and the cathedralesque incinerator towering above. Most of all, I think about the flushers. Somewhere down there, they are chipping away at lumps of hardened fat, pulling out rogue boys now and again. Without them, our cities would be filthy and we would not be in a position to take clean water for granted.

WHAT'S IN IT FOR THE PLANET?

By saving water and using only what you need . . . you reduce the chance of a drought in your area, which will affect the wildlife and environment as well as everyone living there. The need to save water is becoming greater as populations grow, more homes are built and water is divided among more of us. To make matters worse, our bath-time habits are increasingly indulgent, as seen by the popularity of power-showers and whirlpool baths. Smaller households in the UK and the increased numbers of people who live alone have added to the problem – when people cohabit, they tend to share water required for washing up, washing clothes and, yes, even baths.

By being careful what you put down your sink and loo . . . you are helping to cut the chance of a blockage that can send sewage into the overflow pipes. (These lead straight into the river – deemed a better solution than it overflowing into the streets – where it will kill fish and damage the ecosystem.) Sixty per cent of blockages in the sewer happen because of fat and grease.

How to Green Up Your Bathroom

Showers

Generally considered a good thing when it comes to water-saving, a shower will normally use about a third of the water and energy of a bath. This changes if you have a power-shower, which uses up more water than a bath in five minutes. Although a long scrub is important (if not essential) every so often, as a rule of thumb, a short, sharp, non dilly-dallying approach is the most eco-friendly. For those wedded to long showers, there are water-efficient showerheads that feel powerful by creating finer drops but actually use less water. For anyone who needs a 5-minute prompt, other than a shout from the person waiting outside, there are shower timers. Personally, I'm not keen on time management in the bathroom, but then I've never had a problem being a little slapdash in that department.

Baths

You've probably never considered the shape of your bath. But by doing so, you will learn about its water requirements. Tapered or peanut-shaped baths do the best job of providing space for the bather while also using less water. As a traditionalist, I'm more in favour of the basic rectangular tub, but having learnt that this is likely to hold at least 80 litres, I'm aware that it is a water indulgence. To make myself feel better, I wash delicates (jumpers and anything else that doesn't like being in the machine) in the dirty water. Sometimes they even come in with me and we all have a good soak. Obviously this is not as good as siphoning the water with a hose and using it on the garden – an oft-recommended green tip. But much as I'd like to declare the importance of recycling bath water, I've yet to find anyone who has managed it. Even The Greenest Person I Know hasn't, because his bath, like mine, is on the ground floor, and therefore lacks the gravitational effect needed to draw the water down the hose. Mind you, Donnachadh does the same thing in a different way. He showers in a large tub with handles, the water from which is then used for the loo or garden during dry spells. Impressive, but possibly a step further than most of us are prepared to go.

Sinks

Spray heads on your taps is the way to make your sink superbly water efficient. They provide a finer, aerated spray of water. Sadly, they are not to everyone's taste. The fact that we had them in our school loos puts them in a category of green changes that I pretend don't exist, so I don't have to adopt them. Instead I'd rather turn my hand to stopping sinks dripping. A single dripping tap can waste up to 4 litres of water a day, so it's an effort worth making.

Loos

It's funny how easy it is to think about something like putting a brick in your cistern for a long time before you actually do it. It took me a shameful year to spring into action on this. Don't let the same happen to you. Pick up brick, open cistern, fit brick inside. It really is as simple as that. Then, every time you flush the loo, you are saving the brick's weight in water. A toilet hippo does a similar thing, saving you roughly 3 litres each flush (*www.hippo-the-watersaver.co.uk*).

Should you be going through the thrilling procedure of purchasing a new loo, treat yourself to a dual flush model, which allows you to choose between a short flush and a longer one. I'm sure there's no need to remind anyone about the catchy Australian maxim, more recently advocated by London mayor Ken Livingstone: 'If it's yellow, let it mellow; if it's brown, flush it down.'

Try it in August . . .

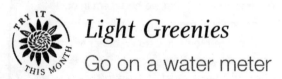

Light Greenies
Go on a water meter

This costs nothing and may save pennies, as well as water. Last year the Environment Minister announced that having a meter cuts water use by 10 per cent per household. Meanwhile, it has been estimated that the average annual water bill for metered homes is £35 less than for those with flat-rate bills. What's not to like? You simply phone your water company and ask to have one installed. The only hitch is whether or not your home is suitable. I was all for it, hoping it would at last bring financial rewards for my stingy habits, but when the Thames Water chap dutifully turned up, he told me my stopcock was in the wrong place, the cheeky so-and-so. Anyway, turns out this is a valve that turns off the water supply and it is also where the meter would be fitted, so that it can measure the water entering your home. Mine was inaccessible, somewhere under our kitchen's front wall, which I was most upset about. So I'm stuck on normal bills with no financial rewards for the brick in my cistern and the water butt in the garden. What made matters worse was being told that I was in a minority. The positioning of the stopcock won't scupper most people's plans, so don't let it put you off. In the future, it looks likely that meters will be compulsory in regions prone to drought, so you might as well prepare.

 ## *Dark Greenies*
Make your own perfume

The eco-friendly have a duty to go around smelling pleasant, but conventional perfumes, the sort on display in department stores and airports, have a poor reputation. When Greenpeace conducted a survey of well-known brands, it found many to include chemicals from the phythalate group that are potentially harmful to heavy users and to the environment. Manufacturers aren't required to reveal exact ingredients – imagine the space it would take up on the bottle and the counterfeit products that would result. Instead they use the generic word *parfum*.

If you take fragrance seriously, another problem with conventional products is that you end up smelling like everyone else. We can all detect Obsession or Poison the moment a wearer steps into a room. 'These perfumes have a chemical, not a natural base,' Celia Lyttelton explains. Celia is author of *The Scent Trail*, a book based on two years she spent on an exotic and sensual odyssey, scouring beaches for whale vomit (ambergris) and Himalayan mountains for jasmine. I turned to Celia after my first attempt to make perfume ended in disaster. Courtesy of Google, I followed a recipe for an alcohol-based perfume that involved mixing 80 per cent proof vodka with essential oils and leaving it for several weeks to develop. Except that mine didn't 'develop'; it simply went off. It reminded me of early attempts to make pot-pourri in the garden. I'd mix rose petals with pond water and leave jam jars of the rotting mixture around the garden.

Similarly with my 'perfume'; it was soon contributing an unwelcome odour to the bedroom. Even the most frowned-upon celebrity scent would have been an improvement. My error might have been that I didn't choose essential oils that worked well together – you have to brush up on your top, middle and base notes for that – and I couldn't resist dripping a bit of my ginger bath oil into the pot. But it's more likely that it was because I couldn't lay my hands on 80 per cent proof vodka – that would necessitate a trip to Siberia, and my carbon footprint won't allow it – so I cheated and used Smirnoff. Anyway, undeterred, perfume number two was based on Celia's recommendations.

The idea is to mix drops of your favourite essential oil with either almond oil or good quality olive oil (perfumes based in oil are popular in Islamic countries because alcohol is *haram*, forbidden). Almond oil is a little greasy, so Celia uses extra virgin olive oil from the first cold pressing of the olives. Unsure if I can lay my hands on that calibre of oil, I make do with organic olive oil and it seems to do the trick. I mix five drops of jasmine essential oil with four drops of orange essential oil, two of lavender (because it's the only other one I have) and mix this with about five teaspoons of olive oil. I manage to pour most of it into a dear little perfume pot that I was given for a birthday present, with the rest seeping down the side of the kitchen table where I use it as polish later (waste not, want not, and all that). Celia says don't worry if it looks more like a massage oil, so I don't. She assures me it will last longer than any high-street fragrance.

And I'm happy with my concoction. So happy I insist on shoving my wrist under people's noses whenever I'm wearing it. I can see that the fiddliness of perfume-making might not suit everyone, and while the smell is pleasant, it doesn't send me into a Proustian reverie. For that I would be better off taking advantage of what Celia calls the 'quiet scent revolution', which is seeing little artisans, such as Diptyque and L'Artisan Parfumeur, challenge the big boys. These places operate by word of mouth, sell proper perfume made with natural ingredients, and spend their budgets on content, rather than packaging and advertising. It's going to cost you more than a few bottles of essential oil, maybe £70 minimum, but the perfume will last longer and you don't risk smelling of homemade pot-pourri.

Eco-Cheats

• When a summer drought is in full swing, keep a bucket near the shower. Since it takes a minute or two for the water to warm up, with a bucket underneath you can collect a drink for your thirsty garden or pot plants. This might seem like a bit of a fiddle, and I can't imagine doing it other than in summer, but, like anything, once you're in the habit and the bucket is in place, it doesn't take long to wander towel-clad from the bathroom to throw the water on the garden.

• Keep a small bag or box in the kitchen, or near your hats and coats zone, for old mineral water bottles, or other drinks bottles that wind their way into your home. When you leave the house, you can grab one and fill it up with tap water, instead of succumbing to another plastic bottle of mineral water later in the day.

• When reservoirs hit rock bottom, don't worry about the sophistication of your water-storing container. Makeshift water butts can be simple affairs. If a summer storm erupts, grab the nearest bucket or washing-up bowl and rush it outside to collect water. All that matters is you dump the collected rainwater on your thirsty plants when the rain has long gone.

How to Use Less Water in the Kitchen

The dishwasher debate

If you're worried that this is the bit when I recommend you give up your beloved dishwasher, and consequently are about to turn the page and get on with becoming a low-water gardener instead, hold your horses.

According to Waterwise, an NGO encouraging us to decrease our water consumption, if 50 per cent more people bought a dishwasher, we could save enough water to supply drinking water to a city the size of Leeds. Why? Because today's dishwashers use an average of 15 litres of water per wash, compared to 50 litres in the 1970s. They are generally water efficient – unlike us when we're let loose with a sink and a bottle of bubbles. While dishwashers have become greener, we have become worse at leaving the taps running and sloshing water down the drain like there's no tomorrow, or at least not one that requires water. Happily for appliance addicts, this dispels the myth that unless you are sweating into the soapsuds, your conscience cannot be truly clean.

Whatever camp you're in, here are some tips on how to be good about it:

Green cleaning by machine

• Cram the dishwasher – not to the point of breakages, obviously – and don't run it if it's half empty.

• Make use of the eco, or economy, setting, if your machine has one. It takes longer but running a slow and steady two-hour dishwasher cycle is superior to rushing through a half-hour one. The economy cycle starts with a cold-water wash and then reuses the same water, slowly heating it up.

• Invest in a water- and energy-saving model, when the time comes to replace your machine. Look for a high score in the obligatory energy-saving label, which rates appliances from A (the most efficient) to G (the least).

• Don't rinse your dishes under the tap and then put them in the dishwasher. As well as being time-consuming, it ignores the fact that most models are designed to cope with some food scraps.

Green cleaning by hand

• Use a washing-up bowl. Sinks hold an awful lot of water and they cool it quickly too. With a washing-up bowl, you can chuck the leftover water on plants and there is less temptation to wash up with the taps running.

• Try not to use too much washing-up liquid, otherwise your soapy subjects will need extra rinsing.

• Use a big bowl for dunking, when it comes to rinsing. That is, if you're not fortunate enough to have a farmhouse-style double sink.

The kettle conundrum

I don't suspect for a moment that this is going to be the first time it has been suggested that you only boil as much water as you need. It's the oldest eco-tip in the book, one that will reduce bills as well as save water. That doesn't mean that we're any better at following it. Odd, really, when you think how it shortens those caffeine-deprived moments that drag out before the kettle boils. It could be a mistrust of the dregs at the bottom that causes us to overfill. In which case, you could start by treating the limescale.

Taking stock

The murky-looking water in which your vegetables have been boiling is not to be sniffed at. It makes flavoursome stock, and has nutrients from the vegetables that have been cooked in it. Add it to any stew or soup instead of water. While on the subject of cooking veggies, remember that separate foods don't always need their own pan of boiling water just because they have different cooking times. A 'one-pan cooking' approach saves energy as well as water. For instance, if you were going for a broccoli, potatoes and carrots medley to accompany your supper, you'd want to get the potatoes boiling first; after 10 minutes or so you could add the carrots, and then finally the broccoli (which is always tastiest when it's bright green rather than disintegrating and turning yellow). The alternative would be to steam them, which is healthier as the veggies retain their nutrients, but you don't end up with vegetable water from which to make stock, so, alas, the water is wasted.

Rinsing recycling

Be creative with old washing-up water and stale water from the kettle by using it to rinse cans and bottles before you recycle them. This is much better than wasting fresh, hot water on the job, which would bring the energy used by your boiler into the equation and make you wonder if your committed recycling efforts were worth it. Whatever you do, don't be overzealous about rinsing. There's no need to get the stuff sparkling, they will most likely be cleaned again before they are transformed for their second life. All you're doing is preventing the items from clogging up the sorting process later on (as well as stopping your green bin becoming a stinky embarrassment to the street). A quick blast from the tap, a shake around in the bottles and cans, and you're done.

Or use the washing-up water on the garden. Water that contains household soaps, washing-up liquid and green cleaning products is harmless to established plants, but don't use water that contains bleach, disinfectant and stronger cleaning products.

Tasty tap water

Drinking lukewarm tap water on a stinking hot summer's day doesn't hit the spot. Instead of running the tap for an age before the temperature plummets to an acceptable level, keep a jug of water in the fridge. Not only will this save all that water wastage, but the chlorine in the water will evaporate after a few hours, leaving the water tasting the better for it.

How to be a
Low-water Gardener

Create your own compost

By now, it is unlikely that you will have failed to notice that compost is the bee's knees. There is nothing bad to be said about the stuff. It is the magic ingredient that all gardens dream of being swamped in. It brings fertility, improved drainage and, of course, those delightful creatures that I raved about in April: worms. To add to its gleaming CV, it is also known for holding on to water. During the summer months, an extra layer of homemade compost will help plants cope with drought.

Make mulch

Flip I may be, but it strikes me that one of the best reasons for using mulch is the excuse it gives you to use the word. Not just because it is childishly fun to say – sounding like something straight out of a Roald Dahl story – but also because it indicates membership of the gardening classes. Lob it into conversation and everyone will know that you have short, muddied nails and know a thing or two about earthy things that go squelch. The proper reason for using it is that it locks in moisture, so you can get away with less watering. A mulch is a layer of loose material placed over the soil. You can make it from all sorts of unlikely bits and pieces: straw, gravel, pebbles, woodchips (often called bark mulch and sold in garden centres), rotting leaves or even carpet. The only limit is whether you mind looking at it when you're out in the garden. I stopped short of using an old bit of orange carpet around the courgettes for this reason. Novice mulchers should note the following tips: make sure you water well before you lay on the mulch. And don't make the layer too thin – as well as water saving, the idea is to block light from the soil to stop weeds growing.

Install a water butt

A water butt is a worthy item indeed. Mine is a solemn, sturdy thing made from recycled plastic and devoted to collecting rainwater from our roof. Just looking at it encourages me to enjoy a moment of self-congratulation (wish I could say the same about the other butt in my life). In the meantime, I'll explain how it works. Rainwater travels from the drainpipe into a large green barrel via a small tube, called a diverter. From a tap at the bottom, you can fill your watering can, and, hey presto, water for nothing, to use on the garden or to wash the car. And not any old water. Rainwater is better for plants than tap water because it is warmer and free of chlorine. Some of my satisfaction with the butt is owed to Gervase and his DIY adviser and friend Tom. Since it was not me who hacked into the drainpipe and built it a stand from old bricks. I had anticipated plonking the butt outside and being done with it. But don't be put off by the thought of installation problems. Despite lots of puffing and blowing and calls for cold beer afterwards, they assure me it was not a complicated operation. Should you not trust yourself with a hacksaw, how about calling on a well-equipped neighbour – in the DIY department, obviously.

Watering hours

When you water is crucial. Tend plants at the fringes of the day to avoid evaporation. Outside of early mornings and evenings in summer, there's no point going out with a watering can. Especially as water heating on leaves can burn your plants.

Be careful that you don't overwater, in a fit of gardening enthusiasm. This discourages plants from putting down deep roots to look for moisture. To get an idea of how damp the soil is, stick your finger in it. You may find the surface is dry but there is moisture deeper down.

Include some low-water plants

Vegetables, as a general rule, require more water than most plants. In the green stakes, they make up for it in more ways than one, so don't abandon your plans for a veg patch quite yet. Instead, complement it with a Mediterranean-inspired theme elsewhere. Herbs such as rosemary and thyme thrive in dry, hot conditions; for splashes of colour, the Environment Agency's list of low-water flowers includes African lilies, lavender, tulips, poppies and French honeysuckle.

Pot-plant care

One problem with container growing is that you have to water plants more often than you would if they were drawing moisture from the soil. To minimize this, don't grow anything directly out of a pot as it will dry out more quickly. Plant into plastic containers. You can always put the container inside a pretty terracotta pot if it's aesthetics that concern you. The first year I grew beetroot, I had them in plastic Evian bottles with the top cut off and holes in the bottom. The beets only ever reached ping-pong-ball size (because their roots didn't have much room), but at least no one could accuse them of taking up more than their fair share of water.

Avoid the sprinkler

It's never easy to give up dancing under a sprinkler on a baking August afternoon. Once you've done it as a child, the temptation is always there. In the city, a lack of privacy holds some people back, but I don't doubt that everyone would be leaping around if they had the chance. What makes it less enticing is news that a sprinkler uses 1,000 litres of water an hour, the equivalent of two days' average consumption by a family of four. Sorry, but you'll have to re-enact your moves under a raincloud instead.

Beware watchful neighbours

Not because they might be peering over at your undignified display (see above), although there is that, but because they could be conspiring with the water authorities and reporting anyone who breaches a hosepipe ban. Curtain twitching is not unknown in times of resource thriftiness.

With the first few tomatoes you grow yourself, you'll want to enjoy them unadulterated, fresh off the vine, with perhaps a little salt to bring out their flavour.

But as time goes on, you'll become blasé. Then it's time to make a **tomato tart**. For learning that such a simple, delicious dish even exists, I have my friend Livvy – also my Worm Ally – to thank. She is queen of such tarts. It is an easy dish because you can use shop-bought puff pastry, spread with a mixture of soft goat's cheese and olive oil. Then you layer on the slices of tomato with some fresh thyme and perhaps a few slices of red onion, and bake the tart for 40 minutes.

For a novel way to enjoy **corn on the cob**, now in abundant supply, I recommend tapping into the Mexican flavours used by chef Thomasina Miers. After stripping the cob of its corn by slicing a knife down it, her recipe suggests frying first onion and garlic and then courgettes and some chilli in butter in an ovenproof dish. Then add the corn, fry for another 5 minutes before transferring to the oven. After 15 minutes, add lots of crumbled feta and bake for another 10 minutes. It sounds a bit odd and fiddly, but trust me, it's delicious. Thank you, Thomasina!

SEPTEMBER

THRIFTY LIVING

MAYBE I AM FORTUNATE TO POSSESS SQUIRREL-LIKE TENDENCIES BUT I CAN'T SAY I mind too much when summer turns to autumn. It is a shame not to be browning your toes in flip-flops and eating Mediterranean-style meals outside. But when you have a stomach-orientated outlook on life, like me, you get over these things. Long light evenings are left behind, yes, but there are winter fruits to gather and chestnuts to roast. I am spurred on by the thought of picking blackberries and hearty winter stews bubbling on the stove.

Lest you think it's only what happens in the kitchen that eases me towards winter without being troubled by seasonal grumpiness, let me attempt to convince you otherwise. Aside from food, embedded in autumnal thinking is something else that I like: comfort. With a nip in the air and a heightened sense of cosiness, September provides an excuse to hunker down and prepare for the dark months ahead.

Comfort and warmth go hand in hand with a drive for rest and replenishment, a chance to take stock, as much as to make it for hearty soups. By late August, I'm already compiling a checklist of important items to have to hand. A snuggly jumper, a teapot and tea tray (best accompanied by scone-making skills) and a roaring fire are always on it, followed by enough apples to ensure a flow of crumbles, pies and puréed fruit (sorry, we are back to food again) and a wicker basket (mainly for aesthetic purposes but also to help with the job of collecting fruit and sustainably sourced firewood). The only thing that remains is somewhere to walk where there are trees and where you can admire the colour of falling leaves.

These are adult pleasures, of course. When you are of school age, they are spoiled by the nagging knowledge that it's curtains for your summer holidays and time to return to school. That is, if you're not already cooped up in a chemistry class by the time the first leaf drops, with only your new pencil case for comfort. Older, and free of these things, I count my lucky stars that I can appreciate the back-to-school feeling without actually having to do it.

Contrary to what you might expect, this shift to the fireside does not trigger overindulgence. Quite the opposite; autumn brings out in many of us the spirit of thrift. There is a natural battening down of the hatches, a save-and-store mentality that kicks in as you prepare for winter. The instinct to fill cupboards with supplies takes over, as if there was a real chance of being snowed in for winter months. I know plenty of people, who I otherwise count as relatively sane individuals, who start stockpiling.

Survivalist strategies are not usually my mum's cup of tea but her winter walnut supply is generally spilling out of cupboards before we reach Halloween, while my father devotes his energy to the practical task of stashing firewood. On a late summer evening, you'll find him peering through the cobwebs into the shed, rubbing his hands together with glee at the thought of the warmth the wood will provide later in the year.

Yes, there is a lot to be said for September. What works against it, in the greener scheme of things, is that it is tempting to splurge on energy in the home. The aforementioned 'nip in the air' becomes less welcome as the season progresses, and a sudden craving for toasty radiators and long hot baths can wreak havoc with attempts at frugality.

I do my best to rise above it. Like a wartime housewife, I pride myself on being economical on the home front. Inherent stinginess, some might call it, but I'd rather call on its more appealing, vintage-clad relative: thrift. With it come thoughts of 1940s austerity rather than plain old Scrooginess.

Habits of my parents that exasperated me as a child have now become second nature. I keep doors shut to lock in warmth, and hold off from turning on the lights in the evening until it is no longer possible to navigate furniture. Since I follow a long line of relatives who would rather take a shallow bath in lukewarm water than admit the immersion heater needs turning on, I have little choice in the matter. Even now, when my mother comes to stay in my flat in London, she looks disapprovingly at the cluster of halogen spotlights in our bathroom (you can't fit them with energy-saving bulbs) and chomps defiantly through a mouldy mango when I suggest chucking it.

On the food front, one of my earliest memories of my (paternal) grandmother is being shown how much more you can get out of an egg after the point that most people toss the shell into the (compost) bin. She taught me to wipe out the last drip of egg white using my finger and I've been compelled to do exactly that ever since. As have I to keep saucers of leftovers in the fridge – some containing as little as a few slices of courgette, half a potato or a dozen pasta shells.

You might imagine that they would never be eaten, but I take enormous pleasure in proving anyone who dares challenge me on this wrong. By bunging them together in an ovenproof dish with some grated cheese on top and posting them in the oven for half an hour, I declare a veggie bake, a new meal from the old. Not something I'd do when people come over for supper but when it's only me and Gervase, I can get away with all sorts of dubious leftover creations.

It was my bad luck that as I reached school age, a health-food shop opened in our village where carob bars and rye breads could be seized upon by my excited mother and her friends. Vegan food became all the rage in our corner of East Anglia. Suffice to say, our lunchboxes suffered. Oatmeal proliferated and carrot sticks and sesame bars became a daily affliction. I decided that being good to the environment didn't taste very nice.

For a while, I thought rebellion might be the best way forward. I could turn against my thrifty forbears, become one of those types to leave the TV on for the cat and fire up a patio heater on chilly evenings. I could throw caution to the wind, eat ready meals and drive an SUV. But it's not easy to turn your back on family tradition. Much as I tried to burn fossil fuels with devil-may-care abandon, I found frugality in the blood.

There were signs all along. Laughably small when you think about it, but noteworthy all the same. As a teenager, I'd watch friends using several cotton-wool pads to remove their make-up, while I carefully reused front and back of one for my entire skincare routine. The thought of splashing out on two pieces of cotton wool every night seemed nothing short of extravagant.

I wanted to be more frivolous about these things. Honestly, I did. I wanted to be like friends who gathered possessions thick and fast, cosmetics, clothes and colourful bangles. But the voice of my mother was always there, asking me if I really needed them, and whether the dress I was about to buy wasn't just like my other one.

Even now, I'm not proud of the fact that I wince when I see friends emptying the leftovers of a dinner party into the bin. I'd rather be nonchalant about food waste. I'd rather not feel compelled to polish off three-day-old curry for breakfast, and of course I can see that popping the final roast potato into my mouth instead of the bin does not make sense. But it's futile. I am condemned to genetic thriftiness. I have no choice but to embrace it.

Once I left school, it became easier. Habits could be disguised as alternative hippy ones, all part of being a skint student, rather than a reluctant teen. They were practical even. I could replicate my mother's cheap bean stews and jazz up my wardrobe for less than a tenner at Help the Aged. I could cope comfortably with a rucksack and limited funds on trips abroad between university terms. Not requiring large quantities of cotton wool wherever I went became an advantage.

Since then, I've noticed that frugal ways such as mine have acquired a following on the internet. A growing online community dedicated to spending less has emerged. Nicknamed 'frooglers', members aim to improve their finances as well as unburdening the planet. They share tips and personal stories on sites such as *www.frugal.org.uk* and *www.downsizer.net*. These forums, and the ideas within them, appear to attract a loose and eclectic network of downshifters, hippies, anti-consumerists and New Agers. Anyone, in fact, who wants to 'reduce debts, save for a holiday, stay at home with your children, live more simply or just beat the system a little', according to Frugal Living (*frugal.org.uk*).

It strikes me as a modern version of the advice in pamphlets distributed during the Second World War that included tips on how to 'make do and mend' and create 'healthy food on war rations'. On the Frugal Living website, there are tips on all aspects of thriftiness, from how to make an eel trap to secure a cheap and tasty dinner to how to cut your children's hair. I'm only glad these forums weren't around when I was growing up. As it was, I still suffered home haircuts – but thankfully did not have to eat eel for supper.

These days, I'm no longer ashamed of being thrifty. And it helps that I have a wormery for food waste and a council that collects the scraps the worms can't manage. It's easier to admit a brown carrot needs to be binned if you know it will be turned into compost rather than sent to rot in landfill.

No one laughs at the leftovers in my lunchbox at work. They are healthy, green and cheap. They gain respect. Sometimes I even show off about them. Guess what went into this soup, I'll say, before reeling off the ingredients: the water yesterday's carrots were boiled in, last Sunday's roast parsnips and some spinach from the garden.

It doesn't escape me that the soup is a close relative of the sort my mother used to make, varying in colour but always confusingly similar in taste. Hearty puddles of puréed vegetables, made to go further with milk. Hardly offensive, but not the thing to make your tastebuds sing. She was never fussed if her soups turned out an unappealing shade of slime-green. Like me, she was far too busy feeling pleased with herself for not letting any nutrients go to waste.

Peeling vegetables off the back of the fridge ('Honestly, they'll be lovely with lentils') is something I have found to appeal more to women than to men. For Gervase, it is a wonder that I could derive even a sliver of satisfaction from storing a teabag on top of the sugar pot to use again later or concocting a meal without going to the shops. Why bother, he'll say. It's a false economy. But I do bother. Because I like to. And because it's what my family has always done.

Making the most of what's in the fridge; straying from the recipe to accommodate last night's leftovers and planning ahead are all important skills for the thrifty cook, helping to cut back on packaging as well as food waste. It helps to have a running idea of what you have in the cupboards so that you know what to use up.

At any one time, I reckon I could give an inventory of our fridge and cupboards. This might be unfair but Gervase, generally, has no idea. If he feels like eating pasta for supper, he buys some in the shop, even though there are three half-full bags in the cupboards.

The other day, feeling every inch the 1950s housewife – hand on hip, with some kind of washer-woman hairdo – I berated him for opening a brand new pack of cheddar when there were two half-eaten chunks in the door of the fridge. He thinks I'm mad, I think he's wasteful, and here we are, back in a familiar conflict zone.

My hunch, I should add, has been backed up by research. Last year, a survey conducted by Leicester University on behalf of Npower announced that men are more likely to avoid day-to-day green tasks, such as reusing carrier bags and turning off appliances, in favour of bigger gestures. So, after a day of saving the world on a shoestring, a woman may return home to find a wind turbine on the roof, but the computer will probably have been left on and it'll be a supermarket lasagne for supper. The male idea, according to the research, is to throw financial caution to the wind and beat the neighbours to the ultimate green accessory. Women, on the other hand, are stuck with worrying about the unglamorous and far less visible minutiae of eco-living.

When I tell you about the relationship I have established with our gas and electricity meters, you'll see what I mean. I can't pretend that peering at meters is a fun green activity, like planting seeds, say, or making chutney, but it has its moments. Imagine that you've received a large gas bill based on an estimate. You check the meter and the naughty gas company is charging you double what you have actually used. That's how it began for me. I located the cupboard that housed our meters and started taking note of the figures. Once I'd established the link between what we use, what shows on the meter and what we are billed, the way I thought about our gas and electricity use changed.

Oddly enough, checking the meters became a bit of a hobby. Let's see how much we've got through this week, I'd think to myself. Will the fact that I changed the setting on our boiler have made a difference? And at what point will Gervase start complaining about his shower going cold? Intriguing questions.

These experiments helped us to reduce our gas bill by almost a third. I'd do a week with the boiler on one setting, taking a reading at the beginning and the end of it, then compare it to the following week, with the boiler coming on for less time.

To most of my friends, I have not admitted this peculiar pastime – it's not the first thing that springs to mind when you're catching up over a glass of wine. But I have one old school friend who shares my interest in energy saving. Jo recently started renting a house that relies on a pay-as-you-go electricity meter. Instead of receiving quarterly bills, she has a key, like a memory stick, that is removed from the meter and taken to a shop (most garages and selected supermarkets accept Southern Electric's version) where the credit is topped up.

Jo and her flatmate, Kate, put £60 on at a time, which lasts them several months. When they return the keys to the meter, it shows how much credit is on it. She says the system makes it very easy to monitor your electricity use because you can see the credits going down as you do different things around the home. Jo has worked out that her washing machine costs about 70p a go. 'When you think about it like that, it makes you careful not to run a cycle with only a few things inside,' she tells me.

Like watching the petrol that you've bought disappear on the gauge in a car, this system exposes the link between the energy you use and the money you spend, unlike the estimate-based approach, which gives you an excuse not to pay attention to what your meter is saying – and therefore what you've actually used.

As you might have guessed from my nerdy interest in meters, I need little encouragement to save energy. I already dart around the place switching things off, like an eco-minded Tinkerbell. Lights mainly. When Gervase is about, we do a little dance around the switches every evening, me following in his wake.

Sometimes, I admit, I am a little overzealous and flick off a light when he's still doing something in the room, which I gather is very irritating. But it's not only because my instinct is to save resources. I'm not a fan of garish lights, or too many of them on at one time. It makes me feel cosy to be in the living room watching a film with all the other lights in the flat switched off. It enables me to hunker down in one spot, and also helps me to ignore piles of papers and washing that need sorting elsewhere. What you can't see, doesn't worry you.

In the same way, when temperatures drop, I would rather use this as an excuse to whip out a fluffy sweater and take a hot-water bottle to bed than blast heat from the radiators all night and wake up with a throat drier than the Sahara.

This is one thing that Gervase and I agree on – hurrah! – that central heating should be used as little as possible. Neither of us like that sweaty, overheated, slightly sicky feeling you get in a house where the central heating has been on too long. Especially overnight. I've realized that when you grow up in a cold house – even if you whinge about it for the first twenty years of your life – you end up ill-suited to hot houses.

Apart from lights and heating, there's equipment in the home to consider. DVD players, Gervase's DJing decks, laptops and mobile chargers, all buzzing, flashing and drawing on the electricity supply if you don't go out of your way to switch them off. If nothing else, it's an unrestful way to leave a room.

And once you are in the habit of turning appliances off at the wall every evening, it takes no more thought and only a fraction more time than not doing it. I see it as putting the flat to bed, as much part of preparing for sleep as a cup of Horlicks or taking the dog out for a pee. It makes up my bedtime ritual. Flick, flick, flick, clean teeth, yawn, bed. Just thinking about it makes me feel sleepy.

Actually, the job of the nightly 'turn off' more often falls to Gervase, who comes to bed later. Along with other manly green tasks such as lugging out boxes of recycling and blowing up bike tyres, it is a predictable example of the division of green labour in the home.

What it is about men and rubbish, I have no idea. Among my friends, I have found that without fail domestic waste management is undertaken by the stubblier sex. Not that I'm complaining. I'm more than happy to delegate – although I notice that in our happy household, waste management is not extended to worm management. While Gervase won't miss a recycling collection, he sees carrying a tub of food scraps to the worms as outside his realm.

But enough quibbles, back to energy-saving for a final word. At this time of year, what's important is that you forge a healthy relationship with it. Equating energy-saving not with depriving yourself but with adding to an autumnal sense of thrift and preparation for winter helps you to look more fondly on it.

Somehow using less energy makes autumn better, more vivid. The cooler weather is invigorating if you let it be, rather than warding it off with central heating. The darkening evenings add cosiness, if you resist lighting up your home like a Christmas tree.

When chilly September evenings arrive, it's time to embrace the spirit of the season. I'm already looking forward to it. But then, given my upbringing and the diet of warming comfort foods on the menu for the next few months, I would.

Storing Garden Produce

The week when my veg bed produces its final round of green beans and tomatoes always seems to be the one when no one is coming for supper and the fridge is already stashed with food. There is only a certain amount of this stuff that Gervase and I can eat, so the rest, I freeze. Most green vegetables should be blanched first – put in boiling water for a few minutes and then plunged into cold water to stop them from carrying on cooking. This is because they contain enzymes and bacteria that, over time, destroy nutrients and alter colour and flavour. By boiling them for a few minutes, you destroy the enzymes before freezing. Once blanched, I load them into the small plastic bags you find at the fruit and veg section of supermarkets and stuff them into the freezer to enjoy over the winter months.

Tomatoes deserve special treatment. Make up a plain tomato sauce to freeze, and use it as the base for pasta recipes.

WHAT'S IN IT FOR THE PLANET?

By saving energy . . . you can reduce your home's carbon footprint. Producing heat, light and power involves burning fossil fuels – namely gas, coal and oil – which adds to the greenhouse gases, especially carbon dioxide, in the atmosphere. With a combination of cutting back on what you use and swapping to a green energy supplier, you significantly reduce your home's emissions. Using only what you need is also part of a wider appreciation of the environment and natural resources.

By saving food . . . given that food waste accounts for one-fifth of domestic waste, you can reduce your household waste and the amount of packaging your home generates. One-third of food bought in British shops ends in rubbish bins, according to the Government's Waste and Resources Action Programme (WRAP). Around half of it could have been eaten, with careful planning and use of leftovers.

Warm and Cosy

Ten ways to keep warmth in: a combination of common sense and Granny wisdom.

• As soon as it gets dark, zip around the house shutting curtains for warmth and extra cosiness. It'll also be good exercise. You want nice thick fabric curtains, running down to the floor, to keep the heat in. Don't let anyone convince you that flimsy blinds are anything like as good.

• Reach for your thermals. If my granny is to be believed, the main thing that young people get wrong – by that she means anyone below the age of 60 – is clothing. We don't know our cotton sweaters from our chunky knits. As with the food we eat, our clothes should also be seasonal, whether we're inside or outside. This time of the year calls for nothing less than wool. Grannies know best.

• Invest in a decent bedspread. Since winter provides an excuse to pile blankets on the bed and curl up under them with a good book, why relinquish this pleasure by cranking up the heating and lounging around in a T-shirt. I found a couple of beautiful crochet blankets on eBay.

• Make a draught-excluding sausage dog. Many years ago, I had the good fortune to watch a *Blue Peter* episode that showed me how. It involved stuffing one leg of a thick pair of tights with old clothes and scraps of fabric before sowing up the end. As I remember, the fun bit was making a face, using buttons for eyes, or felt for a forked tongue if you fancy turning your dog into a snake. At the time, I scoffed at the thought of bothering with all that stitching and stuffing for something you abandoned on the floor. Now older and wiser, I know that 20 per cent of your home's heat escapes through doors and windows and I appreciate the merits of flexing your craft muscles. Should yours be weakened after years of neglect, you can get stylish draught excluders from Cath Kidston and reclaimed fabric company Refab (*www.refab.co.uk*).

• Insulate windows. The obvious way is with proper double-glazing. If that's not possible, there are draught-excluding strips available from DIY stores. My mother swears by using clingfilm for a DIY double-glazing job. I admit I haven't tried it and am not convinced that shrink-wrapping our flat will improve it, but feel free to have a go.

• Insulate your walls. It's not sexy stuff, I'm afraid – cavity wall insulation is one of those terms that could be given out in pill form to help people nod off. But it's important. About 33 per cent of the heat in your home is lost through the walls. Injecting insulation is one of the biggest things you can do to cut your fuel bill and reduce carbon emissions. The only hitch is that properties built before 1920 are likely not to have cavity walls (those built after 1990 will already have insulation by law).

• Insulate your roof, a process also known as loft lagging. Another of those important basics that all green-minded home-owners should do. Loft insulation acts as a blanket to trap heat rising from your living area, stopping you from losing up to 15 per cent of your heating costs, according to the Energy Saving Trust. Think of it as maximizing the cosiness of your home.

• Put silver foil down the back of radiators, attached to the wall. This reflects heat into the room. Ordinary kitchen foil will do, or you can buy specially designed panels from DIY stores.

- Exercise. Spend all year in air-conditioned offices and central-heated houses and you're in danger of leading a lukewarm life. Instead appreciate contrast. Yes, it's cold today, but if you go for a brisk walk in the park before settling down on the sofa, you'll raise your body temperature and feel all the better for it. Now who sounds like Granny?

- Keep doors shut. Obvious but crucial. Enough said.

Try it in September . . .

Light Greenies
Swap to a renewable energy supplier

As far as satisfying and simple green actions go, swapping to renewable energy in your home is a good one. It takes a matter of minutes on the phone and your home won't require any new pipes, wires or meters. Once done, your power points will still be fed by the closest power station, but for each unit of electricity you use, a green supplier will provide the national grid with the same amount from a renewable resource, such as wind, solar and hydro-electric power schemes. That is, if you choose a reliable, dark green utilities company. I signed up with Good Energy because it was a safe bet; it's the UK's only company to offer 100 per cent renewable energy, and it was praised by Ofgem for its commitment to the environment.

There has been much fuss about other supposedly 'green' tariffs. Some offer as little as to plant a tree for every ten customers; the promise of one tenth of a tree surely takes the biscuit as one of the most feeble attempts at greenwash. Because all utility companies must get a certain percentage of their energy from renewable sources, many have been accused of merely selling customers the renewables they are forced to buy by law anyway. So they are not increasing the good they do for the environment, merely repackaging it. At the time of writing, Ofgem was promising to regulate green energy by working with the Energy Saving Trust and awarding the best schemes. When it investigated in 2007, as well as Good Energy, Scottish & Southern's RSPB Energy came out well, as did Ecotricity.

Dark Greenies
Make your own power

For some of us there are enough things to make at home (beds, suppers, packed lunches) without taking these creative urges further. But making your own emission-free energy is, in many ways, the most commendable green leap of all. When you consider that half of the electricity generated at remote plants is lost either in heat or in transmission, it makes sense to do the job at home. As well as reducing your utility bills, solar panels, a wind turbine or even replacing your boiler with a micro combined heat and power unit brings with it a thrill of self-sufficiency, of being able to operate, at least partially, outside of the system. And it's no longer the preserve of hippies. The fact that David Cameron has his own wind turbine is proof enough that generating power has been gentrified.

The cheapest and possibly easiest way to harness the rays is with a solar heating system on your roof, which can meet up to half of a household's hot water needs. It costs an average of £3,000, some of which can be subsidized by grants (*www.lowcarbonbuildings.org.uk*).

If your heart is set on producing electricity rather than plain old heat, look no further than photovoltaic (PV) cells. In defiance of our gloomy climate, they convert daylight, not just direct sunlight, into electricity – although, like all of us, they function better on a sunny day. Without raining on the solar parade, my only concern is that you don't expect immediate financial gain. It takes up to sixteen years to recoup initial costs, say most solar experts.

Wind is a tricky customer. Turbines are suitable for fewer homes than solar panels, since the roof requires higher than average wind speeds, which are often reduced by trees, fences and other houses. Added to which, the companies making them, such as Windsave, are still ironing out initial problems, such as noise from the turbines and their vibrations. It is a tempting prospect, mounting a whizzy little thing on your roof that could provide over a third of your electricity needs, and no doubt it would impress the neighbours (if it didn't keep them awake at night), but it shouldn't be undertaken lightly. If it doesn't work efficiently, you could end up in a situation in which the energy involved in the turbine's manufacturing amounts to more than what it is likely to save over its lifetime. Should you go ahead, like a car, your blades will need care and regular MOTs. And you might look a little foolish if you embark on the big gesture before brushing up on the basic tenets of energy-saving, such as wall and roof insulation. Think laterally: saving energy is only a small step from making it.

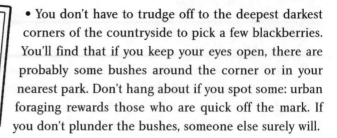

• You don't have to trudge off to the deepest darkest corners of the countryside to pick a few blackberries. You'll find that if you keep your eyes open, there are probably some bushes around the corner or in your nearest park. Don't hang about if you spot some: urban foraging rewards those who are quick off the mark. If you don't plunder the bushes, someone else surely will.

• Do something useful with autumn leaves. Pile them into a black bin bag, add a sprinkling of water, tie up the bag and then pierce a few holes in it. By next spring you'll have mulch, or, more accurately, leaf mould. It'll be rich in calcium and magnesium, nutrients that are essential for healthy vegetables.

• Plant bulbs for next spring – in pots if you don't have any garden space. This is one of the simplest ways to introduce colour and life into your outdoor patch. They are a long-term investment; plant daffodils, tulips and narcissi bulbs roughly four inches deep – make sure you put them in the right way up – and they will produce flowers for generations.

Easy Steps to Stop Energy Gobbling

Turn off mobile phone chargers

These pesky little things find their way into power sockets and carry on charging – drawing electricity – even if they don't have a phone plugged into them. According to the Energy Saving Trust, if one charger in every household is left permanently plugged in for 12 months, the energy wasted nationwide is enough to meet the electricity needs of 66,000 homes for one year. Planetary matters aside, the dangling wires are unsightly, messing up a room's feng shui.

Install energy-saving light bulbs

There has been tremendous fuss about the kind of light these give out, plus the fact that they are more cumbersome, and some say less attractive, than old-fashioned bulbs. But both these things are improving as technology develops. Some low-energy bulbs are scarcely any larger than the old ones and they last, on average, twelve times longer. Some you can depend on for six years if you put them to normal domestic use. To me, that makes them beautiful. Conventional light bulbs (known as incandescent) are soon to be phased out, so the switch to low-energy ones (called compact fluorescent lights) will be taken by all. To get ahead of the game, eco-designer Oliver Heath recommends looking into oversized shades or vintage chandeliers if you want to improve the light they give off. The benefit of these bulbs is that they are much less hot so you can be more creative with your lampshade design without worrying about burning your house down.

Wage war on the stand-by button

However tempting it might be when you're sleepy on the sofa and wanting to get to bed as fast as possible, always switch off idle electronics and appliances. Don't leave them on standby overnight.

Otherwise they will carry on using up electricity, increasing your electricity bill and making you feel guilty when you spot them in the morning, primed for action. A typical combination of TVs, DVD players and hi-fis will cost you an extra £40 a year if you leave them on standby overnight.

Lights out

You may have heard that turning on a light requires a surge of power that makes it worth leaving it on. Well, it's not true, not unless you are coming back to the room within 5 minutes. It is a myth told by people who are naughty about turning the lights off, to make themselves feel better. So spread the word. Here are the facts: it only takes a small amount of energy to power the ballast – the electrical device that starts up the light – not enough to justify leaving an empty room lit up for longer than a few minutes, says the Energy Saving Trust's lighting expert, James Russill. He also says that turning a bulb on and off has no impact on the life of the bulb. So don't let anyone wheel that one out either.

Suss out new appliances

Should the occasion arrive when you have no choice but to buy a domestic appliance that is brand spanking new, take your time. Think about it, talk about it, bore your friends with it, and, most importantly, investigate its eco-credentials.

Go for top grades. By law, all household appliances, including light bulbs, must be given a rating between A and G by the EU, with an A-grade appliance being the most energy efficient. There are also appliances that will have been recommended by the Energy Saving Trust and therefore will carry its logo. The good news is that the latest, sleekest models are often the most energy-efficient.

Check it out on a rating website. The website Sust-It (*www.sust-it.net*) ranks appliances according to energy efficiency, aiming to expose the 'gas guzzlers' of electrical goods. It also lists the cost of using a product by the day or year.

A final note of frivolity: embrace curls

Did you know that half an hour with a hairdryer uses almost the same amount of energy as two hours with a Hoover or 24 hours of a TV blaring? Who needs early mornings spent taming wild locks anyway? Remember, sleep is better than sleek. Dump the dryer and go for a tousled style.

Thriftiness in the kitchen
Last-all-week soups and winter stocks

Learn to love your leftovers

Think of them not as the rejects of one meal, but as the foundations for the next. Even the soggy remains of a dressed salad or a few unwanted carrots will add flavour to a jug of stock or bulk out a stir-fry. I like to make weekend soups and stews using up vegetables left over from the week. In go the last dregs of wine bottles that have been loitering around the kitchen. Gervase does a wonderful thing with leftover risotto, frying it up in patties after poking a bit of cheese into the middle (ideally mozzarella but cheddar will do).

Try out a cooking cycle

For meat eaters, the simplest way to do this is to start with a roast – cook more than you will eat otherwise the cycle won't last long. The following day, the leftovers can be turned into a stew or pie (for the pie, I cheat by using shop-bought puff pastry, simply laid on top of the dish). What's left after that can be bulked out with some rice or pasta and turned into an array of exciting risottos or pasta bakes, before its final incarnation as soup (add some lentils or pearl barley for texture). By which point you'll be bored of anything related to the original dish, so it's time to break the cycle and demand to be taken out for supper.

Shop carefully

According to research done by the Government in 2007, around one-third of shoppers do not check what food they need or take a list (from the Waste and Resources Action Programme, funded by Defra in March 2007). A shopping list is a crucial and underrated part of any eating plan. I'm not saying that every snack should be planned to the last crumb, but thinking about what you need and having a scout around the cupboards before you leave for the shops is not a bad idea. It's better than waiting until you are ravenous and then coming home with an assortment of munchies that you don't really need. Important tips are: check cupboards first; make a list; don't shop when you're hungry; shop alone (so no one can weaken your frugal resolve).

Experiment with sit-boiling

If you're not familiar with the term, it refers to the cooking that takes place after you have turned off the heat. Take broccoli: once it has been on the boil for a few minutes, it can be removed from the hob and left in the hot water to complete its cooking. Not only does this save energy, it reduces the chance you will overcook the vegetables, turning them to mush. It is a form of slow cooking that should be encouraged.

No peeping

Every time you open the oven to prod your supper, it is losing heat and wasting energy. Try to leave things alone. It's hard, I know; if you're a fiddler like me, you'll want to investigate every 5 minutes. A recent and much-needed clean of our oven window – with green cleaning products, obviously – revolutionized my bad habits. Now I can peer through the window and see what what's going on in the oven without opening the door.

Make stock

This is a practice that has come back into fashion, having originally been popular because it makes such good economic sense. From a boiled-up carcass, you can make any number of dishes, and you can use bits of vegetables that you might not want to eat, such as herb stalks and peelings (wash them first). Most vegetables can be added to the bubbling saucepan, except beetroot, which is said to produce a peculiar colour. Personally, I don't mind the idea of purple stock. Probably because, like all stock-making, it appeals to a childish love of potion-making. I like to add leftover wine to mine, gratings of ginger and whole spring onions. Come to think of it, anything I catch sight of risks being popped in the pot.

Use a steamer

In the 1940s, three-tiered pressure cookers and steamers were recommended because they enabled you to cook the different components of a meal on one ring. Steak and kidney pudding in the bottom, potatoes in the next one up, cabbage on top. Steamed meat puddings are out of fashion, thankfully, but this method of cooking is not. Vegetables that have been steamed contain more nutrients. Don't forget that you can put a steamer on top of a boiling pan of pasta to cook vegetables.

Use a lid, and match the hob ring to the saucepan

This piece of advice might be an old favourite, but it is still easy to forget how quickly your food will cook if you put a tight-fitting lid on top. Bringing potatoes to the boil is a classic example, liable to take almost double the time if you do it lidless.

The size of the hob ring should also be appropriate for the size of the saucepan. Cooking will then be faster and more energy efficient. Use a large circle of flame for a small pan and you'll be heating the air rather than your food.

Quick! Make meringues!

A hot oven and some leftover egg whites would prompt this hasty cry from my mother who wanted to make the most of the oven before it cooled. Meringues need a lower temperature than most things, so, provided the oven has been at a high temperature for an hour or two, they will cook after it has been turned off. There is much to be said for making the most of a hot oven. You can use it to warm up pudding, improve slightly stale bread or nuts, or you can pile side dishes into it to keep them warm should you get timing wrong and still be waiting for the main event to cook on the hob.

At this time of year, I become mildly obsessed with **crumble**. I set about trying to find the perfect recipe, altering it according to the texture of the fruit; how many blackberries I've secured from the local park; its flavour and whether or not I'm going to serve it with custard, ice cream or yoghurt. Soggy crumble that sinks into the fruit is my greatest fear when 'crumbling'. I'm never quite sure why it happens but I suspect a combination of not putting the pudding in a hot enough oven and too many juices in the stewed fruit. My failsafe recipe involves some porridge oats or muesli and a generous sprinkle of cinnamon in the fruit. Using cooking apples is ideal as they go beautifully fluffy; if you only have eating apples you might find you want to stew them first. We use the ones on our apple tree – the few that the squirrels have left us – which need a good 10 minutes on a gentle heat before they go soft. However measly the amount of blackberries you have found, drop them in with the apples as they add colour to the pudding.

Here are my crumble quantities. You don't need me to tell you what to do, I'm sure (it's all about your working in the butter with the flour and oats, using your fingertips to make breadcrumb consistency, then adding the sugar). A tablespoon of water sprinkled on top as you put the crumble on the fruit gives it a varied texture.

150g flour	60g butter
50g porridge oats or muesli	90g sugar

OCTOBER

THE OFFICE ECO-BORE

DON'T KNOW WHETHER YOU HAVE EVER HAD THE MISFORTUNE TO DISCOVER AN environmental hazard in your office, but let me tell you, it's not a pleasant experience. When it happened to me, the awful thing was found on my desk. In my mug. Pooled in the bottom, a toxic gunk had built up from the remnants of what once must have been an innocent cup of tea. Over weeks of neglect it had turned green and started to froth a little, adding to the impression that I was harbouring some kind of radioactive waste behind my stapler.

Naturally, to my colleagues in the Body&Soul section of *The Times*, I denied all knowledge of how exactly this eco-disaster had come to pass. But had I been honest, had I racked my brains, I would have been forced to own up to a vague recollection of one particular tea break that involved the guilty mug.

Of course, this kind of thing would never occur in my own home. Or, at least, very rarely. There was the time when I managed to leave a half-finished cup of hot chocolate in the airing cupboard, where it stayed for several crust-forming months before I wondered about the peculiar smell on my pillowcases, but, generally, I am vigilant about toxic remains and other environmental concerns. I only wish I could say the same about my attitude in the office. For some reason, as soon as I spot strip-lighting and banks of humming computers, my tough planet-saving exterior crumbles as quickly as a peanut under a sledgehammer. Especially when I notice that other people aren't recycling or turning their monitor off when they go for lunch. Why should I bother, I think?

Of course, I realize that's not the spirit. Normally I deplore this sort of attitude. My philosophy is to lead by example. I would never slack on my recycling duties at home just because the neighbours weren't dividing up their waste appropriately. But as you can probably tell, I'm suffering from a mild case of green fatigue – a malaise that only strikes during office hours.

There's something about the vastness of an office, the different factors to account for – many of which I perceive to be beyond my control – and the swarms of people contributing to its environmental footprint that overwhelms me. I try to trudge off to the recycling bank in my lunch hour (there are no facilities to recycle plastic in the office) and to bring home the day's banana skins to dump in the wormery (I've given up with teabags, they stain my ruck-sack) but I'm often dwarfed by all there is to do.

Habits I would never dream of adopting at home – such as leaving the computer on stand-by overnight or not bothering to switch off the lights in the bathroom – have been known to creep into my work life. My desk speaks of similar inconsistency. Alongside the toxic tea mug, I'm sorry to admit, there are also several stashes of papers (did I really need to print those emails out?) that I've been meaning to recycle for weeks; plastic water bottles (ditto) and an extensive collection of padded envelopes. My intention is to reuse the envelopes but what is more likely to happen is that the pile will grow so tall I will stop being able to see my computer screen and be forced to throw them out.

Compare this to a neatly organized waste system *chez moi*, with different drawers for plastic bags, elastic bands and reusable envelopes and you'll see what I mean about double standards. The problem, as I see it, is that home life is easy to manage. You set up green systems and stick to them. Fellow occupants might not always follow suit, but at least there are fewer of them. At present, anyway – should children ever brave it into my household, I feel sorry for the little nippers already. Anyway, in the office, I despair. Unlike my own space at home, it resembles a vast, uncontrollable beast I don't think I'm brave enough to tame.

But it is not only the limited power I have over my working environment that causes me trouble. There is something else niggling away. Given that most of us spend more time with our colleagues than our loved ones, I've always tried to draw a firm line at the end of the day, to get home and see my friends or do something different. While there is pleasure in sorting out a green agenda for your home life – you can bunch it together with other dull but important domestic rituals such as sorting out bills and filling the fruit bowl – in the office, everything feels like work, whether it's lobbying for better facilities for the company's cyclists or checking Facebook; if you're in a chair on wheels within metres of a water cooler, it's work. And to offer to be the green champion would surely create more of it, an extra helping of office-based activity.

It would mean staying late to set up new recycling systems and spending lunch times emailing colleagues to remind them to switch off their computers before they go home. People would start dumping padded envelopes and plastic cups on my desk and expecting me to solve their work-related eco-dilemmas. It would be like having another job. An unpaid one.

Martin Gibson, the director of Envirowise, a Government-funded organ-ization that offers free consultations to companies on how to cut environmental costs, thinks I'm getting a bit carried away. He has come in to look around the Body&Soul office and give his verdict on what we could do to improve things. I'm hoping he is also going to help me overcome my block when it comes to drumming up enthusiasm for work-based greenery. His first point is that it doesn't need to involve extra work – that is a feeble excuse.

'If you start by taking responsibility simply for what you bring into the office, you won't be taking on too much,' he says. 'Ignore everything else; just think about your own input. Plastic bottles, Tupperware lunchboxes, takeaway cappuccinos … whatever it is you bring in, you can probably cut down and reuse more of it.' So the plan is this: instead of stressing about what is beyond your control and being overwhelmed by the scale of the challenge, to think about what you can do within the confinements of your desk, lunch and journey to work.

After that, Martin suggests broadening your concerns to account for the input of the people on your team, your floor and then eventually the whole company. Some things, he says, have to come from the top. There's no point trying to transform how a business operates unless the boss is on board. Especially in a big company when you don't always have a say in energy policy; heating; how the lights work, and the suppliers used.

Recognizing when to delegate upwards, he says, will reduce the amount of work you take on and get things done faster. The skill is in doing this without making yourself unpopular and becoming the person your boss dreads bumping into in the lift.

I'm imagining a sort of two-pronged attack: a campaign to inspire collective action among my colleagues, combined with a steady but non-whingy drive to get the 'powers above' involved in the bigger issues.

Having got this far, Martin and I head off to reward ourselves with a Fairtrade latte, a brief moment of celebration that I manage to ruin with my choice of receptacle. I accept a plastic lid and a cardboard sleeve, muttering something about the coffee getting cold, thus revealing the ugly side to my office personality. He brings me up on it and makes a fair point about un-necessary packaging waste – at the very least, I should reuse the cardboard sleeve. I can't help thinking he must be secretly pleased with my display of eco-inconsistency as it illustrates his point about how many easy things there are to change in our own behaviour before we start worrying about other people.

Still on the important subject of office refreshment, we move on to lunch. Impressed by the army of Tupperware boxes on desks and in the fridge in our office, Martin says that this must be something we are good at. Yes, I tell him, trying to redeem myself after the plastic-lid-and-cardboard-sleeve affair, yes, we are good at this. Bringing in a packed lunch is healthier, better for your wallet and it saves on all that plastic used for bought sandwiches and salads. That much we know.

It's the one aspect of office greenery I've always paid special attention to, taking great pleasure in creating lunches from leftovers. Bits and pieces casually slung in a Tupperware tub – with a splodge of hummus here and a handful of home-grown rocket there – often taste better the second time round, something to do with the flavours having had time to develop.

The alternative would be to find somewhere proper to eat, where food is served on a plate. I like this option as it allows you to go in search of a decent hot lunch. Like the French, who, more often than not, enjoy a *menu du jour* at a nearby bistro at lunchtime, if they haven't gone home for a blow-out three-course meal and a siesta. It encourages a civilized way to eat and primes you for the second half of your working day. Unlike a measly sandwich gobbled at your desk, which is hardly the foundation of an afternoon's high achieving – or that's what I would say to any dissenting employer.

Post-lunch – especially if I've taken the Continental route – I generally require a liquid pick-me-up and I don't mean a quick G&T in the pub. It is more likely to be the invigorating embrace of caffeine that I turn to. In the UK, we drink 70 million cups of coffee daily. A large proportion of these, one hopes, are consumed from ceramic mugs at home, but when I'm out and craving a fix, what I end up with is likely to be a paper cup with a plastic lining. The plastic, usually polyethylene, keeps the paper cup intact by protecting it from the hot liquid, but it also makes it unrecyclable. These cups create a mountain of waste that goes to landfill.

In an ideal world, I would take my own mug into work, maybe even my own cutlery. To demonstrate my independence from the disposable variety, I would whip them out defiantly wherever my desire for a cappuccino took me. I would sit quietly, sipping, reading the morning's papers and enjoying the enhanced quality of life that comes with treating yourself to a real spoon instead of swirling a bit of wood or plastic in your drink (which adds an unwelcome flavour that then mingles with traffic fumes should you head out to the street).

Trouble is, like most people, I am often tempted to travel with my coffee

– on to the street and beyond. Instead of sitting still, I try to kill two birds with one stone, to save time by drinking it while I walk to work or while I dash from one meeting to the next. It is this kind of behaviour that has helped us to become mollycoddled by overpackaged hot drinks. Served in splashproof, heat-resistant, throwaway containers, they even have lids through which we can slurp. We might as well be given bibs, it would only be marginally more patronizing.

But you can see why this has come about. Ferrying mugs and spoons around an office isn't always easy. It's a 5-minute walk from the canteen to the desk where I work. Doing it with a full cup of coffee requires skills I haven't used since early attempts at the egg and spoon race. One possible solution is thermos mugs, issued to employees. These are insulated, often come with lids and they are large enough to avoid spillages. Should your boss not be persuaded to bulk buy on behalf of his environmental duties, you can get one for a fiver from John Lewis and most camping shops.

Where's mine? Well, it's on the list. Yes, that's the never-ending list of eco-related domestic kit that tends to be neglected in favour of other more appealing lists. But at least it's there, wedged somewhere between energy-saving bulbs for our weirdly shaped bedside lights and gooseberry bushes for a sparse bit of flowerbed at the back of the garden. I'm on to it, I promise. I like the idea of being special, the only one in the coffee queue with an original receptacle.

Fired up by my caffeine habit, I've been putting some of Martin's other suggestions into practice. I now have a cardboard box under my desk, as do several other people in the office, a halfway house for recycled paper, so that you don't have to trudge over to the big wheelie bin every time your want to throw something away. I've even considered a radical intervention, inspired by something that WRAP (Waste and Resources Action Programme) does in its offices. You take away the bins from under people's desks so they have to take their waste to a communal bin, one for landfill waste, a couple of others for recyclables. Even if you do this for a one-week trial, the idea is to make people think more about the rubbish they are creating at work. WRAP recycles 95 per cent of its office waste, which is something to aspire towards.

The question is whether it is possible to carry out this sort of thing with enough good humour to prevent yourself from becoming that maligned creature, rarely invited for post-work drinks or long lunches on Fridays: the office eco-bore. A misjudgement would not only mean that you end up with a dwindling circle of 'work' friends but also that you inadvertently produce an office full of rebels, who defy the rules and are steadfast in their bad habits.

Influencing the attitudes of colleagues is, in many ways, trickier than getting friends and loved ones to make alterations. Your friends, at least, have chosen you. If you've taken to ranting about the impact of light pollution on glow-worms (if you're interested, it threatens to render them extinct, as males cannot see the flashes female partners give out to attract them), they have only their poor judgement to blame. But colleagues? They have no more chosen you than the dodgy selection of sarnies at the canteen, or the palm-scalding hand-dryers in the toilets. You came with the job. And if you start inflicting your values on people, you won't help your cause.

Considering this, it's a miracle that my attempts to establish various green systems have met with success at all. Since Martin's visit, I have set about improving my relationship with the office environment with renewed vigour. First, a series of makeshift recycling boxes were established. One next to the printer for paper that has been printed on one side and can be put back into the printer for printing on the other side – it would be better still if we had printers that you could set to double-sided printing but, for now, this is our best option. One for plastic bags, so when we take trips to the supermarket in our lunch hour we can take one. And another smaller one for CDs and tape cassettes, which we pile into an old jiffy bag and send off to a CD-recycling company every month or so.

I wouldn't want to compete with the WRAP offices for Eco-Workplace of the

Year quite yet, but we're on our way. What's more, give or take the odd curse when once-used paper jams in the printer on press day, there has been no trouble getting everyone on board. I'd go as far as to say that the changes have been welcomed, even if no one is mad keen to be the one who instigates them.

Martin would have expected no less. He says he never comes across people who are actively against the idea of doing their bit for the environment. It's more that someone needs to take the initiative.

To be quite honest, there's no avoiding that you might lose a few lunch hours if you become that person. On the plus side, it spices up work to be involved with something that is not actually your normal work and it's a great excuse to procrastinate, citing planetary duties. And, while I know this sounds a bit Machiavellian, I suspect that it reflects well on you as an employee as well. I don't like to imagine that all green volunteers in the workplace are secretly after a promotion, but it can't do any harm to your reputation.

Resisting change will do more damage. Take my friend, who wishes to remain anonymous. Let's call her Barbara.

Barbara always had more plastic cups around her desk than anyone else and a bin full of paper that never reached the recycling bin. Colleagues started making jokes about her being the office eco-sinner. It started as light-hearted Friday afternoon banter but the jibes continued. Did she want a patio heater for Christmas? And how did she manage to find room to park her SUV in the staff car park? It wasn't meant badly, but she was secretly horrified. She had become a female Jeremy Clarkson – what could be worse? To shake the title, she now drinks water and hot drinks from the same mug and goes to work by bus. Funnier still is the fact that she has started picking others up on their bad habits.

The conviction of the converted knows no bounds. Like an ex-smoker, there is no one more critical of a weakness than someone who has battled the same one themselves. I've noticed that with all sorts of things. Like food scraps. Having thrown them away for years, now that I compost them, I can barely watch someone dumping a load of onion peelings and teabags in a normal bin. It seems absurd. How can they not compost, I think to myself, forgetting that for most of my life I have done the same.

It riles me on a daily basis that it is not more practical to run a wormery or compost bin at work. We tried it once. For a couple of months, we had a small Bokashi bin in the office but it was difficult to know what to do with the compost we were making. Take it home on the bus? With the Bokashi model, a slimline thing perfect for city composting, you have to sprinkle on a special kind of bran that helps the contents to break down. To make sense of our teabag collecting, my colleague, Angus, made a valiant attempt at an office garden. Salad seeds were germinated on a window ledge and lovingly tended. But in the end, the young plants didn't get enough direct sunlight and grew leggy and weak.

Our composting episode taught me how quickly a form of green policing develops within a work environment. At the end of each day, Angus, who had adopted the role of compost chief, would patrol around the office, poking in people's bins to see who had failed to dispose of their teabags and apple cores properly. I came to dread this moment of truth, when he would march over to my desk and expose the contents of my bin. Had I lapsed and done the wrong thing with my sandwich crusts at lunchtime? Before he started his rounds, you would see people checking out each other's bins and censoring the contents. Those who didn't take to the new waste rules were soon chased up by those who did.

Probably the best thing about my revived commitment to the office is that I've come across other people who are keen to do the same thing. It is not, as I feared, me against the world. It turns out there are all sorts of environmental representatives, green committees and passionate individuals I didn't know about. With a bit of emailing and prodding of management people, I've tapped into an undercurrent of green activism.

It's inspiring stuff; workers of the world uniting under the banner of environmentalism and lobbying for recycled loo paper. More rewarding than you might think, it teaches you not to accept what is the status quo at work but to challenge it.

The other truth that has come to light is that by working on your green credentials, you make your office a nicer place to be. Bring in plants, Fairtrade tea and a responsible attitude to paper use and the atmosphere improves. The alternative creates a downward spiral. The office's short-comings become a reminder of your own. Because you are keen to get home, you don't invest in the environment at work. The less effort you put in, the less you like being there.

For me that would have meant more freelancing, less human communi-cation (talking to the worms doesn't count) and far too much time spent hunched over my laptop wearing pyjamas.

As for the second prong of the campaign, to spark environmental change in the office by delegating responsibility upwards, let's just say that I'm work-ing on it. Doing my utmost to approach the matter lightly but firmly; to show commitment but also humour; to give the impression that while I am not an earth-loving freak – and definitely not a Swampy of the working world, likely to chain myself to the printers unless they are upgraded to double-sided – I won't easily give up. You see the kind of tightrope I'm walking on here?

And it could be paranoia but the other day I'm sure I noticed one of the recipients of my awareness-raising emails leaving the lift for the stairs when I approached. It made me think two things: that I still have a lot to learn about green office politics, and that, given the impact of lifts on a building's overall energy consumption – estimated at between 5 and 15 per cent – it should really be me taking the stairs.

WHAT'S IN IT FOR THE PLANET?

Use your own mug . . . as well as better-tasting coffee, you'll help to reduce plastic waste. Every year, a conservative estimate of 3 billion polystyrene cups are used in the UK. Together these cups use up 24,000 tonnes of polystyrene annually.

Bring in a plant . . . which will breathe in CO_2, improve the air quality and brighten your desk. With any luck, everyone will want one and you'll soon have a healthy jungle of an office.

Turn off your computer at the end of the working day . . . this will reduce your personal contribution in the office and set a good example. Given that each computer on stand-by draws something between 5 and 60 watts, the Carbon Trust has estimated that the average office wastes £6,000 a year by leaving equipment on over weekends and bank holidays.

Learn to be an office activist . . . and you will meet other people in the office; have an excuse to do something other than work and impress your boss. The first step is to set up a green committee that meets to discuss matters such as the purchase of recycled office materials and ways of reducing food waste.

Delegate upwards . . . to tackle problems beyond your control. Explain that going green at work is as important as doing it at home, if not more. According to Government figures for 2004, businesses produce 40 per cent of the UK's overall carbon emissions, compared with 27 per cent produced by households.

Green Office Etiquette

In the same way that advocating green behaviour in other people's homes is something to approach subtly, so too should you tread lightly in the office environment. The result, otherwise, could be resentment and even rebellion. Before you know it, a team of resisters will form, hell bent on thwarting your recycling system and calling you Al Gore's evil twin behind your back.

Here are some tips on the delicate art of greening hearts and minds as well as office buildings:

• Resist the urge to bellow green commandments across the office. Even if you spot someone poised over a landfill bin with a recyclable item, in the long run, the planet will not benefit from bellowers. By all means, rescue it yourself and say something later on, but make sure you do it with plenty of humour.

• Do not dictate what to do. Instead raise problems at meetings and let people come up with their own solutions.

• Lead by example. Concentrate on earning your own halo before you start trying to engineer them for your workmates.

• Point out the varied benefits of going green. Instead of stressing the worthiness, talk about how much healthier you feel after a packed lunch made at home; how much money you are saving, and how much nicer tea tastes from a mug, not a polystyrene cup.

• Provide positive feedback. If the office is producing less rubbish, consuming less paper or generally looking sexier after all that cycling and walking to work, say something. Ask management to let you see the figures so you know when progress is made. Or try an inter-floor energy competition. My friend Sophie works for a PR company that has breakdowns of how much energy each floor is consuming for exactly that reason. For the competitive-spirited, it is an extra reason to turn off the light in the bathroom or corridor, she tells me.

• While encouragement is important and entertaining updates will improve the popularity of the green campaign, don't overdo it. No one wants to receive yet another email to 'all users' with news of the latest brand of recycled toilet tissue being trialled. Email only when necessary.

• Divide up jobs, so no one person is lumbered and everyone feels included. Make a list of office items that need to be collected for reuse or recycling and ask everyone to take responsibility for one thing. If it were plastic bags, you could keep a box somewhere in the office to store them. Other materials might include CDs, books and obsolete office equipment, such as printers.

Things Everyone Can Do in Their Office

Install greenery

Putting a plant on your desk is an easy thing to do. You can't go wrong. It's what people who don't even care very much about the environment but are worried about their own health do. As well as breathing in CO_2, certain plants absorb other toxins and pollutants enabling them to work as air filters. The commonest – and cheapest – is the spider plant, but I prefer dragon trees, spiky-looking palms with pink leaves that can grow up to eight feet tall. Also said to be good at negating indoor pollution are goosefoot plants with their mottled leaves. Whatever you choose, to have green shoots creeping around your computer screen does wonders for your image.

Your computer's lunch break

A full computer shutdown shouldn't be necessary, depending on whether we're talking a long lingering lunch that concludes with a guilty slope back to the office at half past four, or an acceptable hour-long affair. For the latter, it is enough to turn your monitor off – it accounts for roughly 80 per cent of a computer's energy consumption and contributes to a third of the electricity used in a modern office. Those who indulge in the former should shut down their computer fully, although they would be wise to leave a jacket hanging on their chair so that the boss doesn't notice their extended absence.

Lunch al-fresco

As discussed, there are numerous advantages to bringing in your own lunch to work. The problems arise from finding somewhere peaceful to eat it; remembering cutlery; dressing for the occasion (don't let the advent of winter keep you inside), and refining the art of reading your book while balancing your Tupperware box on your knees. All without getting salad dressing on your skirt. Don't think life would be any easier if you'd gone for a takeaway salad. If anything, lightweight plastic boxes and cutlery are even harder to control – so you'd be more likely to resign yourself to lunch al-desko.

The right sort of cuppa

Bring your own mug and see if you can encourage the office kitchen or canteen to offer bowls of sugar rather than sachets; proper spoons rather than plastic stirrers, and jugs of milk not one-portion cartons. To accompany your tea, homemade is best. Should you be inspired to make some cakes or biscuits and bring them into work, you'll never be short of a friend.

Ethical snacking

Evenings spent baking for your colleagues, popular as they might make you at work, are never going to come along as often as you hanker after something sweet halfway through the afternoon. An alternative is Fairtrade snacking. That tea and coffee should feature at work is a given, but did you know that there are 800 certified products available, including flapjacks, cereal bars and cookies? Get in touch with the Fairtrade Foundation and it will help you persuade your workplace to supply its products.

Put the office to bed

However big your company, there is no reason not to treat it as you would your home when you leave for the night. The last person out the door should check computers are shut down and monitors are off, turn off lights and listen out for other humming machines, like printers and scanners, that could be turned off. Tempting as it is to name and shame serial offenders who leave their computers running, it might be better to send round an email reminding everyone before you zero in on individuals.

Promote a greener commute

Some people value their solitude on the way to work but others crave company, especially when the traffic limits their progress to a snail's pace. A lift-share board, where you write up your journey and whether you have any spare space, allows people who come from the same areas to travel together and save petrol. Greener still is any combination of cycling, walking and public transport. Because there isn't a bus direct from you to work doesn't mean you can't cycle to the bus stop. The more cyclists in the office the greater need there will be for decent facilities such as somewhere to change and shower. The next step is a scheme that gives you money off bikes, equipment and maintenance costs.

Try it in October . . .

Light Greenies
Get out at the weekend and learn about mushrooms

The idea of trotting off on a walk with a basket under your arm to secure enough mushrooms to smother several rounds of buttery toast is a seductive one. But the reality? Unless you happen to be with someone who knows their stuff, you end up wondering whether the slimy fungus that you've found nestling among fallen leaves is really edible. I'm lucky enough to be friends with two keen mushroom hunters, who got me started in the first place. Tom and Louise have a certain confidence about their fungi finds, which is contagious. If they're whipping out the frying pan, who am I to turn down a garlicky snack? Alone, though, I look upon even the mushroom counter at Waitrose with a degree of suspicion.

John Wright, a mushroom expert, who leads foraging expeditions at the River Cottage in Dorset, says the best thing to do, after going out with someone who has been picking for years, is buy a book. Naturally, he recommends his own – *Mushrooms: River Cottage Handbook No. 1* – but there are dozens of others, all much of a muchness, which aim to help people with the identification process. 'Even an expert will refer to a book,' John tells me. 'The best approach is to bring back what you find in the woods, then get the book out and start working out what you've got. If you're unsure, don't eat it.' Tom and Louise sometimes use the internet. Sites such as *www.mushroomexpert.com* and *www.mushrooms.org.uk* make the job of working out what you've picked easier, but they reckon a book is still best.

John recommends learning to recognize the five or so most poisonous ones, rather than trying to commit the hundreds of edible species to memory. Then you know what to avoid. Another tip is to take a knife on your walk (and a basket or bag, of course).

If he's not sure what kind of mushroom he's found, John gently levers the whole thing out of the ground. Being able to see what's going on at the base of the stem may be helpful in the deciphering process. If he's certain of its species, this isn't necessary. He simply cuts it off at the base – to avoid getting mud over everything.

For now, I'm sticking with what John calls 'starter mushrooms' that are difficult to muddle up. These include the hedgehog mushroom with its leathery cap and telltale spikes underneath, and the cauliflower fungus, a hideous thing you would never guess was edible, but in fact tastes delicious.

As yet, I haven't picked any by myself. I usually manage to drag someone else out to the woods with me. At least then, should I poison my supper guests, the blame can be shared.

The best way to eat wild mushrooms:

• Brush them with a pastry brush to get rid of any dirt – don't bother washing them unless you've picked them from somewhere really grimy.

• Break them into even-sized pieces so they cook in roughly the same time.

• Heat a mixture of butter and olive oil; throw in a bit of chopped shallot or onion first if you like. Add the mushrooms and lots of thyme. Grind some salt and pepper on them, then cook for about 5 minutes, stirring regularly. Throw in some slices of garlic towards the end, so they don't burn. Turn on to hot buttered toast, with a bit of rocket on it, if you've got any.

Dark Greenies

Cut back on desk hours and do something different

The most common reason people give for not adopting green living habits, such as reusing old materials and growing food to eat, is one simple phrase: 'I don't have time.' It justifies a multitude of bad habits. While I don't doubt that it is often true, it is worth thinking about whether this state of affairs is actually what you want or something you have fallen into. You could have more time to pursue a greener life but you would probably have less money. But you would need less money as you could do things yourself, instead of paying people to do them. This is the 'self-reliance system', famously employed by Richard Briers and Felicity Kendal in *The Good Life*. The opposite is the 'organization system', or so wrote the award-winning economist and environmental thinker E.F. Schumacher in the foreword to John Seymour's *Complete Book of Self Sufficiency*. 'During the last hundred years or so, there has been an enormous and historically unique shift: away from the self-reliance system and towards organization. As a result people are becoming more dependent than has ever been seen in history.'

Becoming more self-reliant is as good an excuse as I've ever heard for working less. There are lots of ways you can shake things up a bit and reclaim your time. Start by working out if you can you afford to work one day less a week. Would your job let you? Have you even asked your boss? You might be surprised how receptive your workplace is to the idea of you doing something different – especially if you have a specific plan in mind for that day. It might be that you would like to volunteer for a charity or go back to college to do a part-time course in permaculture. Another way to approach restructuring your job is to ask about flexible working arrangements, often called flexi-time. Could you work at home one day a week? Could you work late in the office on some evenings and stay at home on some mornings? The point to make is that these alterations will make you a happier and more productive employee. What more could your boss want?

• Propose a green outing at work. When you suggest it, make sure the emphasis is less on the 'green', more on the 'day out', to convince cynics that it will be fun. It could involve a train to the Eden Project; an afternoon admiring the organic garden at Audley End or a visit to the Centre for Alternative Technology in Wales. Who knows, you may return inspired and refreshed, with innovative green ideas for the office.

• For a foolproof method of discouraging someone from wasting electricity by leaving their computer on at the end of the day, there is none as effective as slipping into the offending party's seat and sending rogue emails on their behalf. Once stung, they will never leave their computer up and running, unattended, again.

• It takes a few seconds to put 'think before you print' as the signature on the bottom of your emails – all the better, if your entire company does it. As for double-sided printing, if you discover, as we did, that your printers cannot be set to this option, put a tray next to the printer for paper that has only been used on one side, which can be fed back into the printer.

What to Tell the Boss

- That an eco-consultant will come in and audit your office for free. The results will be as much about cutting costs as improving the company's environmental credentials. Contact *www.envirowise.gov.uk* or *www.carbontrust.co.uk*.

- That the Chartered Institution for Building Services Engineers recommends buildings be no warmer than 21–23°C (70–73°F) in winter and 22–24°C in summer. Any warmer or cooler than this is a waste of heating or air-conditioning.

- That investing in printers that print on both sides saves roughly 40 per cent of paper costs.

- That having a sustainable procurement policy, in other words buying Fairtrade, organic and recycled products, from refreshments to stationery, is exceedingly good for a company's image.

- That the age of cheap oil is estimated to end within thirty years. After that, the rising price of fossil-fuel-derived energy will fall heavily on businesses that have not planned for a low-carbon future. As a first step, encourage your boss to swap to a renewable energy supplier.

- That greener companies have a lower employee turnover. People like working for a company with strong ethics, especially if they are included in decisions. Suggest setting up an environmental committee with staff members from each section of the company.

- That it is pioneering companies who have taken a lead in dealing with climate change that will be remembered in the future. Point out examples such as BP, which, whatever you think about the oil industry, has successfully turned itself from being perceived as an 'oil company' to a relevant player in the future as an 'energy company'.

- That the 'triple bottom line' (in other words, people and planet as well as profit) is increasingly how businesses will be judged. You can quote the entrepreneur who coined the phrase. John Elkington, in *Cannibals With Forks*, said that balance sheets would soon not be sufficient to judge a company's performance; social justice and environmental responsibility would be weighed up, too.

- That a proper break at lunch will ensure better productivity in the afternoon, as well as happy, healthier employees.

How to be a Green Freelance

A couple of days a week, I freelance from home. This suits me very well as I'm a great one for pottering around the house pretending to be processing work-related thoughts.

Whether it enables me to be a greener worker, I'm not sure. There are obvious benefits: not having to travel to work, for one; the use of chipped mugs rather than paper cups for my hot beverages, and a greater awareness of the resources I use – mainly because I'm paying for them (freelancers are less likely to print out gazillions of emails when they've coughed up for the finest recycled paper and a recyclable printer cartridge). But there is also a side to all this that is less deserving of praise. There is only one of you: using lights, cooking lunch and, during the winter months, heating your house. By contrast, office workers, gathered under one roof, are sharing resources.

For the home-bound, here are some tips to make your working life greener:

• Start your day with a walk. I know what you're thinking, this won't directly benefit the environment, but it's nice for you and good for work productivity as it wards off mid-morning sluggishness. It is a psychological start to the day.

• Why are you wearing a washed, ironed shirt? What's the point? That you need fewer clean, washed clothes is one of the greatest eco-benefits of freelancing. I'm not saying you should slob around in pyjamas all day, that would undo the good of your brisk morning walk, but enjoy your freedom from work clothes. And make sure you pull on a woolly jumper in the winter before putting the heating on.

• Find a good spot for your desk near a window. Then you won't need lights on all day. When you stop being able to see the keyboard in the evening, practise your touch-typing skills before reaching for the light switch.

• Aim to keep the house in off-mode as much as possible. Imagine how it would be if you weren't there and try to replicate this by avoiding having appliances, lights and heating on.

• Enjoy your control over purchasing decisions. You can install energy-saving light bulbs, use recycled paper and print on both sides. You can also reuse teabags without eliciting 'eugh!' noises from colleagues.

• Have productive breaks from your desk. A spot of gardening perhaps – you could repot your herbs or plant some winter greens.

• Don't drive to the shops at lunchtime. This will negate the good you have done by not using transport to get to work. Cycle or walk to the shops. Even better, rustle up lunch from last night's leftovers. Having a freelancer in your household should seriously dent your food waste, if they are doing their job properly.

• Enjoy homemade snacks since you are fortunate enough not to be stuck with a vending machine to satisfy your four o'clock munchies. Try toasting nuts and seeds in the oven for 15 minutes. Then drip a bit of soy sauce over them, toss them quickly and put the tray back in the cooling oven to crisp them up. Flapjack, another freelancer's favourite, is quick and easy and a great way of using up leftover muesli or other cereal that has gone stale.

• No need to waste water by being overly meticulous about personal hygiene. The cat won't mind if you whiff a bit.

Seasonal Food

At this time of year, there are those who bang on about the delights of pumpkin pie or pumpkin risotto, but if you ask me nothing beats cubes of the stuff roasted on a tray with a generous coating of olive oil, chilli and salt and pepper. As a side dish, it works brilliantly with a Sunday roast, but I can't think of any meals during which a few chunks of **roasted pumpkin** wouldn't be a welcome addition to the table. Sometimes I peel it first; sometimes I leave the skin on and roast it for over an hour so that the whole lot is edible. Sometimes I go easy on the chilli, crumbling cinnamon powder and a bit of a nutmeg on top instead, to make the dish sweeter; other times, I get carried away with the cayenne paper and it becomes a fire-breathing exercise. This is a lunch in itself, combined with some brown rice and a dollop of Greek yoghurt to cool things down. Instead of chunks you can also cut it into melon-like boats if that floats your, erm, boat. Whatever you do, it invariably tastes delicious.

Oh, and I nearly forgot. I'm always trying to rescue the seeds so I can roast them and store them in an old yoghurt pot to call upon for snacks. I've found it to be a pernickety affair trying to separate them from the stringy pumpkin fibres and washing them, but if you manage it, it's very satisfying. You've got something from nothing. I roast them for half an hour with some cumin seeds and a pinch of salt. It's probably not worth firing up the oven for this alone, so I wait until I'm cooking something else and shove the tray in then.

NOVEMBER

TWO WHEELS GOOD,
FOUR WHEELS BAD

I͟T'S GOOD WHILE IT LASTS BUT IT'S ALWAYS TOO SHORT, THAT AUTUMNAL INTERVAL between summer and winter. Among other things, it offers perfect cycling conditions. Bright days with a nip in the air so you can pedal furiously without breaking into a sweat. Unlike the summer months, when a half-hour journey to work delivers you into the office red-faced and gasping for water, in early autumn cycling is a delight. I wind my way to the office slowly, taking the park route – slightly longer, but you get to zigzag around conkers and stop to snack on blackberries.

Then, suddenly, it's all over. I go from cycling in a T-shirt to wondering if my fingers will remain attached by the time I reach work; from leaping out of bed raring to saddle up, to hiding under the duvet with a bus timetable. The telltale sign that winter is here is when I start to see my helmet not as a safety accessory but as a layer of protection against the elements. That's when I know it's only going to get worse.

Once you've started dreaming of warm buses, trams or trains where you can snuggle up and read the papers, an interest in the trees in the park and the camaraderie between cyclists – which I rave about all through autumn – quickly dissolves. The leaves have fallen, anyway, and the cyclists on the road are increasingly hardcore, less disposed to friendly chat – unless it's about a new range of Lycra vests.

It is at this point that many fair-weather summer cyclists bow out gracefully, to pursue various public-transport options or get the car back on the road. Bikes are neglected, bundled into sheds or out into the garden where they will promptly be forgotten until spring. As an amateur cyclist, my instinct is to follow suit, to hang up my helmet until next year.

And very often, I plan to. I abandon my bike for a couple of days, thinking I'll be better off finding covered transport. Something more cosy. But cosy is not the word for a jam-packed Tube or commuter bus in London. Crammed would be more suitable. By comparison, sardines would count themselves lucky.

I am quickly reminded of the bleary-eyed Tube creature I used to be, of the groggy mornings when, having dozed on a stranger's shoulder for a large part of the journey, instead of swatting up on the day's news, as I should have been, I would arrive feeling more like going back to bed than embarking on a day's work.

Of all the disadvantages of abandoning the bike, the lack of fresh air in the morning is the one I notice the most. The malodorous consequences of overheated public transport combined with commuters wearing their heavy-weight winter coats a little too soon gets me back in the saddle faster than anything. As does the fact that none of my friends are wimping out yet. Compared to them, there's no doubt I bring up the rear of our cycling team – both in terms of skill and commitment. To give you some idea, I still get off and push at London's biggest roundabouts, whereas none of my friends would think anything of whizzing around them. But I'd rather tag along at the back than give up completely.

So, after a few days of public transport, I crawl back to my bike, apologize for my annual crisis in confidence and assess whether it will survive another winter on the roads. It was originally bought for my sister, you see, second-hand in 1993. Given its age, it's not doing badly, give or take the slipping gears and the brakes that require significant forethought if you want to stop any time over the next mile. On the plus side, it seems to be thief-proof. Try

as I might to have it pinched (so I have a decent excuse to upgrade), occasionally, usually drunkenly, leaving it unlocked outside our flat, it is always where I left it, waiting for me, like a faithful dog. And for that, I love it. Reliable, eco-friendly and good for my thighs – what more could you want from your transport?

My only previous experience of cycling as an adult was at university in Oxford. We all got around the city on two wheels. It is an ideal stomping ground for bad cyclists, wobbling off to lectures and winding around cobbled back streets to reach the best pubs. But it is a world away from taking on rush-hour traffic in a big city. The more I cycle, the more I realize that this should be avoided at all cost. Pleasurable cycling in town is about cycle paths and back routes. When a scenic moment arrives, you appreciate it all the more. When, suddenly, you find yourself freewheeling alongside a canal, or breezing through a park, that feeling of carefree pleasure that defined my university cycling days, in fact my student days altogether, takes hold.

Cycling always helps you get to the best spots. By bike, I can reach five different parks within 15 minutes of leaving my flat. And there's a fantastic pub near me that is frequented almost entirely by cyclists since it's inconvenient to reach any other way. Turn up in the evening and you'll find bikes racked up on the rails outside, helmets flung on tables, and a crowd with flushed cheeks and slightly sweaty backs slurping pints.

Gervase has always got around on two wheels. He thinks nothing of cycling from one side of London to the other. Back when I was a Tube girl, he used to tell me what he liked best was the feeling of getting around under his own steam, moving from A to B without relying on anyone or anything. He said there was an element of activism in choosing to cycle. At the time, I thought he was being unnecessarily political about it, but now I can see what he means. You are outside the system when you cycle. You are your own boss and it is empowering. If you can make it across the city, it is as if you are able to exert some control over it.

But what if you're not in a city? You might be lucky and find there's a tangle of cycle paths in your area. According to Sustrans, 75 per cent of us live within two miles of a National Cycle Network route (*sustrans.org.uk*). But many people find the opposite, that a burgeoning commitment to road-building has not been complemented by appropriate provision for bikes. In the countryside, there appears to be more stacked against cyclists. First, there are fewer of them, and with cycling, there is always safety in numbers. Plus, the distances are greater, and the roads, while empty, are often winding. Motorists little expect a bicycle to be around the corner.

Hence, people become increasingly reliant on their cars. When I talked to David Lort-Phillips, an organic dairy farmer who lives on an idyllic patch of land overlooking the Cleddau estuary in the Pembrokeshire National Park, he said transport was one of the main challenges that people living in remote areas faced when wanting to do their bit for the environment. I was there to find out how rural communities plan to tackle climate change. David is embarking on a sustainable housing project in the nearby village, along with introducing green measures on his farm.

He wants the countryside to keep up with environmental campaigns in the city. Given the stunning countryside around us, the herd of Jersey cows grazing in the distance and the fresh organic milk in my coffee, it is easy to forget that life in the countryside isn't automatically green. 'Private transport is an important part of rural life,' David told me. 'City-dwellers have to accept that. You can't expect a farmer to cycle 15 miles to the closest town, or wait for a bus.' David won't give up his car but instead he drives a Toyota Prius, which has a hybrid low-emission engine. The other cars on the farm run on liquefied petroleum gas (LPG), which is cleaner than petrol or diesel. To account for the methane emissions from his cows, his plan is to ferment manure by trapping it underground in the new dairy building and then using the gas this emits as fuel. In other words, making energy from flatulent cattle.

I like the idea that if you can't do one thing, you can make up for it by doing something else. It stops the looming sense of failure when you realize you can't do without a car for your job or you need to fly to America to see your relatives. It shows that there's no reason to give up on the environment completely. Instead, like David, you can find something you can do.

By contrast, in the city, public-transport networks are better, and it's petrol-heads who have a hard time. There are bus lanes, pedestrian zones and extortionate parking fees, plus, in the capital, the congestion charge. It has made it easy for people like me and Gervase to shun cars and get around by bike, bus and Tube. Tempting as it is to pretend that we have made an admirable green decision by not buying a car, to be honest, it was not concern for our carbon emissions that clinched it. Keeping a car on the road in London is expensive, laden with hassle and ultimately pointless if you don't have children to ferry around or desperately need one for work. That's not to say I can't envisage a time when we might consider buying one.

Already we have progressed from occasionally hiring a car for long weekends to joining a car club so we can borrow one at less expense and more regularly (see car club section on page 318). There's no point denying the joy of piling camping stuff in the back of a car, rather than lugging it to a train, or the safe and cosy feeling that comes from having your own protective bubble to take you wherever you want to go. But I like to think our years of public transport have toughened us, heightening the pleasure when we do borrow a car. We have become resourceful as a result, better at packing lightly and knowing when to leave the hula hoop at home.

But we may yet join the ranks of car owners, or even, gulp, van owners. Gervase has always wanted to do up an old transit van, an idea that appeals to me even though I know it would do serious damage to our carbon footprint. A diesel-guzzling giant vehicle is hardly the obvious choice for someone worried about the environment. Then again, it would be fun. We could sleep in it at weddings and parties. We would use it to get around the UK for our holidays, for camping trips and visiting friends. It would double as a holiday home so maybe I could justify it by comparing its emissions with those from taking flights abroad.

Of course, neither of us would drive the van around London on a daily basis. That would be polluting and expensive. We would carry on cycling to work, if nothing else because we both enjoy membership of the cycling classes. I'm flabbergasted that I get away with it, that no one has spotted me as phoney, or that a Lycra-clad enforcer of cycling standards has not taken one good look at my shoddy bike and dodgy indicating skills and forced me to hand over my bike lock. With my tendency to wobble along a main road like a drunken bluebottle, that I can be part of the urban bike clique gives me great hope. It suggests that cycling has moved beyond its status as a minority sport for super-greens and fitness fanatics to something that anyone can do.

Gervase is the only person who doubts my rights to membership. He doesn't rate my road skills, finding it virtually unbearable to cycle with me. He worries I'm going to do something disastrous every step of the way, which I find, in equal parts, sweet and irritating.

He's been on at me to do an urban cycling safety course. These are growing in popularity and sometimes offered at subsidized rates by city councils. Since I have subjected myself to the streets of London with only a cycling proficiency certificate awarded aged ten, I can see his point. I speak to a friend at work, Lucia, who did a day course last year, organized by Cycle Training UK. She says it helped her to become an 'urban warrior on wheels' rather than a 'puny cyclist'.

Mind you, it sounds like Lucia already had some urban warrior leanings. She'd been cycling in London for several years and wasn't scared to run the odd red light and assert her presence on the road. The good thing about the course, she says, was this confidence was bolstered by knowledge of what she should be doing in each scenario, according to the Highway Code. Of the softer, more psychological tips, the most useful was to make eye contact with drivers. 'At the very least it reminds them that you're a human,' says Lucia, 'and that you know what they look like if they knock you off.'

The problem with many city cyclists, especially women, is that they're apologetic for being on the road. Sorry about little me, we think, I'll just squeeze in here next to the gutter. But this isn't right at all. Lucia's course stressed the fact that you have every right to be on the road and you shouldn't allow cars to bully you. Instead of creeping along close to the pavement, you should be bold, even if it means holding up a car behind you for 50 metres. Hugging the gutter is ill-advised because a driver might not see you and once you're there, and cars are overtaking you, it becomes difficult to move back into the traffic. Within reason, I suggest behaving like a car. Obviously that doesn't mean creating a queue of cars for the sake of it, but making your presence felt on the road is a good idea.

The sheer number of cyclists on the roads in London helps to make me feel safe. I'm aware of the dangers, of course. Of the collisions my friends have had, most have been with pedestrians. Touch wood, I have only fallen off, unspectacularly, while stationary on the pavement (don't ask). However, I'm terrified of motorists suddenly swinging open the doors of parked cars as I'm whizzing past. And I don't much like the long bendy buses popular in London. Sometimes they frighten the life out of me by squeezing me against the pavement when they turn left.

This may sound enough to keep most sensible people in their cars, but it's not much different from the hazards of being a pedestrian in London.

You may have noticed that I haven't mentioned the fitness benefits of going by bike yet. That's because I don't see cycling as exercise. If I did, it would probably put me off. Of course, when I started, I was all too conscious of it, huffing and puffing up the slightest inclines. And when I've been out of the saddle for a week or two, I feel the strain in my thighs. But it's incredible how quickly your body adjusts and you stop noticing that you're cycling at all. I drift off, think about all sorts of things; mainly what I'm going to have for supper. Cycling gives you the appetite of a rhinoceros, while cleverly preventing you from resembling one after all the food.

I've also been avoiding the problem that I mentioned at the

beginning of the chapter: what to do when the weather does its worst and cycling is about as appealing as snail porridge for breakfast. For such a dilemma, I turn to proper cycling nerds, the sort you see whizzing past with the most upmarket gear and flashiest lights, who most certainly don't give up just because there's black ice on the roads and several inches of snow bunched around their bike tyres.

Last year, I managed to lure them all on to my blog by writing a post about how to make cycling bearable in November. With my minimal experience, I came up with a dozen or so tips, including wearing two pairs of socks and tracking down some lobster gloves (so-called not because of chapped, red hands but because they are claw-like: a happy compromise between a mitten and a glove, which gives you control over your bike).

The invitation for cyclists to share how they cope as temperatures drop was leapt upon. I learnt about neck gaiters (like scarves but closed ends so there's nothing to flap about); fenders (curved metal things that go round the upper portions of the wheels to prevent mud being thrown up by the tyres) and studded tyres (to help your wheels grip on ice). I also learnt that no one, however committed, enjoys the first 100 metres on a cold day. Your muscles are cold and it's always going to be hard work. Stick it out and things quickly get better. Some people say they prefer winter cycling to summer, since you get less sweaty and the roads are emptier.

But it also made me think about the tendency for any sport to become engulfed by the massive industry that sells us the latest clothes technologies and accessories that cost a fortune and weigh down your wheels. The refreshing thing about cycling, compared to other sports such as climbing, is that you don't need much gear. 'I don't have any fancy clothing, just plenty of layers and two pairs of socks and gloves when it's extra cold,' writes Karen, who cycles throughout the year. Her words are refreshing, compared to the recommendations for the latest breathable microfibre sports vests and neoprene overshoes. Another tip I liked came from David. 'If you're caught short on a cold day ... insert a couple of pieces of paper (A4) into your helmet,' he advises. 'This creates a layer of insulation.'

It goes without saying that it is much greener to make do with what you have and improvise than go out and plunder a sports shop for all the latest gear. The only concession I make is a fluorescent stripe that I wear for safety reasons, and, on dark winter nights, a similarly dazzling waistcoat. To my surprise, I'm quite taken with the fluoro gear: a touch lollipop lady, a touch 1980s raver. Otherwise, while obviously avoiding trouble-spots like floaty scarves – an invitation for spoke disaster – I stubbornly refuse to stop wearing skirts and dresses. I would rather sacrifice my entire winter tights collection, which I do anyway by cycling in them, than allow the way I get around the city to have a dreary impact on my clothes.

While I'm not sure about putting paper in my helmet, you won't catch me getting carried away in a cycling shop. Mainly because I wouldn't want to see all that money that I've saved by not running a car or buying bus tickets being frittered away. Ever faithful to my frugal roots, I'm more likely to be in there sweet-talking the nice chap with oil-stained fingers into pumping up my tyres. It's not that I can't do it myself, I hasten to add, but they do it so well in bike shops, with a special automatic pump. I'm always very impressed and make all the right noises about what a good bike shop it is. After all, what's the point of being a member of the cycling classes if you don't get special treatment?

WHAT'S IN IT FOR THE PLANET?

Hop on a bike . . . and you can get around without having to worry about transport emissions. Cycling also reduces noise pollution and congestion. According to Sustrans, you can park ten bicycles in the same space taken up by one car. And, as it points out, bicycles are kinder to animals, with much less chance of road kill.

Take public transport as much as possible . . . if you don't trust yourself on two wheels, find out about bus and train options that will lessen your carbon footprint. In turn, this will reduce the UK's overall CO_2 emissions from transport. These were measured at 22 per cent of total CO_2 emissions in 2005 (by Defra), compared to 37 per cent from energy industries and 15 per cent from domestic energy use. This suggests that it is as worthwhile focusing on how you get around as on how much energy you use in your home.

Primp Your Bike

Stuck with an old shopper you inherited from your mother or picked up for a bargain price? Don't worry, a few tweaks here and there and the prospect of riding it in public will vastly improve. If it's the only vehicle you own, you might as well make it look good. Not too good, mind, or it will get nicked. Here are some tips:

1 **Be creative.** You want to aim for the kind of look that bike thieves tend to avoid. Flowery garlands, glitter on the handlebars and colourful stripes are a good start. Don't ride with anything trailing, however, in case it gets caught in the spokes. Expect all this bike preening to be frowned on by the Lycra-clad cycling brigade who wouldn't introduce a millimetre of ribbon for fear it might slow them down. But it's fun if you are trying to encourage kids to cycle, or on a weekend bike ride, a festival trip or to make your point vividly at an anti-climate change protest.

2 **Invest in a decent seat.** This will boost comfort levels no end if you're making do with an old bike. I've got myself a squidgy gel model especially for women and it's a delight to sit on.

3 **Make sure you have a bell.** Just as every car should have a horn, so every bike should be able to say tinkle-tinkle now and again. To warn of your presence behind pedestrians or other cyclists, it is crucial. The fun is in choosing the sound. I'm rather taken with something called a trumpet bulb hooter that you can fix on to your handlebars, although I wouldn't want to give anyone too much of a fright.

4 **Choose your waterproof seat covering carefully.** The obvious makeshift version is an old plastic bag, tied under the seat to keep it dry when you leave your bike outside – to avoid the wet-bum-on-arrival look, which is not a good one. Don't use any old flimsy thing, however; choose a nice-looking carrier bag that fits the overall colour theme of your bike. I've started using a shower cap: the elasticated band is perfect for keeping the rain out. A good reason to pocket the ones offered in hotel rooms.

5 **Don't scrimp on lights.** Invest in really good quality, bright ones that are easy to attach to your bike. As soon as the batteries start to go and the brightness fades, replace them. For this, the green option is to invest in a recharging device so you don't have to keep on buying new batteries and chucking the old ones. There is also a new generation of battery-free LED lights coming on to the market (*www.ecoutlet.co.uk*).

Walk More

Walking is good for you. We should all leave the car behind and get wherever we want to go in slower, healthier, not to mention greener, fashion. The 'good for you' bit doesn't always do it any favours, though, making walking sound like beansprouts or Pilates. That's not how walking really is. For me, it's crucial to thinking. Sometimes I have to pace about the flat just to work out my next sentence. It's as though there's a switch that only flicks when I'm in motion. It's actually rather inconvenient. I have to take scraps of paper and a pen with me on walks.

One thing I will say is that walking affects your footwear. You can't expect to be one of life's walkers in Vivienne Westwood heels. I don't know which came first for me: a taste for comfortable shoes (Ugg boots, Birkenstocks, you name it, if there's an inelegant footwear trend, I'm for it) or a belief in getting around under my own steam. Either way, it hastened my love affair with the sort of shoes that make each foot resemble the snout of a duck-billed platypus.

Ten reasons why I walk

- To save money.

- To feel and look healthier.

- To slow down.

- To get perspective on my problems.

- To make room for a teatime slice of cake.

- To see what's going on outside.

- To appreciate the changing of the seasons.

- To unwind – literally, to release the tightened muscles in my neck.

- To hone the art of doing nothing, while doing something.

- To spend time with someone, or sometimes the opposite: to spend time alone.

Try it in November . . .

Light Greenies
Get to know sloes

These bitter little purple fruits, dangling in clumps from blackthorn hedges, aren't much on their own, but submerge them in sugary gin and they transform the liquid into a sweet heady liqueur. It's the stuff that drunken winter evenings are made of. Mix it with tonic for a colourful alternative to the traditional aperitif or serve it neat in a shot glass to knock friends off their perches at the end of a meal.

Don't laugh, but I'm a big fan of *www.sloe.biz*. The internet has become a place for brew-your-own fans to discuss technique; and it's a good way of clearing up what exactly a sloe is before you start raiding bushes. You will also find recipes for sloe jelly, blackberry brandy and other more desperate attempts to exploit autumn hedgerows.

What I like best about this website is that it opens with the words: 'Take a litre bottle of gin, and drink half of it.' You have to make room for the sloes, you see, which by this point should be washed and spilling over the kitchen table. Some might see it as a fiddle, but I enjoy pricking each sloe with a skewer or fork before filling the half-empty bottle of gin almost to the top; then you add half a mug of sugar, more if you want a sweeter drink, before making sure the lid is airtight – I often use wine bottles, so I find a cork that fits. The alternative is to freeze the sloes, which means they will break down when they hit the gin, in the same way as if they'd been pricked. It's a shortcut, but I like the pricking process for the same reason that I like podding peas. It's active relaxation.

Your drink will be ready to quaff by Christmas, but it'll be even better by next Christmas – although I defy anyone to resist cracking open a bottle to taste some.

By all means, experiment with different ways of drinking sloe gin. For an indulgent cocktail, you can't beat sloe gin and champagne, with the gin employed as you might use crème de cassis in Kir Royale. I was convinced that we were the first to create this drink, at my friend Jo's hen party in Wales, christening it the Sloe Downfall. But since then I've heard the combination mentioned by others, and I've come to accept we were probably not the first to be undone by its potency.

Dark Greenies
Treat yourself to an electric car

There are some 'buts' to this recommendation. The big one is that it's obviously better not to drive a car at all. But I'm a realist. Fact is lots of people do and if you switch to an electric one, while also swapping your electricity provider to a green one, voilà, you have a zero-emission vehicle fuelled by renewable energy. An electric car uses energy sparingly, by drawing on its battery only when it is in motion, not when you're sitting stationary in traffic or at a red light. For city driving, it is very efficient. But this leads me to my second hesitation. I would not inflict a G-Wiz, the UK's most popular electric vehicle, on anyone but a city slicker looking for a way of scooting around town. At 8 foot 8 inches long, with maximum speed of 50 mph – and that's only if you happen to be on a downward slope – it is not a car for the countryside.

That said, the financial benefits are impressive. After waving goodbye to £6,999 to buy the thing, you pay no tax; you can squeeze into small spaces; park for free in some parts of London, and you don't have to pay the congestion charge in the capital either. You plug it into a three-pin socket and over six hours it will charge to give you a range of 40 miles.

On the flipside, there have been serious concerns about its safety. The body of the car is not as solid as that of ordinary cars, which has led to it performing badly in safety tests. In its defence, it's not supposed to be like normal cars, nor is it intended to be driven at high speeds. I've not driven one myself but those who have say it's a nifty little thing, perfect for running around in the city, so long as you don't mind the odd burst of laughter from people on the street taking in its dwarf proportions.

• If you're in the habit of hopping in the car at the weekend to do your supermarket shopping, what about trying an online delivery service? With Ocado, the favourite of well-heeled professionals, you can opt for a green van delivery, which means you will be allocated a van that is already in your area. Each van is said to replace up to twenty cars on the road.

• For extra motivation to encourage you to walk rather than drive, visit the Walk-It website (*www.walkit.com*). Here you can type in your journey details and find out exactly how long it would take you to go by foot; how many calories you would burn and the CO_2 avoided.

• Don't chuck those last few slices of stale bread. Instead make a simple version of bread and butter pudding with them. I line a dish with sections of old bread, after wiping it with an old butter wrapper. Sprinkle the bread with sugar, raisins, cinnamon, specks of butter and finally pour in some milk, and ideally a splash of cream. Bake for 20 minutes for a comforting pre-bedtime treat.

Share Lifts

There's nothing better than disguising a guilty habit with a green one. OK, so you're a car driver, but if you team up with someone who lives and works near you, that makes you a 'car-sharer', which sounds a lot better.

Informal car sharing

This revolves around establishing a loose network of people who make similar journeys. You take it in turns to drive, choose the music and provide éclairs on the way home. If one of your party doesn't drive or have a car, it's not a problem. Contributions towards petrol can be made. One reason why more people don't do this is that not everyone wants to be sociable at 8 o'clock in the morning. The process of getting from A to B serves as time out, to think, to have your own space. The last thing you might want is someone keen to chat about the weather or force Radio 1 on you. The key to getting around this is to warn fellow car-sharers what to expect. 'By the way, I'm not a morning person,' usually does the trick.

Formal car sharing

By registering with websites such as *www.liftshare.org* and *www.nationalcarshare.co.uk*, you can be put in touch with other car-sharers in your area who do the same journey as you. The idea is to get extra bums on seats for journeys and to share the petrol. After signing up online, you type in your intended destination and request either a driver or a passenger to share the cost of the journey. The only hitch I've found with the system is that there are often far more people looking for lifts than there are drivers looking for companions. That and safety. Some people might be concerned about hooking up with someone they hadn't met before for a long-distance car journey. But to register on these sites, you have to give your address and full personal details, which are checked, thus making it difficult to remain anonymous. I'd say it was no more or less safe than going to someone's home to pick up something you've acquired through Freecycle or eBay. If you're uncomfortable with the idea, you might be better suited to the concept of a car club (see below).

Join a Car Club

If you're happy to share a car but not to spend long journeys making polite chit-chat with people you don't know, a car club is a good option. We joined City Car Club (*www.citycarclub.co.uk*), which is much like Street Car (*www.streetcar.co.uk*) and operates in towns and cities all over the UK.

Find your nearest car club on *www.carplus.org.uk*.

Here's how mine works

Like all these things, the **signing-up process** is the worst bit. The company has to check your driving licence and take all your details – most of which can be done online. Then it issues you with a swipe card and a pin number, which will give you access to any of the club's cars. There are hundreds around London, parked in bays, often in residents' parking. You book your car on the website, and, so far, I've not had a problem with availability. At this point, you state how long you want to borrow it for – which could be for as little as an hour or as much as a couple of weeks. Keys are kept inside the cars and you get in with your car club card, swiping it on the front windscreen in James Bond fashion, before entering your pin number into another spectacularly futuristic gadget that lives in the glove compartment.

Payment How much you pay is based on how long you have the car for, how much petrol you use (again, you pay for petrol with another card stored in the car) and your membership rate. We chose gold membership, which means we pay £15 a month, which also covers insurance. On top of that, we pay £38 for the first day that we borrow it; £19 for the subsequent days. If we wanted to borrow it on an hourly basis, it would cost £3.80 per hour. This works as long as you borrow a car for roughly ten hours or more every month. If you're going to use the club less than that, it would be better to choose bronze membership, which only costs £5 a month but you pay slightly more per hour/day. We reckon our membership still saves us masses of money that we would be spending if we were keeping a car on the road in London.

Benefits As well as being cheaper than hiring a car, it is also more relaxing. You don't have to queue for hours in a grim car-hire depot, only to realize that you don't have the card you used to book the car so you're not going anywhere. Nor is there the drama of trying to get the car back at the right time, with a full tank, to avoid being charged for an extra day. If you're running late, you can simply phone the car club and extend your booking. And nobody checks the car for scratches that may or may not have been there at the beginning of the weekend, which makes the process of driving more pleasant.

Drawbacks Make sure that there is a car close to you as some of the benefits of the club disappear if you have to trek across town on public transport to reach the car. That's when you realize why people like to own their cars, so they can keep them outside their house.

Can't Part with the Car?

Then become a greener driver. The Environmental Transport Association says that just by changing the way you drive, you can drop your fuel consumption by as much as 25 per cent. So-called 'eco-driving' is not up there in the green stakes with walking or going by bus, more a pale turquoise than a dazzling emerald, but it's a good start.

• **Drive smoothly.** Speeding, rapid acceleration and sudden braking is not only unrestful for your passengers, but it also increases fuel consumption. Imagine a cup of tea is balanced on the passenger seat and then try not to spill it. Girl racers, take note, revving also wastes fuel, as does staying in a low gear, and getting too close to the car in front, which leads to sudden braking. Instead, try to maintain a steady speed.

• **Cool carefully.** Air-conditioning makes a car less fuel-efficient. Unfortunately, so does opening the windows. Which is best depends on how fast you're going, according to the Department of Transport. At slow speeds, it recommends having the windows open; once you are doing speeds of 50mph or more, switch to air-con, if you're lucky enough to have it.

- **Monitor how you are doing.** Keep a pen and a homemade notepad (staple together some scraps of paper) in the car. Every time you buy fuel, write down your mileage and how much fuel you've bought. In no time at all, you will have built up an idea of how much you are using and what kind of driving is most fuel-efficient.

- **Keep your tyres pumped up.** Under-inflated tyres increase something called rolling resistance between the car and the road, which forces the engine to work much harder. Pay regular visits to your garage to check on your tyres, or, if you can, delegate this boring task to someone else.

- **Spring-clean your car.** Given that anything that adds weight increases fuel consumption, it's worth clearing out the boot once in a while. That pile of books you've been meaning to take to the local library will be upping how much you spend on petrol.

- **Cut out small journeys.** A car creates the most pollution when it is going at less than 15mph. Those 'just popped out for a pint of milk' journeys are the ones that do the damage. And couldn't you walk? Your cuppa will taste superior, with an extra dash of smugness, if you've collected the milk on foot.

For more green driving tips, check out the Environmental Transport Association's website (*www.eta.co.uk*).

Choose a Greener Car Next Time Round
When to ditch your rusty wheels?

In most cases, resisting the pressure to upgrade to a superior model is the right approach to your belongings. Cars, however, are an exception. Old ones are seriously bad for the planet. I'm not talking middle-aged models here (from the late 1990s), rather the exhaust-belching relics of earlier decades, manufactured at a time when emissions were much less of a big deal than they are today. The average life of a car in the UK is about thirteen years. Unless you do a very low mileage each year, running a car that is older than this is unwise if you care about your carbon footprint. A Fiesta from the 1970s is said to have an environmental impact that is seventy times greater than a brand new one. Obviously there are manufacturing costs and waste implications involved in upgrading, but it is the driving of a car that accounts for 85 per cent of its total energy footprint. Only 10 per cent comes from manufacturing and 5 per cent from disposal (according to the Energy Saving Trust). As for scrapping an ancient car, it's not such a bad idea. Modern scrapyards, officially known as Authorized Treatment Facilities (ATF), do an impressive job of recycling the components, leaving you to worry about finding a low-carbon alternative.

On the hunt? Look for the best rating

Now you know about the dangers of driving old bangers, you have an excuse to choose a modern car, although second-hand is obviously still best. Bear in mind the following: look out for a car with good fuel consumption (anything above 60 miles per gallon is not bad going). It's also worth knowing that diesel cars emit less carbon dioxide, which is good for climate change, but more smog-forming particulates, otherwise known as diesel smoke. Cars registered since 2001 will be graded on a scale from A to F, based on carbon dioxide emissions. The greener your car, the cheaper it will be to tax it. Electric vehicles, in category A, pay zero tax. By contrast, four-wheel drives such as the Land Rover – rated F on the Department of Transport's A–F fuel-economy rating – which spew out over 185g of carbon dioxide every kilometre, cost £195 a year in tax (in 2007). To work out your car's rating, use this online calculator: *www.vcacarfueldata.org.uk/ved.*

Here are a few green wheels I like (but can't afford)

• Ruling supreme in the green garage is the **Toyota Prius**, bathed in the glory of its celebrity connections: Leonardo DiCaprio, Cameron Diaz and Meryl Streep all have one. It is not the only hybrid car to combine petrol power with an electric motor – there's a Lexus and Honda model too – but it is the least polluting, emitting 104g of CO_2 per kilometre. I borrowed a Prius for a weekend to see what all the fuss was about and after cruising around in this eerily quiet but luxuriously powerful car, it was hard to give it back.

• A word of caution on **biofuels** (which include biodiesel and bioethanol). They are increasingly controversial. Fuel made from crops and trees planted on a large scale has come under fire because it leads to deforestation – in itself one of the biggest causes of CO_2. Huge areas of forest are cleared to grow the crops that can be converted into fuel. There is also the food versus fuel debate: should developing countries be growing crops to burn rather than to eat?

• A **Citroën C1** is neither a hybrid car nor does it have a special kind of low-emission fuel, but it still manages to have carbon dioxide emissions that rival the Honda and Toyota hybrids, for which it deserves special attention. It travels 61.4 miles to the gallon, with CO_2 emissions of 109g per kilometre, which means your tax and insurance will be low.

• Again in the realms of normal cars that most people drive, Volkswagen has come up with a concept called **BlueMotion**. It is an environmental series that will consist of the most efficient model of each car range. So far (on publishing) a Polo, a Passat and a Passat Estate wear the BlueMotion badge. Soon, a Golf will follow, becoming the most economical model in the range (emitting 119g of CO_2 per kilometre and doing 62.8mpg), though not the greenest. The Polo retains that title, creating 99g of CO_2 per kilometre. It is currently Britain's greenest car, but soon enough I've no doubt it will be overtaken.

Seasonal Food

Parsnips, those pallid root vegetables, appalled me as a child: chewy, fibrous and not as comfortingly bland as potato. I'd groan when I noticed my mother tucking them down the side of a roasting chicken. Perhaps if I'd tried them in chip form, it would have been different. A bowl of **parsnip chips**, served with ketchup or a spicy guacamole and a cold beer, make the perfect snack while you're watching a film or needing something to keep the wolf from the door. Peel the parsnips first, then cut them into thick, oversized chips (they will shrink when you roast them). Toss them in some olive oil and salt, adding a shake of cayenne pepper if you like a kick, then lay them out on a baking sheet to roast in a hot oven for 30 minutes.

DECEMBER

STEPPING OFF THE
SEASONAL TREADMILL

As far as I know, few people reach December without being swept up, at least momentarily, in the 'getting ready for Christmas' frenzy. Really, though, this national obsession gets under way long before Advent. Somewhere in late autumn when leaves are still falling and the last tomatoes are turning red, the first few shops launch their Christmas displays, cunningly designed to trigger an onslaught of nostalgia for twinkly lights and sleigh-bell-festooned chocolates.

At these times, what is required, I have found – to help with the job of ignoring piles of chocolate money strategically positioned at till counters – is a certain moral fortitude: a seasonal resistance strategy.

My own, I'm sorry to say, is feeble. While I manage pretty well to resist buying what is crowding shop shelves, I am easy prey to the emotions that the season – and the high street – set loose. At the slightest whiff of tangerine peel, I drift off into a reverie of Christmases past. By the time I spot decorated trees peeping from behind curtains, I am beyond help. I will be rummaging in my cupboards to look for mangy bits of tinsel and racking my brains to remember how to make mulled wine.

Part of the problem is that my family – actually, make that just my mother – does not so much prepare early for Christmas as remain in a constant state of anticipation throughout the year. It begins on Boxing Day, when the holiday sales provide an unmissable opportunity to stock up on discount crackers and tree chocolates (which will have gone white at the edges by next year but since the dog is the only one to eat them, no one minds).

Over the following months, stocking gifts are squirrelled away (yes, in the magic cupboard, see January), and a slow build-up of fruit jellies and dates amasses in the kitchen.

Of course, there is nothing wrong with a bit of planning. It is to be encouraged; an important way of avoiding last-minute dashes to the shops that yield misjudged gifts and excessive quantities of food. The only problem I've experienced when I've accumulated gifts early in the year, with no clear idea of who is going to receive what, is that I've ended up with a hotch-potch collection of items, none of which are suitable for anyone.

This kind of balls-up paints an accurate picture of my hit-and-miss attempts to weave principles into my Yuletide behaviour. On some things, however, tradition and nostalgia override any attempt at ethics. A real tree is non-negotiable. My heart sinks when I read in the *Green Guide for Christmas 2006* (one is published every year to help people resist seasonal excess) that I shouldn't be having one, or sending Christmas cards, or even travelling any-where over the festive period – unless I can get there on my bike.

'Advances in modern communication technology make it possible to see and hear your kith and kin via the internet,' says the guide; '. . . investing in a simple webcam set-up can bring you closer, if not physically.'

If one thing is likely to provoke a sudden episode of depression in early December, it's the thought of spending the pending holiday rigged up to my laptop bonding with my family via MSN messenger. It is too grim to con-template, especially if you throw in having no tree to cheer you up, nor a stash of absurdly jolly snowman cards to be written. That's all wrong if you ask me. You must be able to be environmentally aware at this time of year without hav-ing to frown on anything that sounds remotely fun.

To find out, last year I pledged to follow the greenest possible approach to sourcing a tree. If I'd known it would lead me to a wood in Sussex on a wild and windy day in mid-December, where, equipped with a spade, I would dig my own tree, I might have taken the easy option and done what I do most years. Nipped out to the Christmas-tree man who lurks on a junction in North London, flogging very possibly stolen trees at discount prices.

I did ask him once where the trees came from and he replied, with a smirk, 'A wood!' He didn't have a clue. Chances are he nicked a load off a lorry coming from Scandinavia. I found out later that over 15 per cent of our trees come from Denmark, and another significant chunk from Germany. This time, I would settle for nothing less than a British tree, grown in sustainable fashion; responsible for minimal transport emissions. But could I really justify chopping one down, only to chuck it in January?

According to the Royal Horticultural Society, so long as you compost your tree in the New Year, or get the council to pick it up and turn it into wood chippings, you're not doing badly, environmentally speaking. One up on that would be to get a tree with roots attached; keep it well watered over Christmas and plant it out in the garden afterwards so it carries on absorbing CO_2.

With this in mind, I set about finding a supplier on the British Tree Growers Association website (*www.christmastree.org.uk*). Pines and Needles, a family-run business that delivers trees to the London region, caught my eye. It gives 10 per cent of its profits to Great Ormond Street and offers to collect your tree in the New Year for recycling.

For time-poor Londoners, who would probably pay someone to clean their teeth given half the chance, there is even a service that includes instal-lation and decoration.

Instead I borrowed a car from our car club to drive to Wilderness Wood, in East Sussex. Not because, at a couple of hours' drive away, it was the closest place to pick up a British-grown tree, but because I was impressed by its green credentials. It helped that I could combine my tree-hunt with a walk in the Sussex High Weald, one of England's most enchanting bits of woodland.

Set in 61 acres, Wilderness Wood, a family-run working woodland recognized as a Centre of Excellence by the Forestry Commission, has won countless awards for its environmental commitment. It's doing all the right things in terms of sustainability, but it is also a nice place to hang out. There are nature trails, an adventure playground and bug hunts for children, plus a cosy café with a log fire that sells local cakes.

You don't have to dig a tree yourself, there are plenty of pre-cut ones, but I wanted the full harvesting experience. I wanted to feel mud under my nails and pine needles in my hair. Or at least, I wanted to supervise these things. Thrusting the spade into Gervase's hands, we marched into the wood just as it started to rain. Sensibly, most people had stayed at home, waiting for a crisp blue sky under which to harvest their tree, but there were a few others tramping around in wellies as darkness fell.

'It's only a tree,' one man bellowed to his anxious-looking wife, as she circled the field for the umpteenth time. 'They all look the same.' But I sympathized with her. With 650 potential festive centrepieces closing in on you, finding the right one, the one that reflects you and your aspirations for the Christmas period, becomes of the utmost importance.

We settled on a bushy five-foot number that looked manageable enough. It was a Norway Spruce, a popular variety – in some ways, the sparrow of Christmas trees. In its short life, it would have provided year-round cover for small birds and animals. Goldcrests and long-tailed tits would have found shelter and food in its branches, I discover from the Forestry Commission's website.

On bug hunts in the summer, children are encouraged to shake the evergreen trees at Wilderness Wood. It's a good way of finding insects, explains Anne Yarrow, who has run the place with her husband, Chris, for twenty-seven years. She tells me that in the spring the Christmas tree plantation hosts the best display of bluebells. The trees need lots of weeding, so woodland flowers are given the opportunity to flourish around their roots.

As we hacked at our chosen spruce, I did wonder fleetingly where the bugs and birds would go now. Wrenching a tree from the ground is a surprisingly brutal process. Was I really doing the right thing destroying bug homes?

Anne was reassuring. For every tree taken away from Wilderness Wood, another will be planted, making the process as carbon-neutral as possible. In fact, they plant more than they sell to allow for growing hiccups.

The other benefit to planting Christmas trees, pointed out by Guy Barter, head of advisory services at the Royal Horticultural Society, is that younger trees have been shown to absorb more CO_2 than older trees and leave more carbon in the soil than other crops.

As we finally severed the roots of our tree, heaved it out of the ground and bundled it into a black bin bag, secured with string, I hoped it had done its job of locking carbon into the ground. However, concern for my tree's role in climate change was soon replaced with a growing excitement about getting it home and festooning it with fairy lights.

There is nothing more thrillingly festive on a December evening than carrying a Christmas tree along a country lane. If you can avoid doing it yourself but instead be the one who admires it from a few paces behind, all the better. The prickly feeling of pine needles on your neck and the substantial weight of the tree on your shoulder detract from the feel-good glow, according to Gervase.

Back home, we replanted it in a large flowerpot, covered the kitchen floor with soil, watered our new arrival and tied gold ribbon around the grubby pot. Then we stood hands on hips to admire it. It was a beauty, no question about it. We chose well. Back when I picked one up from the dodgy tree-dealer, I'd never felt this proud.

Our success with the tree is proof that a green Christmas can be fun. Of course, I get why some people have given up on it. They cite commercialism and media hype as having hijacked the whole affair and refuse to be sucked in. But, if you ask me, that is a cop-out, like not bothering to acknowledge Mothering Sunday because you don't like the tacky cards on display in high-street card shops.

Instead, by stripping away the bits you don't like, the consumer froth, pointless spending and hideous polyester Santa outfits, you are left with the proper stuff. Simple things, like spending time with different generations, going on walks, slowing down, eating well and being nice to people.

Christmas, after all, is based on tradition. It is a time when you recycle old recipes; wheel out the same tree decorations and after-supper games and watch repeats of the films you've sat through year after year. There is even someone in most people's families who can be counted on to tell the same old stories – some would say a less welcome aspect of Christmas recycling.

Take decorations. Clearly, this is not the time to follow fashion. Imagine how boring Christmas trees would be if they all had tasteful white lights and expensive glass beads. It would threaten the season's kitsch swing and put a whole lot of tinsel out of a job.

As for complicated colour themes that account for table linen and whether your napkins complement the cheese board, don't even go there. What you've got is just fine. Clashing colours, remember, is an approach taken by people who are so inherently stylish they can get away with it.

It's also a sign of being concerned enough about your environmental impact that you don't want to splash out on needless bits of plastic – when you've already got some needless bits of plastic that you splashed out on years ago.

Like many families, we rely on the contents of our Christmas box, an ancient trunk that resides in the attic cupboard next to the boiler, eleven months of the year. Mid-December, its moment arrives. We drag it downstairs where the contents spill out on to the carpet and the cats start their annual ping-pong tournament with the baubles. Over the years, some of the nicest pieces, an angel passed down several generations and a string of tinkly bells that hung from the ceiling, have been lost or broken by curious paws – of children as well as pets. The multicoloured plastic snowflakes given out by Shell garages in the early 1980s, however, have mysteriously reproduced and by the time we've finished flinging it all at the tree, it usually resembles a 1980s office party: brash with excessive sparkles.

But if you ask me (and I'm sorry if I'm being shamelessly sentimental, I warned you that I was prone to nostalgia at this time of year), this is how Christmas should be. Outside of normal style rules, hopelessly unchic and full of family repetition. The last few years, I've found myself looking fondly upon our trashy tree decorations. When the ghastly reindeer antlers, which my mother thinks are hilarious and insists on making me wear during Christmas lunch, emerge from the trunk, I barely even wince.

That's not to say a small amount of updating stock isn't sometimes necessary. When only half the tree lights manage a flicker and the old boot from the Monopoly set is the only piece that remains, it is time to find some replacements. This requires gearing yourself up for a trip to the shops, something that shouldn't be undertaken lightly at this time of year. In my experience, if there is one thing likely to shatter the magic of Christmas once and for all, it is spending too much time on the high street.

Yes, I know the twinkling street lights are supposed to be one of the season's wonders and the whole festive cheer, chestnuts-at-the-roadside thing is supposed to make you feel as though you've stepped out of *A Christmas Carol*, but the fact is you could not be in a worse place to indulge Dickensian fantasies. Homogeneous streets, packed with corporate chains and stressed shoppers, blow away any vestiges of the nineteenth century.

They also yield depressingly predictable trappings. They are the least likely place that you will find inspiring and inventive presents. Any originality is usually of the pointless gimmick variety. A battery-operated pepper grinder; a food spiralizer perhaps (to make decorative swirls from your cucumber), or a Santa outfit for your dog, one of Selfridges' top-selling items a couple of years ago.

Obviously, it depends where you live. As you might have guessed, my cynicism stems from being stung by central London for several years. Any tenderness I once felt towards the build-up to Christmas in the capital has been beaten out of me, along with the lingering hope that shopping for gifts is an enjoyable experience for all. You lose that when you've seen men skulking miserably in the lingerie department of John Lewis, pained expressions on their faces, as if it was them who were going to have to wear the pencil-thin lacy thongs they've got their eye on.

The last time I braved it, several years ago, darting from Portobello Market to Regent Street, I absentmindedly left all my bags on the Tube on the way home. What happened to the set of twirly pasta forks, bath smellies and other goodies, I have no idea. I overcame my loss surprisingly quickly. Not being able to bring myself to repurchase everything, that year I made do with makeshift presents, homemade affairs like chutney and lemon curd, and items from my present drawer, wrapped up extra prettily to disguise their humble contents.

No one seemed to mind. On Christmas Day, I studied my family's faces for signs of disappointment. Nothing. Except, what was that? A flash of relief? A sign that a meagre present can come as a relief to someone who is worried about their own offerings not measuring up? That's when I realized that the cliché about it being the thought that counts is probably true. Since then, I have nurtured my own tiny rebellion against present buying. I still buy gifts but I see them more as tokens. There has been a shift in my attitude.

I have also begun to appreciate the emotional minefield that is gift-giving. Members of my family have been known to burst into tears at the end of Christmas Day, not because the most thrilling holiday of the year, the annual extravaganza of gifts, food and booze, has reached its conclusion, or because they are disappointed with their booty, now laid out on the bedroom floor, but because they sense that their own offerings have been substandard. Because they have received nicer gifts than they have given. This is the trauma of the failed gift-giver. Naturally, it is all in their mind, no one really thinks this, but it causes distress nonetheless. For them, it's as if the whole thing is a competition, or, worse still, an exam, and your relatives are going to give you grades on Boxing Day for gift quality and effort.

To get away from all this – as well as to save some pennies and cut down on unwanted stuff clogging up our homes – we have tried several times to 'not do' presents. The trouble is getting everyone to stick to it. My sister and mother are liable to whip out 'just a little something' gifts, which then make everyone else who has obediently stuck to the rules feel terrible. It's very hard convincing someone that you honestly, really, promise, don't want anything.

Emboldened by my makeshift gifts – the year that the Tube line swallowed the rest – the following year I boycotted the shops again, but this time I turned to a few of my favourite online stores, selling ethical gifts and those made from recycled materials (see page 377 for list). It seemed a good opportunity to support the shops whose principles I admire. It also fits with my ethos that you shouldn't have to give up the fun bits of Christmas, but instead adapt them to reflect ethical considerations.

The thought of receiving an ethical gift might once have been met with the grim resignation reserved for Brussels sprouts, but times have changed. Over the past decade, offerings have become more abundant, more glittering and less predictable. The Give-a-Goat phenomenon has seized imaginations with its option of giving money to charity – nominally for an animal or useful medical supply, although in most cases the money is spent where it is most needed. It has become a popular alternative. Name your charity and it will have its ethical gift guide.

I don't have a bad word to say about this. The only reason I don't give goats myself is because I like something to wrap, something to physically give, other than a card that says where the money will go; and because I think it's fairer to ask to be given a goat yourself than inflict one on someone who might have been longing to receive an MP3 player.

Anyway, that year, the one of the ethical gifts, I ended up wrapping a range of peculiar items on Christmas Eve: Fairtrade mittens, reclaimed fabric cushions and photo frames made from recycled cardboard and plastic. Again, the following day, no difference in the 'just what I wanted' and 'really, you shouldn't have' noises made by my nearest and dearest. I concluded it must be one of two things: either I'm lucky enough to have relatives who grin wildly and heap praise on anything I decide to wrap, or they are relieved to have received a modest gift, nothing too hideous or difficult to transport, with an interesting story behind it.

The elephant-dung notepads were an instant hit. In the excitement of reading about how the dung is dried to turn it into paper, and other manufacturing information, everyone forgot that they had received something as mundane as a notepad. And that goes for all presents made from recycled materials: there is an element of gimmickry – 'What! This is made from that!' – which is always popular.

Had I the good fortune to live close to a small market town, instead of in a sprawling capital city, it might have been a different story these past few years. I might never have sought refuge in ethical catalogues and recycled products. There's no doubt about it: weekend markets across the country, where local goods and crafts are sold, provide fertile and ethically robust shopping ground.

Last year, I spent an afternoon at the Saturday market in Cambridge,  sampling British cheeses and hot-spiced ginger cordial, an ideal companion for whisky, or so I was told as I bundled a couple of bottles into my rucksack. There was entertainment – jugglers in Father Christmas outfits followed by carol singers; the crowds were bearable, and with the stalls packed together all in the market square, I picked up several gifts without having to walk for miles and still had time for a cup of tea and a mince pie at the end of it all.

Most of my haul, I realized back home, were things I could

have made myself: jars of preserves and boxes of fudge. But there is only a certain amount of Christmas creativity you should allow yourself. Go overboard, start thinking you should make your own crackers and show off a talent for fussy table decorations, and you'll pave the way for your own miserable Christmas, spent wondering why the crackers didn't go bang and no one appreciated the holly-decked candles. Relaxing in front of the fire (with the heating turned down) and watching your favourite films should take priority. Unless, of course, you are über-talented and can do both at the same time.

Avoiding overpackaged items and trips to the shops by producing homemade gifts is all very well, but it's not worth sacrificing sanity in the process. Truth is, I always intend to do more, pulling out magazine cuttings that explain how to make chocolate truffles and glittery snowflakes for the tree. I love the idea of being homespun, digging out my hoarded scraps of wrapping paper, ribbons, glitter and buttons and piling it all on to the kitchen table.

But when it comes to what I can be bothered to make – homemade Christmas cards? A nativity scene made from scraps of fabric with a baby Jesus made from buttons? – anything more than a few oranges studded with cloves and wrapped up in ribbon to make the house smell nice and some gift tags made from last year's cards is unlikely. What is more probable is that I'll pour myself another glass of mulled wine and relish the whole Christmassyness of the scene, deeming this to be more important than being productive.

The good news is that you can contribute homemade touches without coming over all domestic-goddess about it. While I am distinctly uncomfortable in my capacity as an arranger of elegant displays of seasonal greenery, there is nothing I like more than hauling vast clumps of holly and mistletoe into the house and hoisting them up on the ceiling. On a frosty morning, with the hedgerows glittering in the low winter sun, snipping at them, along with other rogue bits of evergreen, is one of the nicest tasks imaginable.

The same applies to gifts. You don't have to slave over the fudge or truffles yourself. You can buy someone else's and find an old glass jar to fill, wrapping the whole thing in ribbon. Shortcuts are crucial if you take the creative route.

For this year's presents, I'm not sure what my long-suffering relatives have in store. One idea I've had is to visit an official Christmas Fayre, a seasonal market. There are many that take place in towns around the country, presumably different from a 'fair' because of the ye olde world vibe and traditional slant on gift-giving, which would suit chutney-givers like me down to the ground.

It's a good excuse for a day-trip anyway. Hop on the train, escape the London crowds. I could take in a city like Canterbury, or a town like Ludlow I've never visited. But rustic goodies only get you so far. To supplement them, I'll no doubt be browsing *www.recycledproducts.com* looking for quirky and innovative items that use ingenious waste materials to amuse the relatives on Christmas Day.

Gervase is the only one whose present escapes eco-spin. In a bid to make it up to him, to show I'm not all bad, as the curtain falls on another year of him suffering my peculiar brand of eco-fascism, I do my utmost to give him a decent present, something he really wants – regardless of whether it's made of recycled materials. We go our separate ways on Christmas Day, him to his parents, me to mine – which is handy, as the rest of my family won't witness this aberration. If they did, I wouldn't hear the end of it.

Perhaps when we are older, or married, or proper grown-ups, we'll spend Christmas together. But I'd probably miss the drama of a Christmas spent alongside different generations, with scrappy decorations and arguments over whether it's acceptable to brush up on the Trivial Pursuit questions before a game. It would be a shame to send my increasingly bizarre array of gifts by mail, not to heap them under the tree on Christmas Eve.

Worse still, not to be able to study the expressions of family members the following day when they open this year's bags of worm compost or recycled hemp underwear. And no, before you mention it, I would not consider doing this via webcam.

WHAT'S IN IT FOR THE PLANET?

Shop carefully because . . . by taking a plastic bag to the shops, you can reduce the amount of plastic waste generated at this time of year. Plus, by giving a 'to do' present such as theatre tickets, or homemade items and carefully chosen ethical gifts, this won't fill your home with plastic packaging – according to Friends of the Earth, about 125,000 tonnes of the stuff is thrown away every Christmas.

Recycle because . . . we create 3 million tonnes of waste every Christmas in the UK (according to *www.wasteonline.org.uk*), so if there is one time of year when it pays to be vigilant about reducing, reusing and recycling, it is now. To give you an idea, 20 to 30 per cent more glass and cans are collected over the festive period. Don't forget to recycle your tree, too. More than 7 million trees are sold in the UK every year, but only 10 per cent are recycled. The rest create unnecessary waste in landfill sites.

Choose local food . . . to avoid totting up unnecessary food miles. The Environment Agency says that a typical Christmas dinner made from imported ingredients travels more than 24,000 miles – that's once round the globe. A similar dinner made from UK farmers' market produce travels a mere 376 miles.

Be energy aware ... because it is when you are home all day that it is tempting to crank up the heating, leave the TV on and light up the whole house like your Christmas tree. Speaking of which, fairy lights might not be the patio heaters of the festive season but a typical string will produce 1.44kg of carbon dioxide (if left on for ten hours a day), which is roughly the same as two dishwasher cycles, according to the Energy Saving Trust.

The other thing about Christmas is that it is always going to be a touch chilly. You're not supposed to be swanning around the home in a T-shirt. You're supposed to be snuggling down in the living room with a rug on your lap and taking a hot-water bottle to bed.

Green Up Your Style on the Slopes

How to be a responsible skier

Can I mention one thing before we start? I'm being kind. Because it's cold and dark and you have to take your pleasures where you can in December, I'm not ruling out skiing altogether. I'm not pointing to figures that show alpine areas are now receiving 20 per cent less snow and that within fifty years all ski resorts below 1,200 metres will go out of business. Nor am I directing you to a miserable dry ski slope or demanding that you cancel your flight to Grenoble. Tougher eco-types would have none of it. They would say that jumping on a plane to get to an overcrowded mountaintop that has been levelled out by industrial machines and where energy-gobbling ski-lifts trundle up and down is not exactly a responsible winter activity.

Instead, I gently put it to you that you consider adapting your holiday. Think of future generations who might also like to sample the sport and do your best to preserve the world's snowy wonderlands.

- **Ask about an eco-policy.** At every stage of the booking process, ask about the environmental impact of skiing and if your hotel/chalet/ski school is doing anything about it.

- **Go by train.** By far the most relaxing way to start the holiday, and Eurostar has special ski-trains (*www.eurostar.com/ski*).

- **Find a green resort.** Try *www.skiclub.co.uk/skiclub/resorts/ greenresorts*, where you can find out which ones recycle, use renewable energy and have a green building policy.

- **Avoid skiing in places that rely on artificial snow.** It damages vegetation and decreases bio-diversity levels. You might not care much for small mountain shrubs, but if you've ever spent spring or summer near the mountains when they're in bloom, you'll realize how important it is to preserve them.

- **Try a different winter sport.** When you get there, instead of plain old skiing – so last century – why not give snow-shoeing or cross-country skiing a whirl, neither of which need maintained pistes or lifts.

- **Look out for sustainable accommodation.** Whitepod, a high-tech eco-camp in the Swiss Alps, leads the way with its dome-shaped, low-impact tents, designed to blend into the mountain environment. Inside, guests stay toasty with sheepskin throws and wood-burning stoves. Fingers crossed the resort's popularity will encourage others to follow in its snowy footprints.

To Tree or Not to Tree

No tree, no Christmas. It's as simple as that. I shan't be bullied by anyone into making do with a cardboard version, or dressing up a pot plant, another miserable alternative offered by eco-obsessives.

Proper versus plastic

The only thing on the side of plastic trees is that you can reuse them every year. Even so, I don't believe they will last a lifetime. Give one a couple of years before it's chewed by the dog or replaced by a superior model and bundled into the attic. I'm also suspicious of what gives its fake pine needles that glossy sheen and splattering of fake snow. When the British Christmas Tree Growers' Association carried out analysis on a number of artificial trees, it found PVC and twisted metal were the main players, both of which are unrecyclable. Obviously the BCTGA has plenty to gain from turning us against fake trees, but the point that they will sit in landfill sites for many yuletides to come is worth making. If you ask me, a real tree wins hands down. My vote goes for the smell of pine needles over PVC. Find a British-grown tree with its own roots so you can plant it out in the New Year (*www.christmastree.org.uk*).

Decorations

Not everyone is happy with the ancient, usually broken, family heirlooms that are dusted off every year. To update your stock, limit yourself to ethically made and Fairtrade decorations, of which there are many, sold by companies such as the Natural Collection and Traidcraft. Some people bake biscuits and then, while they are still soft, stab holes in the top with a skewer so ribbon can be threaded through them and they can be hung on branches. Sounds delightful, unless you have pets that prowl around the tree. For me, I rather suspect this falls into the 'making crackers' category of Christmas creativity – in other words, lovely idea, not a hope in hell of me doing it. Reviving paper-chain making with old wrapping paper and finding bits of ribbon to tie around branches, on the other hand, now there's a thought.

Twinkle twinkle

If Christmas isn't complete without a tree, then a tree isn't complete without a string of fairy lights draped around its branches. Ninety per cent of households, according to the Energy Saving Trust, leave their tree lights on 24 hours a day. While I understand this is magical for people like me who take midnight strolls and peep in at twinkly trees, it isn't strictly necessary. Much better to put them on only in the evening when you can see them properly and turn them off at night, or put them on an automatic timer so they flick off when there's no one awake to appreciate them. Even better, when your old lights pack up, invest in some LED ones. Their efficient beams use a quarter of the energy of normal ones and last longer.

Aftercare

With a real tree, the best thing you can do is plant it in the garden afterwards – and don't forget to water it, especially during the summer months. There it will obediently carry on absorbing carbon dioxide. If you don't have a garden for replanting, offer the tree to a friend. Or, as a last resort, your local authority can make woodchips and firewood from it. Trees are classed as garden waste by most councils. They should either collect from your door or arrange a local collection point (check on *recyclenow.com*).

Try it in December . . .

Light Greenies
Eat at a green restaurant

Celebrating Christmas revolves an awful lot around the kitchen. It is here that mince pies emerge from the oven, brandy-spiked mulled wine simmers on the hob and endless family dramas unfold, like rolls of marzipan for the Christmas cake. It's a wonderful thing, this intense culinary activity, but sometimes it's a bit relentless. Especially if you're the one running the show. With something constantly needing to be chopped, stirred, cleared away or eaten, it is a good idea to escape, at some point, to eat somewhere else, where someone else does the washing up. And what better opportunity to try out a green restaurant, one of the growing number of eateries that reflect our efforts to care for the planet. Find somewhere dedicated to composting, recycling and local sourcing. To do this, you'll need to ask around, look on the internet or check out the restaurants listed by the Green Tourism Business Scheme (*www.green-business.co.uk*).

Leading the pack is a dockside-eating complex in Bristol, Bordeaux Quay. Everything in the restaurant, brasserie, bakery and cookery school is sourced from within 50 miles to cut transport costs. A vast skylight reduces the need for lighting and a solar water-heating system sits on the roof alongside a rain-water harvester gathering water to flush the loos. Other green touches include eco-friendly cleaning products and a delivery van that runs on biodiesel. In London, there are also rich pickings: the first Soil Association-certified organic pub, The Duke of Cambridge; Acorn House, a restaurant with a wormery and herbs growing on the roof, and Oliver Rowe's restaurant Konstam, in King's Cross, where ingredients are sourced from within the M25, among others. Any restaurant that has its own veg garden or allotment – such as Due South, in Brighton, and Raymond Blanc's acclaimed Le Manoir Aux Quat' Saisons – is worth visiting. And for somewhere that has taken the link between growing food and serving it a step further, try the Field Kitchen at Riverford Farm, in Devon (HQ of the organic box scheme). Here guests are packed off on an obligatory tour of the farm before they are allowed to eat dishes made from what's out in the fields. It's a clever concept, not least because after working up an appetite on a two-mile farm tour, what you eat invariably tastes delicious.

Dark Greenies

Indulge in some geek chic

Over the past few years, the green movement has been in the throes of a sneaky shift of allegiance. Once suspicious of technology – blaming it for simply creating more waste and requiring more energy to power soon-to-be obsolete gizmos – it associated itself with all things natural, traditional and slow. More recently, it has recognized the environmental benefits of being technologically savvy. Not in all its forms, but when it comes to renewable energy in miniature form – in other words, wind-up and solar-powered gadgets. For this, we have a geek revival to thank. It might not be techno-geeks who are living sustainable lives in the woods, but it is their research that has enabled wood-dwellers to create their own energy.

Another case in point is the clutter-free life of those who embrace technology, who have learnt how to download, upload and subsequently unload while the rest of us were still learning to Google. There's no need for shelves groaning with soon-to-be-discarded CDs if you've mastered the first two. The fruits of this green geek crossover come in handy as gifts at Christmas, especially for gadget-lovers and hard-to-please men. There are watches, torches, radios and bike lights powered by solar energy and wind-up technology. Much of it you can see on *www.treehugger.com,* a website that helpfully plucks out what is cool and eye-catching in green-geek world and tells us about it. The good thing about these green gadgets is they are as much about showing off as obeying the eco-agenda.

Eco-Cheats

• Don't chuck your old cosmetic bottles: they can be used again to store travel-sized amounts of shampoo and face cream. I fill spray bottles with soapy water to douse on plants susceptible to greenfly and with plain water to keep the leaves of indoor houseplants moist.

• An easy way to make your own candles is by melting the remains of old ones in an empty tin can, placed in a saucepan of simmering water. Then pour the wax into a jam jar – it might be a murky colour if you've mixed different candles, so it might be better to heat them separately so you can make stripes by letting one layer harden before adding another. You'll need to buy wicks from a craft shop or candle-making supplier. A word of warning: don't let the wax get too hot, as, like chip fat, it is flammable.

• If you're sending gifts in the mail, make your own protective packaging by shredding unwanted post and other paper waste – with the kitchen scissors if you don't have a proper shredder. Scrunched-up balls of paper protect equally well, although you might not want to use your old letters for this, unless you are happy to reveal your secrets.

Giving Cards

To reduce paper waste, some people are happy to send E-cards via email; others appreciate the excuse not to bother at all, muttering 'I'm saving trees', and the rest of us find ways to justify the tradition, preferring seasonal greetings that plop on to our doormats than ping into an inbox. Anyway, it is Christmas. Time to relax the rules a bit, loosen your belt and indulge in a seasonal sin or two.

Here's why it's OK to send cards:

• **It provides an opportunity to support a charity.** The Charity Advisory Trust suggests boycotting any card that gives less than 10p out of every £1 to charity (see *www.charitiesadvisorytrust.org.uk* for a report on who gives what).

• **You can buy them directly from a charity.** By doing this, you bypass the middleman altogether.

• **You can buy cards printed on recycled paper.** If we all did this, it would improve demand for recycled paper and increase the value of what is collected from our recycling bins.

• **You can recycle them afterwards.** Either by reusing them to make gift tags for next year's presents or by finding your nearest card recycling bank – often in supermarkets, but check with your council. You can reuse old envelopes or even send Christmas postcards should you still feel guilty about paper waste.

- **You don't need to send a card to everyone.** It sounds a bit mercenary but my policy is to choose people who will appreciate one. Relatives, older folk and friends who live far away. I know, for instance, that my 97-year-old granny takes enormous pleasure in counting how many cards are on her mantelpiece each year. For that reason, how could I neglect my duties?

Wrapping Presents

If anything is pushed on us at this time of year, it is shiny batons of wrapping paper, shrink-wrapped and waving everywhere you look in shops. Why? Because if they weren't, we might come to our senses and realize what a waste of money and materials they are. The fact is you can use anything to wrap presents, and it doesn't necessarily look shoddy. Glossy pages from magazines, brown paper for an old-fashioned look or even bits of old fabric. My materials of choice are the free posters given out in newspapers. They are the best thing that ever happened to my wrapping-paper supplies: bright, cheery and made from good quality paper, perfect for the job.

Here's how to be a green wrapper

Avoid Sellotape if you can. It makes wrapping paper unrecyclable. Put it in the green bin and paper mills will not thank you as it has to be filtered out.

Reuse any metallic or glittery paper. Like Sellotape, this can't be recycled. Instead, designate somewhere in the house, a drawer or part of a cupboard, where you can store it for next year – call it vintage if it makes you feel better.

Be creative. Demonstrate artistic prowess by using silver spray stencils, ribbons and anything else to jazz up newspaper or other plain alternatives to shop-bought wrapping paper.

Keep an eye out for paper that donates money to charity. This is a good option for purists who hate using second-hand wrapping paper and like their presents to look slick. For the last few years, John Lewis has offered designer paper that gives 25 per cent of each roll to a charity.

Presents

It is often assumed that either you give lavish gifts and are eagerly invited back next year, or you take an ethical, more commonly known as worthy, route, offering something oatmeal in colour and forgotten by the time thank-you letters are written. Well, here's some news. Things have changed. There are vast numbers of ethical gifts – and alternative approaches to present-giving – that will have a reduced impact on the environment.

Choose from the following:

'To do' presents

As well as dispensing with packaging and wrapping paper, this sort of gift offers an experience rather than cluttering a home. It could be

theatre tickets, gallery membership, a meal out or a spa weekend –
or, more affordably, a single treatment, such as a pedicure followed
by a cocktail. Or maybe just the cocktail.

What I like best about these presents is the giver gets to go along
too, a cunning way of giving and receiving simultaneously. And
having something fun to plan in the New Year is a sensible way of
brightening the less fun half of winter.

What to do: Write down the details in a card, or create an elaborate
homemade gift voucher if you are that way inclined. And whatever
you do, make sure you carry through. Ideally, book the tickets or
event before you give the card, or promptly afterwards when you've
found a suitable date. Don't leave it for months. There's nothing
worse than being offered a fantastic evening out only to hear
nothing about it again.

Homemade presents

By now, you'll know what I think about ambitious plans to crochet
cardigans and sweat over saucepans of jam days before Christmas.
That doesn't mean I won't turn my hand to some of the more simple
creations that can double up as gifts. I reckon you could put almost
any festive food – fruitcake, mince pies, gingerbread biscuits,
chocolate-coated brazil nuts – in a pretty box or large jam jar,
decorate it with ribbon and make someone very happy.

A couple of ideas: It depends how far in advance you want to make
the gift. Months before, you could cook some Christmas chutney,
flavoured with cloves and cinnamon and chillies. If you want it to be
ready to eat in December, you'll need to have it in jars by the end of
September – this gives it enough time to soften and lose its vinegary kick.

Since I've had a wormery, I've been longing to give out small ziplock bags full of rich compost, along with a couple of bulbs and a decorated flowerpot.

For a last-minute gift, you could make some lemon curd. As Delia Smith, my trusted friend in the kitchen, says, it's so simple to make a child could do it, and it is delicious on toast, scones or even dolloped inside the lid of a mince pie. I follow her recipe and add two eggs and the juice and grated rind of a lemon to a bowl of 3oz (75g) of sugar, then drop 2oz (50g) of butter in small pieces on top and place the bowl over a simmering pan of water. For the next 20 minutes expect to be loosely tied to the hob as you have to stir regularly waiting for it to thicken. These quantities make enough for two small jars.

My friend Sophie won last year's prize for the simplest and most inventive edible gift, arriving for lunch with a box of tiny Christmas puddings made out of marzipan. Inspired by the Portuguese obsession with fruit-shaped marzipan sweets – and a particular chap called Pablo, I gather – she came up with the idea herself. You make small balls out of marzipan (buy it in block form) and leave them to soak in a bowl of brandy for a minute (don't leave them for too long or they'll start to dissolve). Dipping them in melted chocolate is the trickiest bit. Sophie says you'll need two teaspoons for the job and a swig of brandy to steady your hand. Then fashion small leaf-life lumps and balls out of the marzipan, dye them red and green with food dye and fix them on to the top of the balls so that they resemble holly and berries, vaguely. Put the balls in the fridge and turn back to that marzipan-infused bowl of brandy. It would be an eco-sin to waste it.

Online Shops

Buying online saves time and it also prevents those sneaky trips to the shops when you go in with one or two things in mind and come out laden with goodies. So, without further ado, I present my top ten ethical online gift shops.

- *www.ecotopia.co.uk*: good for gadget lovers, there are solar chargers for iPods and mobiles, eco-kettles and wind-up radios and bike lights.

- *www.biomelifestyle.com*: champagne flutes made from recycled glass are one of its top sellers, along with lots of bamboo products for the home and handmade teddy bears made of unwanted clothes from charity shops.

- *www.ecocentric.co.uk*: co-founded by eco-designer Oliver Heath, you'll find LED crystal fairy lights, cushions that were once seatbelts and lots of light shades.

- *www.peopletree.co.uk*: deeply ethical clothes, many of which are certified Fairtrade and organic, along with a range of jute bags for collecting newspapers, plastic bags and other recyclables.

- *www.goodnessdirect.co.uk*: assemble a Fairtrade hamper for a friend, choosing treats such as cashew butter and organic champagne truffles.

- *www.greenpeople.co.uk*: popular for its eco-make-up. Organic lipstick made from earth minerals and other chemical-free cosmetics.

- *www.adili.com*: showcases the most stylish ethical clothing out there.

- *www.escortoys.com*: for little 'uns below the age of eight, wooden toys made from FSC (Forest Stewardship Council) certified wood.

- *www.divinechocolate.com*: the best place for Fairtrade chocolate advent calendars and stocking goodies, such as chocolate money.

- *www.naturalcollection.com*: old-timer in the world of ethical gifts, this nine-year-old company covers all areas of green living, from recycled aluminium foil to tree decorations.

Etiquette when Giving a Goat

Adding to the global goat population is a popular way of doing your bit, but it is not for everyone. And it's not just goats. Now there are fast-breeding supergoats, along with cows, camels, ducks and sheep. In 2006 Oxfam Unwrapped kept ahead of the game by introducing extra-virile rams to boost sheep numbers across the globe. Before you invest your money in livestock, you might want to consider the following.

Find out where the money is going. It doesn't necessarily buy the animal you choose. Buy a goat, calf, donkey or camel and your gift could also be used to fund the livestock most appropriate to the individual community, depending on circumstances and local environment.

Make sure you wouldn't prefer to make a simple donation to charity. Once you know that your goat could end up being a pig, the concept might not appeal. However, in its defence, goat-giving is a refreshing change from reaching for the chequebook. It might essentially be another vehicle for giving, but it's a light-hearted way to do it and to get others involved.

Test the water first. If you know your brother is longing for a proper present, a share in a mango plantation will evidently disappoint. As my friend's father said after she had painstakingly explained how the Good Gift catalogue works: 'But what do I actually get for Christmas then?' To avoid tears under the tree, you could supplement your charitable gift with a conventional one; even if it's just a little something.

Volunteer yourself. If you think these kinds of charity donations are a smashing idea guaranteed to leave the recipient with a feel-good glow, suggest that your friends give one to you. This seems fairer than taking away someone else's right to a box of smellies.

Save it for anti-Christmas types. The charitable donation approach is perfect for tricky customers. The ones who complain about the loathsome chocs-and-socks routine and plead every year not to be given anything. Perhaps they mean it: here is your chance to find out.

Where from: *www.oxfamunwrapped.com*; *www.farmafrica.org.uk*;
www.goodgifts.org; *www.sendacow.org.uk*; *www.presentaid.org*.

Christmas Dinner

A year's worth of eating is a lot of meals. Especially if, like me, you
are as likely to skip one as you are to say no to a mug of hot
chocolate on a cold winter's day. But of all my 365 dinners, there is
one that will always stand out. Christmas dinner with all the
trimmings is the centrepiece of festivities. Being a meal that requires
planning and preparation, and which is likely to feature a fowl of
some sort, it is important to consider the eco-dimension, as well as
how your belt can be adjusted to cope.

Fowl play

Whatever fowl ends up at the triumphant heart of your feast should
have the opportunity to frolic, in free-range fashion, before it
pleasures your digestive system. Try *www.farmer.org.uk* to find
farmers' markets and farm shops where a meat supplier can order
one for you.

Turkey trouble

As the old joke goes, it's turkeys who get least out of Christmas.
And they don't exactly have a ball beforehand either. Like intensively

farmed chickens, non-free-range turkeys will have been cooped up in sheds, where they suffer indignities such as having their beaks trimmed (to stop them pecking each other) and coping with breast blisters from the crowded environment and bad sanitation – you may be able to see these blisters under the wings of a poor quality turkey in a shop. Since you don't want to ruin the Meal of the Year with a miserable-looking animal, make sure you give yourself enough time to find a local, free-range turkey farmer.

Cooking your goose

Under the direction of Hugh Fearnley-Whittingstall, who professes to favour goose over turkey, many people now plump for this slimmer, more elegant bird. It has become the chic choice. One advantage is the rich pools of fat it creates while cooking. Potatoes can be roasted in it and frugal cooks can save it up in jam jars to eke out its flavour for future meals. We failed miserably to eke anything much at all from our goose when we abandoned turkey one year. Instead we managed to roast the living daylights out of the thing and it was as dry as a ship's biscuit. Turns out we had taken the free-range thing too far, sourcing a wild goose that had flown around too much. It wasn't that we had cooked it for too long, we assured my mother, more that it was a tough old bird from the start.

Geese have the advantage of being the toughies of the bird world. Not docile enough to be intensively reared, like, say, ducks or turkeys, they demand a free-range lifestyle. So it's easier to lay your hands on a right-on retailer than you might think.

Sprouts and other vegetables

Seasonal greens are the order of the day. Forget mangetout and beans, it's the season for cabbage, sprouts and root veg. These get along famously with a roast bird, although not everyone is a fan of tender flesh soaked in gravy. There is always some poor vegetarian, promising not to mind, who gets stuck with a nut roast or an extra portion of sprouts, or else ends up exceedingly drunk having been unable to indulge in all the meaty nibbles – sausages wrapped up in bacon and devils-on-horseback – that everyone else has lined their stomach with while the turkey takes its time in the oven. Since it's the season of goodwill, I recommend taking advantage of the winter root vegetables available and laying on something special for veggies. Parsnips, carrots, sweet potatoes, even lesser known – and liked – varieties of suede and turnip, once roasted with a dousing of olive oil and balsamic vinegar and a generous sprinkle of salt, become sweet, crispy and delicious. Roast for 40 minutes and then add a layer of halloumi before returning to the oven for 5 minutes or so. Once on the table, you'll have to watch out that the drunken meat-eaters don't dig in first. (This also makes a nourishing, light supper, served with couscous or baguette, in the days following Christmas when you might be grateful for a meat-free meal.)

Leftovers

Don't think you can get away with roasted vegetables every night. There's the rest of the bird to think about. You might barely be able to look at it right now, but a few months down the line, you'll be ready to face a stew or curry from the freezer.

Here are a few ideas:

Turkey salad Not one for the freezer, but you should be able to stomach this lighter way of eating turkey quite quickly after the excess of Christmas Day. It's all about throwing together chunks of turkey with strips of cucumber and spring onions, salad leaves, tomatoes and coriander; then adding a dressing of lime juice, soy sauce and black pepper. Round off the meal with a tangerine, from your interminable supply – not likely to be grown in the UK, I know, but essential nevertheless.

Christmas dinner pie Here's a way of using abandoned veggies, old mashed potatoes and whatever meat you have left on the roasting tray. Shake some flour over small chunks of meat to thicken the sauce, add the veggies and a little stock – made from the carcass obviously – and fill a lasagne dish with it. It's up to you whether you want to top it with mash and grated cheese, or layer some pastry over the top. Bake in the oven for 45 minutes. If you decide on pastry, you can mash together the potato with leftover sprouts and heat it up in the oven (with a splash of milk to stop it drying out) for a bubble-squeak side dish.

Curry Make a paste with tomato purée and spices such as garam masala, turmeric, chilli powder and grated ginger. Fry some onions and garlic, add the paste, then the chunks of leftover meat and any veggies knocking around and some stock. Good for the freezer. Bring it out in a few months' time when it's not so obvious that it's leftovers.

There's nothing like baking homemade mince pies for making you feel as though you've conquered Christmas. It's under control, your home is smelling sweetly of spices and a smudge of flour is artfully adorning your face – or, if you're like me, you're more likely to have lumps of pastry attached to your ponytail. One problem with this vision of domestic bliss is that pastry-making is a bit of a bore. As for complicated recipes to make your own mincemeat, it's enough to drive anyone straight to the shops for a dozen of the deep-filled, overpackaged variety. Instead, I cheat. Twice. I make **Double-cheat Mince Pies** by using a ready-made roll of pastry and a jar of shop-bought mincemeat. Double-cheating doesn't stop you from customizing them, sprinkling ground almonds on to the rolled-out pastry and adding extra dried fruit to the mincemeat. As well as adding to the illusion that you have slaved over your Christmas duties, this also makes the materials go further. My mother would never start a jar without first padding it out with extra raisins, finely chopped apple and a couple of slugs of brandy. One for the mincemeat, one for the chef.

To accompany the pies, what about a saucepan of **Hot-spiced Devon Cider**? Of course, the cider doesn't have to be from Devon, although it helps with your halo if it's as local as possible, and definitely British. Here's what to do: heat up 1 litre of cider with a can of dark ale (yes, yes, British too), a couple of cinnamon sticks, some cloves and perhaps a bit of nutmeg if you have any, plus a tablespoon of dark brown sugar, half a sliced lemon and some chunks of apple. Simmer very gently for about 20 minutes to let the flavours infuse – don't let it boil, though. Anyone who says they prefer mulled wine can be punished with a detailed explanation of food miles and the importance of supporting British breweries.

Sources and Green Directory

Each chapter is divided into two resource sections. The first consists of the sources that provided some of the information I have used. The second is simply a stash of websites and information that have helped me over the years in my efforts to live a greener life. By no means would I wish to suggest it is comprehensive.

JANUARY

Sources and further reading

Local Government Association figures www.lga.gov.uk

Waste and Resources Action Programme www.wrap.org.uk

'Clothes line', Michael Durham, *Guardian*, Society, 25 February 2004

'The secrets of used clothes', UN Chronicle Online Edition
www.un.org/Pubs/chronicle/2006/issue3/0306p33.htm

'The great charity shop con', Sophie Parkin, *Daily Mail*, Femail, 22 May 2006

BBC *Real Story* about overseas dumping of recycled waste, aired
5 December 2005

For more info about the Materials Recycling Facility in Greenwich, see
www.greenwich.gov.uk/Greenwich/YourEnvironment/RubbishRecycling/RecyclingIn
Greenwich/TheRecyclingProcess/MRF.htm

Friends of the Earth
www.foe.co.uk/pubsinfo/briefings/html/20011220155157.html

Wasteonline www.wasteonline.org.uk/resources/InformationSheets/Plastics.htm

Other useful information

Swap shops and exchange networks
www.freecycle.org, www.gumtree.com, www.letslinkuk.org, www.swapshop.co.uk

The etiquette of online swapping
www.freecycle.org/faq/faq/faq_guidelines

DVDs, CDs, cassettes and VHS – how to recycle them
www.thelaundry.biz, www.london-recycling.co.uk, www.polymerrecycling.co.uk,
www.therecyclingpeople.co.uk

TVs
www.icer.org.uk (Industry Council for Electronic Equipment Recycling – it has a list
of companies that will recycle all types of electrical and electronic equipment);
www.restructa.co.uk

A word on electrical and electronic stuff
A new set of European rules, known as the WEEE (Waste Electrical and Electronic
Equipment) Directive, has made those who make and sell all kinds of such goods,
from low-energy light bulbs to printers, responsible for recycling them. Check with
the manufacturer and the retailer; they might take back your waste electronic equipment, or be able to point you towards your nearest recycling centre

Broken appliances and white goods
www.recyclenow.com to find your nearest recycling centre for electrical goods
www.icer.org.uk has a list of companies that deal in used electronic items
www.environment-agency.gov.uk/weee has info about the WEEE Directive

Mobiles

www.actionaidrecycling.org.uk
www.oxfam.org.uk/get_involved/recycle/bringbring.html
Many mobile phone companies now run in-store recycling programmes –
check with yours

Computers

www.free-computers.org
www.computeraid.org
www.digital-links.org

Eco-auditors

www.3acorns.co.uk
www.carboncoach.com
www.beyond-green.co.uk
www.ecoauditor.co.uk

FEBRUARY

Sources and further reading

Wardrobe refashion blog www.nikkishell.typepad.com/wardroberefashion

The Compact http://sfcompact.blogspot.com

Adbusters' Buy Nothing Day www.adbusters.org/bnd

'Fashion victims', War on Want 2006 report:
www.waronwant.org/Fashion%20Victims%2014524.twl

'Let's clean up fashion', Labour Behind the Label 2006 report:
www.labourbehindthelabel.org/images/pdf/letscleanupfashion.pdf

World Health Organization (WHO), for figures on health problems related to
pesticides used by cotton farmers

The Energy Saving Trust on washing machines and how much you can pile into them; www.energysavingtrust.org.uk

The Low Carbon Diet, Polly Ghazi and Rachel Lewis, Short Books 2007

Other useful information

Ethical fashion shops
Howies www.howies.co.uk
Adili www.adili.com
Natural Collection www.naturalcollection.com
Kuyichi www.kuyichi.com
People Tree, www.peopletree.co.uk
Edun www.edunonline.com
Equa www.equaclothing.com
Tonic T-shirts www.tonictshirts.com
Seasalt of Cornwall www.seasaltcornwall.co.uk
American Apparel www.americanapparel.net
Frank and Faith www.frankandfaith.com
Traid www.traid.org.uk
Oxfam clothes www.oxfam.org.uk

Campaigning bodies
International Labour Organisation www.ilo.org
Labour Behind the Label www.labourbehindthelabel.org
Clean Clothes Campaign www.cleanclothes.org
Make Trade Fair www.maketradefair.com
War on Want www.waronwant.org

Clothes-swapping information
www.swishing.org
www.StyleWillSaveUs.com
www.hybird.co.uk

Call in a wardrobe therapist
www.kirajolliffe.co.uk
http://raejames-personalstylist.com

Read about it

Not Buying It: My Year Without Shopping, Judith Levine, Pocket Books 2007

MARCH

Sources and further reading

International Scientific Forum on Home Hygiene www.wwf.org.uk/chemicals

Friends of the Earth on home chemicals
www.foe.co.uk/resource/newsletters/safer_chemicals_update_4.pdf

Air fresheners research published by team from University of Bristol in Archives of Environmental Health, 19 October 2004, reported in *New Scientist* magazine

'Triclosan targets lipid synthesis', McMurry L.M., Oethinger M., Levy S.B., reported in scientific journal, *Nature* 394 (1998)

More research on Triclosan
www.beyondpesticides.org/pesticides/factsheets/Triclosan%20cited.pdf

'Chemical world: the definitive guide to your home and garden',
Lauren Steadman, *Guardian*, 22 May 2004
www.guardian.co.uk/chemicalworld/story/0,,1219558,00.html

Other useful information

Green cleaning products
Ecover www.ecover.com
Bio-D www.naturalcollection.com
Fresh and Green https://shop.wwf.org.uk
E-cloth (a general purpose cloth that absorbs dirt and grease and can be used without any cleaning products) www.e-cloth.com

Naturally Inspired stockists Marks & Spencer's
Method stockists John Lewis, www.methodhome.com

To find out where you can refill your Ecover bottles
www.ecover.com/gb/en/WhereToBuy

Useful online eco-shops selling cleaning supplies
www.goodnessdirect.co.uk
www.naturalcollection.com
www.summernaturals.co.uk

Eco-paints
Ecos Organic Paint www.ecospaints.com
Earthborn range by Oliver Heath, www.earthbornpaints.co.uk
Auro www.auro.co.uk

Recycle old paint
www.communityrepaint.org.uk

DIY/redecorating
The Green Building Store www.greenbuildingstore.co.uk

Buying good wood
www.foe.co.uk/campaigns/biodiversity/resource/good_wood_guide
http://environment.independent.co.uk/green_living/article2657753.ece

Greenpeace's garden furniture league table
www.greenpeace.org.uk/blog/forests/garden-furniture-guide

Forest Stewardship Council
www.fsc.org/en

APRIL

Sources and further reading

The Vegetarian Society www.vegsoc.org

Friends of the Earth www.foe.co.uk/resource/briefings/food_climate_change.pdf

Rowett Research Institute, Aberdeen; www.rowett.ac.uk

'Overview of Cruel Practices – luxury foods come at a high price for animal welfare', Compassion in World Farming
www.ciwf.org.uk/campaigns/other_campaigns/exotic_foods.html

'What is ethical veal?', BBC News 24, aired 21 January 2008

Bread, Eric Treuille and Ursula Ferrigno, DK Publishing 2004

Other useful information

Worm chat – vermiculture forums
www.lowimpact.org/topics_worms_and_vermiculture.htm
http://compostcompulsion.tribe.net

My worm hotline
www.wigglywigglers.co.uk; 01981 500391

General composting info
www.recyclenow.com/home_composting
http://www.gardenorganic.org.uk

Read about it
Nose to Tail Eating: A Kind of British Cooking, Fergus Henderson, Bloomsbury 2004

Visit a nose-to-tail restaurant
www.stjohnrestaurant.co.uk

Green pet products
www.ecoutlet.co.uk/shop
www.worldsbestcatlitter.com
www.biobags.co.uk

MAY

Sources and further reading

Friends of the Earth on garden products banned because of pesticides
www.foe.co.uk/resource/press_releases/hundreds_of_pesticides_ban.html

Friends of the Earth on imported cut flowers
www.foe.co.uk/resource/briefing_notes/50_climate_top_tips.pdf

'Drained of life', John Vidal and Ochieng Ogodo, *Guardian*, 14 February 2007

Other useful information

Read about it
21st Century Smallholder, Paul Waddington, Eden Books 2006
Urban Eden, Adam and James Caplin, Kyle Cathie 2004
Bob Flowerdew's Organic Bible, Kyle Cathie 1998
Flower Confidential: the good, the bad and the beautiful in the business of flowers, Amy Stewart, Algonquin Books 2007

Learning to grow
www.rhs.org.uk/vegetables
www.gardeningpatch.com/vegetable
www.mytinyplot.co.uk
www.gardenorganic.org.uk
www.selfsufficientish.com

Learning about permaculture
www.permaculture.org.uk
www.naturwise.org.uk
www.spiralseed.co.uk

Allotments
www.nsalg.org.uk
www.allotment.org.uk
www.allotments-uk.com

Guerrilla gardening
www.guerrillagardening.org

Wwoofing
www.wwoof.org/wwoof_uk

Green flower suppliers
Wiggly Wigglers offers next-day delivery bouquets using what is available locally and seasonally, www.wigglywigglers.co.uk
Moyses flowers sells seasonal bouquets and focuses on the ethical side of floristry, www.moysesflowers.co.uk
A flower-growing co-operative of 40 families grows scented narcissi in the Scilly Isles, www.scentednarcissi.co.uk
Farmers' markets are a good place for local blooms, visit www.farmersmarket.net

JUNE

Sources and further reading

www.confetti.co.uk published research in February 2007 suggesting that UK weddings on average cost £18,490

'What is and what ain't fair trade', Jane MacQuitty, *The Times*, 24 February 2007

Cafod report, **'Counting the cost of gold'**, May 2006
www.anglogold.com/NR/rdonlyres/C23B6899-8CB3-485B-AFBB-
2B7B467370FB/0/CAFODUnearthJusticeExecutiveSummary.pdf

Other useful information

Meeting greens
Green Drinks www.greendrinks.org
CSR Chicks http://groups.yahoo.com/group/csr-chicks

Dating websites
Love is Green www.loveisgreen.org
Natural Friends www.natural-friends.com
Green Singles www.greensingles.com

Seducing greens
Soya wax candles and organic massage oil www.botanicals.co.uk
Organic bedding www.greenfibres.com
Solar-powered sex toys and natural lubricants
www.lovehoney.co.uk
www.sextoys.co.uk
www.organiclubricant.com
Fairtrade wooden spanking paddle www.coco-de-mer-shop.co.uk
Vegan condoms www.britishcondoms.com/vegan-approved-condoms

Marrying greens
Build your own website to help with travel details
www.theweddingtracker.co.uk
Choose a venue with experience of green weddings
www.penrhos.co.uk
www.hazelwoodhouse.com

Find your nearest Oxfam with a bridal section
www.oxfam.org.uk/shops/content/shopfinder.php

Wear a once-worn wedding dress
www.houseofcouture.co.uk
www.thedressmarket.net

Wear an ethically made wedding dress
www.enamore.co.uk
and shoes
www.beyondskin.co.uk

Choose non-chemical confetti
www.confettidirect.co.uk

Presents
Choose a charity list over presents, or do both
www.weddinglistgiving.com
www.oxfamunwrapped.com
www.goodgifts.org
or make up a present list of gifts made from recycled materials
www.recycledproducts.org

Honeymoon by train, or travel responsibly
www.seat61.com
www.responsibletravel.com

JULY

Sources and further reading

Greenpeace www.greenpeace.org.uk/tags/british-airways

'UK carbon emissions by source', Defra, published 2006
http://news.bbc.co.uk/2/hi/science/nature/6955009.stm

Intergovernmental Panel on Climate Change, Aviation and the Global Atmosphere www.grida.no/climate/ipcc/aviation/001.htm

'Africa – up in smoke?', second report of the Working Group on Climate Change and Development, New Economics Foundation, 2005

'Save the planet: cancel that flight now', Camilla Cavendish, *The Times*, 15 March 2007

'What is the real price of cheap air travel?', Tom Robbins, *Guardian*, 29 January 2006

Aviation Environment Federation
www.aef.org.uk/downloads/Howdoesairtravelcompare.doc

'IDB America', an article from the magazine of the inter-American development bank http://grupobid.org/idbamerica/index.cfm?thisid=3193

Statement from Friends of the Earth, Greenpeace and WWF about carbon offsetting www.foe.co.uk/resource/briefings/carbon_offsetting.pdf

Other useful information

Be persuaded to fly less here
The Art of Travel, Alain de Botton, Penguin 2003
www.cpre.org.uk/campaigns/transport/airport-expansion

Or not at all here
Heat: How to Stop the Planet Burning, George Monbiot, Allen Lane 2006
www.planestupid.com

About carbon offsetting
Tourism Industry Carbon Offset Service www.ticos.co.uk
climate care www.climatecare.org
carbon neutral company www.carbonneutral.com
green campaign statement about the value of carbon offsetting
www.foe.co.uk/resource/briefings/carbon_offsetting.pdf

Responsible tourism websites
www.responsibletravel.com
www.tourismconcern.org.uk
The Association of Independent Tour Operators has a good section
on tips for travellers: www.aito.co.uk

A handful of travel companies that have won responsible tourism awards
Tribes www.tribes.co.uk
Intrepid www.intrepidtravel.com
Geckos Adventures www.geckosadventures.com
Biosphere Expeditions www.biosphere-expeditions.org
Guerba www.guerba.com

Get inspired about camping
Cool Camping, Laura James, Harper Collins 2006
www.go-camping.org

AUGUST

Sources and further reading

The Dirt on Clean: An Unsanitized History, Katherine Ashenburg, Farrar Straus and Giroux 2007

'Working up a healthy lather', Liz Gill, *The Times*, 13 May 2006

Directgov www.direct.gov.uk/en/Environmentandgreenerliving/ Energyandwatersaving/DG_064370

'Water meters on the way', Valerie Elliott, *The Times*, 31 January 2007

'Hazardous chemicals in consumer products', September 2003 www.greenpeace.org.uk/MultimediaFiles/Live/FullReport/6043.pdf

The Scent Trail, Celia Lyttelton, Bantam Press 2007

Waterwise www.waterwise.org.uk

Other useful information

Advice about how to use water carefully

Water UK www.water.org.uk
Bag it and Bin it Campaign www.bagandbin.org
Find out about going on a water meter www.uswitch.com/Water

Low-water gardening information

Environment Agency advice www.environment-agency.gov.uk/subjects/waterres
(then choose 'Are you saving water?' section)

How to find an energy- and water-efficient dishwasher

www.sust-it.net

Where to buy proper perfume

Diptyque 195 Westbourne Grove, London W11 2SB, 020 7727 8673
www.spacenk.co.uk
L'Artisan Parfumeur www.artisanparfumeur.com/uk

Create your own scent

Creative Perfumers School of Perfumery 21 Arlington Street, London SW1,
020 7629 8468. Courses cost £550 and last either two full days or five evenings

SEPTEMBER

Sources and further reading

Adrian White, psychologist from University of Leicester, published a study on **GNA**
(Green Net Aptitude) in conjunction with npower, November 2006

'Love food; hate waste', WRAP campaign, launched December 2007
www.lovefoodhatewaste.com

'Reality or rhetoric: green tariffs for domestic consumers', Virginia Graham,
National Consumer Council 2007
www.ncc.org.uk/nccpdf/poldocs/NCC144rr_reality_or_rhetoric.pdf

'Green energy deals mislead customers', Martin Hickman, *Independent*, 8 March 2007

Energy Efficiency Partnership for Homes
www.eeph.org.uk/resource/facts/index.cfm?mode=view&news_id=56

'Standby and electricity', *Which* magazine report, 5 October 2006

Other useful information

Favourite froogler websites
www.frugal.org.uk
www.downsizer.net
http://sfcompact.blogspot.com
www.hintsandthings.com
www.moneysavingexpert.com

Recipes for using leftovers
www.lovefoodhatewaste.com
www.leftoverchef.com
http://thefrugalcook.blogspot.com

Information about green energy
www.foe.co.uk/campaigns/climate/issues/green_energy

The greenest green energy companies
Good Energy www.good-energy.co.uk
Ecotricity www.ecotricity.co.uk
RSPB Energy www.rspbenergy.co.uk

Generating renewable energy in your home
Grants
The Low Carbon Buildings Programme www.lowcarbonbuildings.org.uk
Solar
Solar PV Grants and Info www.solarpvgrants.co.uk
Solar Century leading company selling panels www.solarcentury.co.uk
Wind
Wind turbine info www.lowcarbonbuildings.org.uk/micro/wind

The British Wind Energy Association www.bwea.com
Windsave company selling turbines www.windsave.com

For courses about DIY energy generation
See the **Centre for Alternative Technology** www.cat.org.uk

Logos to look out for when buying electrical appliances
The Energy Saving Trust's Energy Efficiency Recommended Logo
www.energysavingtrust.org.uk/energy_saving_products
The EU Energy Label from A (best) to G (worst)
www.energylabels.org.uk/eulabel.html

OCTOBER

Sources and further reading

Envirowise www.envirowise.gov.uk

Energy requirements of lifts
www.energydesignresources.com
www.energydesignresources.com/docs/end-30.pdf

Wasteonline
www.wasteonline.org.uk

The Carbon Trust map showing CO_2 emissions for different sectors
www.carbontrust.co.uk/energy/startsaving/carbon_news_summer_07_business_
footprint_map.htm

The New Complete Book of Self-Sufficiency, John Seymour,
Dorling Kindersley 2003

A Crude Awakening: the oil crash, documentary released 2007, featuring
Colin Campbell, co-founder of Oil Depletion Analysis Centre

'The end of oil is closer than you think', John Vidal, *Guardian*, 21 April 2005

Other useful information

Organizations that will help you green the office
The Carbon Trust www.thecarbontrust.co.uk
Envirowise www.envirowise.gov.uk
Friends of the Earth online audit www.green-office.org.uk
Global Action Plan www.globalactionplan.org.uk

Those serving a specific function
Fairtrade at Work www.fairtradeatwork.org.uk
Save-A-Cup (recycles polystyrene cups) www.save-a-cup.co.uk
Fonebak (recycles mobile phones) www.fonebak.com
Shred-It (recycles sensitive documents) www.shredit.com
Waste Traders (provides help dealing with difficult materials, such as
hazardous materials) www.wastetraders.com

Buying recycled products in the office
The Green Stationery Company www.greenstat.co.uk

Recycled products
www.recycledproducts.org.uk
www.recycled-paper.co.uk
www.remarkable.co.uk
www.greeneyedfrog.co.uk

Learn about mushrooms
Mushrooms: River Cottage Handbook No 1, John Wright, Bloomsbury 2007
For info about John Wright's fungi forays, www.mushroomhunting.co.uk
Mushrooms and Toadstools, Brian Spooner, Collins Wild Guide 2005
Comprehensive site with identification key (but please use a book, too!)
www.mushroomexpert.com
A visual guide www.mushrooms.org.uk

Work less, live more
www.thedownshifter.co.uk
www.downshiftingweek.com

Read about it
The New Complete Book of Self-Sufficiency, John Seymour,
Dorling Kindersley 2003
How to be Idle, Tom Hodgkinson, Hamish Hamilton 2004

NOVEMBER

Sources and further reading

My blog post on cycling in November
http://timesonline.typepad.com/eco_worrier/2006/11/ten_ways_of_mak.html

Sustrans www.sustrans.org.uk

'2005 emission estimates for greenhouse gases in the UK', Defra,
31 January 2007 www.defra.gov.uk/news/2007/070131a.htm

Crash test performed on G-Wiz exclusively for *Top Gear*, May 2007
www.topgear.com/content/news/stories/1832

Environmental Transport Association
www.eta.co.uk/pages/going-green-during-the-journey/ggduring/default.htm

Commission for Integrated Transport www.cfit.gov.uk

Autocar **magazine** www.autocar.co.uk

The Energy Saving Trust www.energysavingtrust.org.uk

EU's renewable energy targets published June 2007

Other useful information

Brush up on cycling basics
Cycling to Work: A Beginner's Guide, Rory McMullan, Green Books 2007
Sustrans UK's leading sustainable transport charity www.sustrans.org.uk

Advice and jargon busting
www.whycycle.co.uk
London Cycle Campaign www.lcc.org.uk

Cycle shops
www.evanscycles.com
www.cyclestore.co.uk

Buying a second-hand bike
Bumblebee Auctions UK-wide auctions of police property, including bikes
www.bumblebeeauctions.co.uk
The Bike Man Cambridge-based company specializing in doing up used bikes
www.thebikeman.co.uk

Buying cycle gear
Lobster gloves www.wiggle.co.uk
No-battery bike lights and **padded cycling pants** www.ecoutlet.co.uk
Trumpet bulb hooter www.sbrsports.com

Cycling safety courses
Based in London, but it provides instructors for courses all over the UK
www.cycletraining.co.uk

Sharing lifts
Liftshare www.liftshare.org
National Car Share www.nationalcarshare.co.uk

Car clubs
City Car Club www.citycarclub.co.uk
Street Car www.streetcar.co.uk

Tips on greener driving
Environmental Transport Association www.eta.co.uk
Green Car Guide www.green-car-guide.com
Independent guide to green cars www.whatgreencar.com

DECEMBER

Sources and further reading

British Christmas Tree Growers Association www.christmastree.org.uk

Forestry Commission www.forestry.gov.uk

'Dreaming of a "green" Christmas?' Friends of the Earth's twenty top tips, 15 November 2005

The Energy Saving Trust www.energysavingtrust.org.uk

WasteOnline
www.wasteonline.org.uk/resources/InformationSheets/ChristmasRecycling.htm

Other useful information

Green restaurants
Konstam London, 020 7833 2615 www.konstam.co.uk
Duke of Cambridge London, 020 7359 3066 www.dukeorganic.co.uk
Acorn House London, 020 7812 1842 www.acornhouserestaurant.com
Bordeaux Quay Bristol, 0117 9431200 www.bordeaux-quay.co.uk
Due South Brighton, 01273 821218 www.duesouth.co.uk
The Star Inn Helmsley, 01439 770082 www.thestaratharome.co.uk
Le Manoir Aux Quat' Saisons 01844 278881 www.manoir.com

Christmas markets in the UK
Christmas market locator www.christmasmarkets.com
Portsmouth www.christmasfestival.co.uk
Bath www.bathchristmasmarket.co.uk
Winchester www.winchesterchristmasmarket.co.uk
Ludlow www.ludlow.org.uk
Bury St Edmunds www2.buryfreepress.co.uk/christmasfayre

Giving a goat
www.oxfamunwrapped.com
www.goodgifts.org
www.farmafrica.org.uk
www.sendacow.org.uk
www.presentaid.org

The tree
British Christmas Tree Growers Association www.christmastree.org.uk
LED fairy lights www.lights4fun.co.uk
Pines and Needles London www.pinesandneedles.com
Wilderness Wood East Sussex www.wildernesswood.co.uk

Green skiing
Getting there www.eurostar.com/ski
Finding a resort www.skiclub.co.uk/skiclub/resorts/greenresorts
Luxury sustainable accommodation www.whitepod.com
About other winter sports, such as snowshoeing
www.responsibletravel.com
www.jonathanstours.com/snowshoes.html

Index